50 Years of
Motorsport Marshalling

50 Years of Motorsport Marshalling

George Copeland

Best wishes

George

Published by British Motor Racing Marshals' Club Limited

www.marshals.co.uk

ISBN 978 0 9561756 0 1

Cover design by Clare Brayshaw

Cover photographs – Northern Marshals John Philips, Mike Pratchett and Phil Eddowes run for cover under attack from wayward Ginetta but return to douse the driver, Hunter Abbott.

Photos by Paul Lawrence

Set in Optima 11pt

Prepared by:
York Publishing Services Ltd
64 Hallfield Road
Layerthorpe
York
YO31 7ZQ
Tel: 01904 431213
Website: www.yps-publishing.co.uk

Author's Note

The thought of writing a book to commemorate the Marshals' Club's 50th Anniversary first came to me during the latter end of 2005. I was gradually disengaging from the variety of advisory and Non-Executive Director positions I had taken on since selling our plastics manufacturing business in 1994/5. What was I going to do to fill my time?

At around that time, too, Marshals' Club Council was looking at ways in which to record our 50th anniversary. As the longest serving member of Council, I was perhaps best placed to record what history there was of the past fifty years and I felt I should give it a go. It proved to be a daunting task!

The purpose of the book was to record fifty years of the Marshals' Club. It is not a well documented history and I spent most of the first few months simply contacting people I knew to tap their memories. Keith Douglas, one of our founders and struggling with ill-health at the time, was the first to respond. His memories of those early days and involvement in all things marshalling ever since, proved invaluable. Other responses were hard to come by and my resolve wavered a bit in those early months.

Then we moved home in early 2006 which left all my office papers in boxes for six months or more while we built an office at the new place. Other Clerk of Works duties at our new home took me away from the project for much of the next twelve to eighteen months. During this time, though, information started to trickle in, as folks learned of the project and shared their memories with me. By this time it was well into 2007, our anniversary year, and clearly as a 'virgin author' I was going to struggle to put together anything worth publication in time for our official birthday that year. However, 2007 was proving to be an eventful year for the Marshals' Club and marshalling generally and I felt it might be worthwhile delaying publication to incorporate some of the changes these events might bring, as part of our history. So, the whole project started afresh in late 2007.

Inevitably, the book is a series of anecdotes gleaned from those who remember those early days – or knew a man who did! Whatever comes of this tome, whether it sells one copy or 1,000, 50 Years of Marshalling will have been a labour of love. I have enjoyed enormously my time with the Marshals' Club and feel I have been more than adequately rewarded for any effort put in by the enjoyment I have experienced and the friends I have made through marshalling.

I have nothing but happy memories of my almost forty years as a member of The Marshals' Club and as a marshal generally. Yes, there has been the sadness of colleagues and driver friends lost to the danger of the sport but even here there were tales of camaraderie that say all there is to be said about the folks who go marshalling. They come from all walks of life, don't care if others are better/worse off than themselves, come with or soon learn the caustic sense of humour common to marshals everywhere and very quickly become part of the marshalling family, a great bunch of people.

If this publication is to be dedicated to anyone, it is to this fine bunch of men and women who have given so much to motorsport and who have been such friends to me these past forty years. Special dedication should be to those who take on committee duties within the Marshals' Club. This must often seem a thankless task but the regional committee structure is one of the strengths of the BMMC and we should be grateful that so many have been prepared to volunteer their services over the years. Thank you all for your friendship and for the many contributions to these memories of 50 Years of Marshalling.

All profits from the sale of this book will go to Marshals' Club funds for the benefit of all marshals.

Acknowledgements

I have tried, wherever possible, to record in each chapter who contributed to that chapter. Other contributions have been included verbatim. The Mike Abbott and Tony Hodgetts contributions so captured the mood of the time, as the Marshals' Club got started, that any editing might have spoiled them. Ken Cowley's path into marshalling echoed the path taken by so many of our marshals that this too warranted direct quotation. Chris Whitlock's series of They Do it Differently articles reminded us that ours is not the only way!

I felt, too, that the contributions from John Baker and Steve Tarrant, survivors of two of marshalling's most serious on-track incidents, deserved to be in their own words. How John and Steve recovered from their dreadful accidents should serve as an inspiration to us all.

Race Gypsy's article provides an excellent guide for anyone who wants to marshal abroad and encourages everyone who wants to marshal abroad to – Nike style – Just Do It!

Separately, I would like to record thanks for Keith Douglas's unique memories of how the Club started and for Keith's lifelong dedication to the Marshals' Club and all it stands for.

I would like to thank Jim Bamber for the excellent cartoons I have used within the book and for his support of the Marshals' Club in recent years.

Thanks to Roger Emery for his early memories of ES at Silverstone and to Bob Sketchley for his frequent reminders of anecdotes, some of which made the book, others that would have landed us both in hot water were omitted!!

Where I have been sent photographs and included them in this book, I have always tried to find the original photographer and give credit where due. I do apologise where I have not been able to identify the source.

Finding the right publisher was probably the single biggest task I faced. It seems publishing is much more specialised than I envisaged and one publisher or another dropped out at frequent intervals when it was discovered they could not give me exactly what I wanted at a cost I could afford. Then John and Catherine Newman came to the rescue. Catherine's Mum had just published her own book, using York Publishing Services. YPS proved to be just what the Doctor ordered and I thank David, Clare and Amanda there for initiating me into the terminology of publishing and for turning a fairly basic manuscript into what I hope most will find to be an interesting history of motorsport marshalling.

Special thanks to Eric Ridler for all his artistic and creative help in designing various sales leaflets to promote this book.

Like all good men, there is an even better woman behind me, my wife! We are close to celebrating our own 50th anniversary and through all this time June has encouraged me, our son and daughter and now four grandchildren to get on and do things! She can always see the bright side in any situation and has constantly urged us all over the years to keep going, even when the initial enthusiasm has waned a little. I love her dearly and I hope, like the Marshals' Club, we will have many fruitful and enjoyable years ahead of us after we celebrate our own 50th Anniversary!

I would like to thank all those who contributed to this book, some with memories of the time, others with the odd comment of encouragement. It all helped and I am grateful to one and all. Preparation of this book was over a two-and-a-half year period, during which time we moved house, sold a business, had storm damage that destroyed my computer memory and my own shortcomings in the memory department will not have helped. If I have missed anyone, please forgive me.

Dedication

This book is dedicated to all Marshals' Club members over the years and to marshals everywhere. However, it is especially dedicated to two people I believe epitomise all that is good about marshalling.

Keith Douglas

Keith Douglas, who sadly passed away on 24th August 2005, was one of the founders of the Marshals' Club and a constant supporter of all things marshalling right up until his death. He was behind many of the developments over the years that helped make the Marshals' Club what it was. He worked constantly and effectively behind the scenes within motor sport's hierarchy to gain distinctions for our Club that we would otherwise not have gained. Keith became friend and mentor to me during my thirty plus years as a Director of the Marshals' Club. I valued his advice and direction, especially on taking a more statesman-like approach to bureaucratic problems within the sport than is my natural inclination – although I cannot honestly say I always showed the patience he felt I should!

John Baker

John Baker, happily, is still with us, albeit a little shorter than he used to be! John was grievously injured in the terrible accident at the Marshals' Club 21st Anniversary Meeting at Silverstone in 1978. As local Chairman at the time, I became closely involved in his fight for life. His life hung in the balance for several weeks afterwards and his fight back to full health was long and agonising. John was never a very outgoing person but his sheer doggedness and resolve to get better impressed me then and does now. He endured a long fight back to being able to walk again but was back to marshalling before he could walk unaided. He came out of that a couple of inches shorter than he was. Fortunately, he can still see over the flag post and is back to being a regular flag marshal at almost as many meetings as before.

There are chapters in the book on each of these fine gentlemen. This dedication is to recognise their particular contribution to marshalling folklore.

Foreword

The Joy of Marshalling

An interesting response from Sir Jackie Stewart within his contribution to the book was a reminder of what an enjoyable job marshalling can be. It was a timely and appropriate prompt. Inevitably, the book will record many of the issues that have frustrated us over the years, the bureaucracy that has impeded us on occasion and the lack of real consideration at times. Hopefully, the book will also remind us all of happier times and why we still marshal.

Why do we do marshal? We do it because we enjoy it. Many I am sure would like to have driven but could not do so for a variety of reasons. Many more, though, marshal just to be involved.

In the early days many friendships were formed and, rather like schooldays, we never seem to forget those we marshalled with in the early days of our marshalling careers. Meetings then were often very well subscribed, which helped greatly with the social side. You met new people every week and very quickly found a new circle of friends to meet at different circuits all around the UK. The marshals' camp sites at major events became great social occasions.

There was often the satisfaction of a job well done – the incident marshal who had safely removed a driver from his wrecked car or the flag marshal who had just had a great day on the blue flag in long distance racing and got a wave of acknowledgement from grateful drivers at the end of the day.

As marshalling numbers dwindled, some of the social attraction went too. Being the lone marshal on a post out in the sticks somewhere does not have the same appeal as a day on post with a bunch of marshalling mates. Thankfully, we have seen numbers increase over the past two or three years and it is obvious from some of the postings on Ten-Tenths Marshals' web site that the social side of marshalling has seen a welcome resurgence of interest. Long may this continue.

Some of the Alternative Marshalling Method proposals will help with manning levels and should help to eradicate too many single-manned posts, even when short-handed.

What we must not forget is that we do this job for fun. If it ceases to be fun, try to find out why and improve the situation if you can. If you cannot, don't just vote with your feet, speak to someone, a Marshals' Club member if possible, and see if the Marshals' Club can help. That is what we are here for!

HEROES ALL

What is a Marshal?

I suppose the first thing to do in a book on motor sport marshalling is to define just what a marshal is and what he or she does.

Technically, they are the unpaid helpers who allow motor sport to go on. Marshals organise the competing vehicles in pit and paddock on race days at circuits and *parc fermé* areas on rallying. They organise the start procedures and thereafter look after all the relevant safety on track or *en route*. On rallies, they have the extra task of crowd control on open stages. Not usually such a problem on closed race circuits that today are more and more enclosed by safety fencing pretty well all around the circuit.

Most important of all, the marshal is an enthusiast. Some are frustrated drivers but many, many fewer than you might imagine. The vast majority of marshals just want to be involved in their sport of choice and, as in so many other sports and leisure activities, volunteer their services where they can.

There is a camaraderie among marshals that has not lessened over the years, although single manning of posts as marshalling numbers dwindle, has not exactly helped the companionship side of marshalling. The Marshals' Club became aware of this fairly early on and have worked since with circuit owners and 'the authorities' to remedy this situation. The Alternative Marshalling Methods report completed during 2007 was another Marshals' Club first; is designed to improve efficiency from reduced numbers but also to restore some of the companionship sadly missing under present arrangements. The proposal is currently before the MSA and the FIA for implementation.

As part of this change, we have incorporated some changed titles for circuit marshals that are in some respects, perhaps more meaningful than before. The Observer now becomes Post Chief. The Post Chief is in charge of the post and with his or her team, continues to act as the eyes and ears of the Clerk of the Course for that particular section of the track (hence the previous title of Observer). The Post Chief will report any incidents to Race Control, by telephone or radio and written report if serious, including reports of any driving thought to be less than considerate to other competitors – otherwise anarchy reigns!

The Flag Marshal and Course/Incident Marshal are now combined as Experienced Marshal, able to do either job as required, to make best use of the fewer marshals available to us on many occasions. They will be backed up in the near future by a much improved system of light signalling instead of (some) flags and fast response vehicles in the case of serious incident.

Also on circuit, you will find the Rescue teams in properly equipped rescue vehicles. Rescue Marshals are assessed and tested annually and are trained to a very high standard, capable of handling all sorts of emergencies, as later chapters will show, when some of our Rescue Marshals acquitted themselves well at a major air crash. Rescue vehicles also carry a licensed paramedic and/or doctor on board and a prescribed list of emergency medical equipment to enable them to deal with any emergency they are likely to encounter.

Pits, Paddock and Startline Marshals continue as before, performing a critical task in ensuring that race days run to timetable. This is especially critical in the current climate of high circuit hire costs, which means the organising clubs have to include as many races as they can to keep the cost within reach of the average competitor. Slick work in pits, paddock and startline is essential to ensure that everyone gets a race and no races are cancelled towards the end of the day where track curfews apply.

In addition, we have marshals who help out around Race Control, the nerve centre of any race day, and other doctors and medical staff who are there to deal with any emergency aid required by competitor, official or spectator. Many of the medical staff join the Marshals' Club for the camaraderie and feeling of belonging that the Marshals' Club engenders.

This then is a brief note on what and who marshals are. Enthusiasts first, volunteers second and vital to the running of any motor sport event. Marshals do it for the enjoyment, try to remain detached from the politics of the sport and remain at the very heart of motor sport.

Marshalus Orangus By Paul Newns

Species: Marshalus Orangus

Habitat: Open spaces incorporating tarmac and grassy areas

Appearance: Bright orange coat; athletic build; moves quickly over ground.

The Marshalus Orangus is a friendly creature which responds warmly to affection.

It is inquisitive and will often be found staring at odd pieces of metal, and is an avid collector of a variety of things which may be generically called "freebies".

DO NOT FEED THE MARSHALUS ORANGUS!

The Marshalus Orangus needs a carefully balanced diet. Please do not be tempted to feed it or you may upset the balance, which can be fatal unless an antidote called "Alcohol" is administered quickly.

A related species is Marshalus Blackus which can be found in a colony called "Silverstone" in middle England. This can be identified by its black coat and orange stripes.

Pre-Marshals' Club

There is not a great deal on record of marshalling activities prior to the formation of the Marshals' Club in 1957. What memories I have been able to uncover point to a haphazard system, to say the least.

There were no qualification procedures. Not surprisingly those most closely connected with the organising club became the senior officials. Everyone else who turned out to marshal seemed to mill around Race Control and, rather like the old Dock Labour Board process, would eventually be assigned to various jobs by the Clerk of the Course or some other senior official.

Again, this was a bit of a haphazard process. Those known to Club officials were appointed first; those that remained were often given spectator marshalling duties. This was seen as a marshalling post of last resort but it must have had its moments! All that separated spectators from racing machinery was often a few straw bales and a single-strand rope fence. Quite large crowds came to many of the more popular race meetings of this time and the rope fence could sometimes be something of a moveable obstacle, as pressure increased from those at the back who wanted a better view of cars drifting through the corner. I should imagine a spectator marshal's job could be quite lively at times, more so than now when duties involve merely patrolling between well-defined steel barriers and fences.

From my own experience of race spectating in the early 1960's, I can recall the rush across the fields at Silverstone Club corner to get the bonnet of our car as far under the rope barrier as we could. We would very often then sit on the bonnet or in front of it with our sandwiches to watch the racing!

On circuit, flag marshalling was often assigned to ex-drivers or drivers "resting" from competition – apparently not a very successful exercise, it seems! Whatever the truth of this, flagging soon became a serious marshalling role, the first, perhaps, to employ an element of selection by experience. Flag marshals were often issued with white coats, to better distinguish them from others around the straw bales that provided a platform for flagging and the only barrier between competing cars, the rest of the marshals and the crowd!

Given this potentially dangerous situation, it is remarkable there were so few serious incidents of marshal or spectator injury. Marshals seemed not to give the danger a second thought and very often treated their day out as a social occasion. Food and drink hampers were much in evidence; marshals were out to enjoy themselves, while still providing a valuable safety service on circuit.

In that rein, they were not too different from today's marshals. In the days when we could rely upon a full complement of marshals at every post, marshals would often arrange to marshal on circuit as a group. Often a larger group of friends would marshal consecutive posts – and rib each other mercilessly if they missed an obvious blue flag situation or otherwise cocked up! No alcohol would be on post but evenings would be spent "socialising".

Despite the fine aims and levels of enjoyment for the marshals in the 1950's, it was a fairly haphazard situation. Marshals were picked at random for a variety of tasks for which they may have had no previous experience; training did not exist. Gaps in marshalling strength would often be filled from volunteers from the crowd – who did not even get their admission refunded!

As the number of race meetings increased during the mid-1950's it was perhaps time for marshalling to be better organised. A group of enthusiasts from the Stoke-on-Trent area identified this need and in 1957 did something about it. Sadly, none of the original founders is still with us but if they are looking down on what they created, they should be very proud. Marshalling in the UK has become very professional, despite the marshal's true amateur status in an increasingly commercialised sport. The Founders would surely have been very proud of this achievement.

Marshalling in the Fifties

by Tony Hodgetts

Let me try to describe for you what it was like to act as a marshal at a race meeting fifty-plus years ago. For a start, many of the venues were temporary; the circuit to be used had been laid out on the day before by volunteer labour, who had to take it down again and return the site to an operational airfield by the end of the weekend. The race meeting would probably be held on a Saturday, as the Sunday Observance Act put severe restrictions on the charging for spectator admission (even the British Grand Prix took place on a Saturday) and the Lord's Day Observance Society kept a very beady eye on any transgressors with a view to reporting them for prosecution. You probably went in past the Guard-Room, complete with RAF police, to find your way to signing-on, which was probably in a tent. Race Control would usually be in an old double-deck 'bus, with the Clerk of the Course downstairs and the timekeepers and commentator on the top deck, the whole lot being driven to the circuit with ropes, stakes and signs filling every space available. Timekeeping by clocks, results courtesy of typists, "skins" and Gestetner.

The volunteer crew had to set out fire extinguishers (usually one per post, ordinary water based red ones), field telephones and their attendant wiring, almost entirely Army surplus stock, right back to the exchange switchboard, which, if you were lucky, was plumbed into the 'bus so that the wiring runs could be connected to a permanent board with access from outside. They had to run a rope and post barrier all round any spectator areas, to keep the punters back from the racing cars; that was the only barrier separating the bodies from the action, and the prohibited areas had to be patrolled by spectator marshals to dissuade the 'loonies' from sitting on the edge of the tarmac for a better view. That, you will appreciate, was a very thankless task, and usually fell to the newest recruits to the crew of marshalling hopefuls, which makes it very surprising that any of us survived and went further. It also usually happened that whatever you did on your home circuit, when you went to a new venue you ended up patrolling a rope when you tried somewhere new. It gave you a crash course in crowd psychology and how to handle stroppy idiots who wanted to endanger themselves and everybody else for a better view. The worst were the press photographers, who considered themselves above any reasonable regulation.

So you signed on and were allocated to a job and a post – knowing beforehand what you were going to do was for the friends and regulars – and collected kit as appropriate, being careful to check that you'd got all the flags you needed, and that they were fastened to the staves. It's a bit embarrassing when you wave your blue flag at a driver and it shoots off the stave and wraps itself round his head. And of course he won't give it back to you, so you're a bit hampered. When you got to the post, you check that your phone works, which was by no means certain, and check that your fire extinguisher feels as though it's loaded, and if it's not and your phone worked you report it and hope for the best.

You knew that you'd got to the right place because there was a straw bale there. A straw bale (singular), placed about a yard in from the tarmac. Now you might think that this was generously provided for your protection, but was really there to act as an aiming point so that the drivers knew where to start turning; they'd have used you as the target, but you might move and upset their calculations! It paid to check that your straw bale was a stout and secure one, because one of its uses was as a launch pad if a car got too close and you had to jump over it as it goes through your "post". This only worked for single-seaters, so the technique for errant saloons involved moving towards them to narrow the angle, then swerving to safety when you were sure of their trajectory. You get quite skilled in predicting the behaviour of an errant car on your allocated corner. You have to be. You also got quite adept in predicting whether the driver was going to make it on this lap while he was still on the approach; this mattered most when you had assessed the ability of the various drivers as compared with the brutality of their cars. Fifty years ago the standard of preparation was not as good as rules in 2005, and several car/driver combinations were definitely 'too fast for chassis'. Sadly in many cases their limitations proved lethal. If you were lucky enough to have a well-staffed corner (three – an Observer, a Flag Marshal, and a Track Marshal), you all kept lookout for certain drivers whenever they appeared, and yelled a warning for anything unusual.

You might well be short-staffed, particularly if you were round the back of the circuit, out of sight of the crowd. If there were two of you, you could cope, as one could wave a flag and ring race control while the other dealt with the practicalities; but if you were by yourself, then you had to make a swift assessment of priorities and finish up standing astride an unconscious driver whose TR3 had rolled and deposited him in the middle of the track, waving a yellow flag madly. On that occasion the entire field, from battling leaders back to the novices at the rear, slowed down to a walking pace. In those days there was no provision for stopping the race other than the chequered flag.

Training was quite definitely a matter of doing the job you were given and keeping your eyes open, in case you were suddenly given something else to do because of shortage or necessity. If you worked hard and showed an aptitude, promotion could be quick. The nearest thing I ever got to formal training was a visit to Silverstone to act as Assistant Observer to Squadron Leader Alan Brittan, which was very instructive as well as being a very busy day at Woodcote. I worked very hard, and actually got a mention in the "Autosport" report on the day's racing for my efforts in clearing oil and wreckage from the course during racing.

You were very close to the drivers, both physically and in comradeship, and quite often the great and famous would appear at a club meeting at a temporary circuit. It was very noticeable that the stars were warm in their thanks to the flag marshals, and Graham Hill, Innes Ireland and Jim Clark were among those who slowed down after the flag to call thanks for good blue flag work. I also recall a little white-faced lad in his brother's red E-type Jaguar, who could barely see over the steering wheel, giving a sound thrashing to the local talent; that was the first time I saw Jackie Stewart, and from that day we'd got him marked down to go far.

A few years later I was acting as Chief Observer at an Oulton Park meeting when a rather startling telephone report came in from Druids that a car had gone off in a rather spectacular fashion and disappeared. When I collected the report of the incident, it concerned Jackie Stewart in the Ecosse Cooper Monaco, which had gone along the bank, over the Flag Marshal and Observer as they dived for cover, got airborne and finished up perched in a small willow coppice, six feet off the ground. I took back the report to Race Control; it described the incident in impeccable Civil Service reporting style and immaculate copperplate writing, and concluded "I am, by the grace of God, K. Gibson, Observer".

The first time I went to Oulton Park in 1954, the crowds on the straight between Druids and Lodge were two feet from the track, and the trees were not much further back. I recall that if you flagged at Cascades, your first job of the day was to take the shovel and tidy up the trench at the edge of the track, so that you could dive in if danger threatened; I had to use it when Peter Kaye's Mini rolled over the top of m, when he lost it coming down from the Avenue. The flag marshal at Esso used to stand behind a mature oak tree for protection, until a Lotus F3 car hit it, with fatal results – the marshal was unhurt, but never came back. There used to be a small pond at Cascades, which was filled in after Graham Hill rolled his Jaguar and went into the water upside down, and Brian Vaux plunged in, got a door open, and fished him out. It's all rather hairy stuff, but we rather took it for granted that we were involved in a dangerous sport. Bear in mind that we'd all come through a war, when almost anything could happen without warning, and many of us had been in the Forces in one capacity or another and were accustomed to doing as we were bid without argument.

Even at the Grand Prix the atmosphere was totally different from the current separation. I can remember walking down the pits after practice and examining closely all the works Maserati team cars, lined up unattended in front of their pit. On a later occasion I was crawling under Graham Hill's red Speedwell A35, when I came face to face with John Sprinzel, who was crawling from the other side, both of us bent on finding out what had been done to make it corner so well. When I was acting as a "gofer" for an F3 team at the 1958 GP, the next paddock space was occupied by a rather scruffy area for the Lotus 16 works team cars, with the mechanics working under planks, leaning on the back of the open lorries that were acting as transporters, as they had no ramps. At the same meeting we found ourselves allocated the Ferrari pit for our race, and when we carted all our kit in, there were Peter Collins and Mike Hawthorn sitting on the pit counter relaxing after finishing third and first in the GP; and they stayed chatting with us for twenty minutes until our race started.

All that is concerned with racing; the contrast with then and now is much more marked in that field. Rallying has changed, for back in the fifties road rallies and night navigation from OS maps ruled, but the move into the forests has kept the rally marshals and spectators much more in touch with the action. I can remember the entire crew of our passage control on the 1959 "RAC" going to the aid of young Mr. Stuart Turner, navigator for Wolfgang Levy, to replace a flat tyre on the DKW, without need for a jack, in a windy wood north of Ingilston – they just picked up the back of the car with the driver still in it. And the crews still rely on the enthusiasts in 2005 if they go into a ditch.

To go on about what fun it was back then would be counter-productive; but all the rather eccentric happenings that I have mentioned happened to me, and more beside. I've gone up in the air and seen my straw bale taken from under me into the lake at Mallory Park by David Prophet's Kincraft, and then tried to explain to Race Control that I needed a straight tow and please could I have a new straw bale! For those with a critical eye, the flag post at Gerard's Out used to be on the inside of the circuit.

How the Club was Formed

I am indebted to Cliff Hammond of North Region for the following notes on John Ashton, one of the founding fathers of the Marshals' Club.

John Ashton was born in Newcastle-under-Lyme on 7th May 1914. He was educated at Newcastle High School and left at the age of eighteen, going into his father's firm, Beck & Moss Limited. He joined the RAF Reserve early in 1939 and was duly called up the day war broke out. He went to Tern Hill to finish training as a Sergeant Pilot and was duly gazetted on completion.

After Advanced Training School (which consisted of one week's conversion course from Hawker Harts to Hurricanes) John was posted to Lille, in France, to join 85 Squadron with the British Expeditionary Force. Later he took part in the Battle of Britain from Tangmere and in 1941 was posted to Hornchurch as a Flight Commander of 64 Squadron.

There followed tours of duty abroad, in Egypt as Squadron Leader, taking part in the El Alamein advance in October 1942; then to Malta as CO of a Spitfire Squadron and later in command of an Air/Sea Rescue Squadron. The following year, 1943, saw John back in Egypt as a Flying Instructor, followed by service in the Balkans and Italy. In 1944 he was promoted Wing Commander and when war ended he was commanding 339 Wing at Leghorn in Italy. Demobilisation followed in December 1945.

John had several near misses in his flying career – a crash landing in a field on the Isle of Wight following a one-sided battle involving eleven British fighters and 150 German fighters! He had done the same thing on an earlier mission shortly before the Dunkirk evacuation, when he was shot down over Belgium. John was Mentioned in Despatches and won the Distinguished Flying Cross for valour.

After demobilisation, John rejoined the family firm, continued to fly with the RAF Reserve, competed twice in the King's Cup Air Race and twice in the Daily Express Round Britain Air Race. He flew on for many years and trained RAF cadets at weekends. John died in 1988, aged 74.

John's memory of the birth of the Marshals' Club is in his own words, from an article in North Region newsletter while John was Club Chairman.

My interest in motor sport started purely as a spectator before the war, watching those fabulous and superb German Mercedes and Auto Union cars at Castle Donington, driven by such masters as Nuvolari, Lang and Seaman, etc. Alas, the war came before I could make more of it and to my sorrow I had to sell my two-litre Lagonda and go to see the Germans being active in other ways!

After the war I divided my time between motor sport and flying. The flying part was part RAF Reserve and part civilian. I had the good fortune to be asked to be the pilot to a friend who owned a Miles Messenger. We flew on many air rallies in Northern Europe and once by good fortune, we won a closed circuit competition and an excellent crate of champagne to go with it!

When I heard the North Staffs Motor Club was being formed, I rushed along and got my name tabled in the first few. I was keenly interested in the Club, competing in various events and organising others. At this time, I joined the MG Car Club, Midland Centre, the Nottingham Sports Car Club (who organised races at Gamston) and the Shenstone and District Car Club. In 1949, I was co-driver with Bill Lamb in the second Tulip Rally, driving a Healey Silverstone sponsored by Donald Healey. We had a lot of mechanical bothers and finished 62nd out of 320 starters.

The • NSMC had many drivers keen on racing, including Harold Greenwood who organised NSMC races at Silverstone, an event which gained great popularity over the years. In about 1952, I became Chief Marshal for this event and each year my secretary and I used to hunt through the masses of letters we had written to people and each year we would scratch our heads wondering what job to give to which person. This nightmare continued until one year Jack Banister, a very active member of the NSMC, joined us in this onerous task.

Amid much blasphemy, I said to Jack that we ought to make a register of Marshals and note against each name the person's capabilities. We both thought this was a good idea and I thought nothing more of it until Jack rang me a few days after, saying, "I've done it; I've got all the paper work out to start the Marshals' Club. What shall we call it?"

We spent many hours both at Jack's house and at my office discussing details and each time Jack would rush away and come back in no time having achieved an almost superhuman amount of work and organisation. I spent most of my time saying "Hum" and "Ha" and sitting with my mouth open, completely aghast at the rapid pace Jack was making.

All plans completed, we were posed with the difficult question of how to launch the Club. We had the good idea of inviting Roy Taylor to dinner at the North Stafford Hotel in Stoke. Roy's tremendous knowledge of motor sport was invaluable and he suggested we held a meeting in Birmingham inviting one member from each of the recognised Motor Clubs in the country who promoted race meetings. Roy promised to come along to help us manage the meeting and Jack once more rushed off to get the letters in the post as quickly as possible.

Jack and I drove over to the Queens Hotel in Birmingham, both feeling a little nervous. However, the room we had reserved was in order, the drinks lined up and tables laid for dinner. Our guests that night included Keith Douglas, John Holmes, Bunny Ransom, Ian Lunn, Alan Atkinson, Graham Peacock and Tony Bird, all of whom became household names within the new British Motor Racing Marshals' Club, which was formed that night.

Roy Taylor begged to be excused from joining the Committee but we will always be grateful to him for his wise counsel and help in forming the BMRMC.

From here on, I rely upon various notes provided by Keith Douglas who, of all the founders, was the one who stayed the course and continued to help marshals throughout a long and varied (part-time!) career in motor sport.

Winning support for this new organisation for marshals was not so easy. Several 'in authority' suspected it would become a marshals' union, likely to down flags and fire extinguishers if things were not to their liking. Union power and strikes were a fairly constant part of business life at that time and the first hurdle to overcome was to convince those in authority that a properly formed Marshals' Club would be good for marshalling and for sport as a whole.

During 1956 an article appeared in one of the motor racing magazines, advertising the proposed Marshals' Club and inviting people to join. Whether the Club existed at that time is a moot point. The governing body at the time was the RAC (prior to the RACMSA and then the MSA) and it was very difficult to get any new racing club registered, let alone one that smacked of being a marshals' union!

Nevertheless, Jack Bannister and John Ashton persisted. Some volunteers appeared but no one is sure just how many, probably not as many as public proclamations suggested! However, there were enough to set up a steering group. Keith Douglas, by then sometime race commentator, sometime marshal and sometime club rally driver, expressed an interest and was immediately invited on board as the Nottingham Sports Car Club representative.

Also on the steering group, Keith remembers, were Jack Bannister and John Ashton, from North Staffs Motor Club, of course, Alan Atkinson from Mid-Cheshire Motor Club, John Holmes from a London-based club, Ian Lunn from the Civil Service Motoring Association and Bill Hawkins from the Essex Motor Club. So, some heavy hitters from the race organising clubs of the day, set about the formation of the British Motor Racing Marshals' Club in late 1956, early 1957.

It is interesting to note the varied backgrounds of those involved. Jack Bannister ran a plant hire business, John Ashton was a distinguished member of The Few who fought the Battle of Britain, rose to the rank of Wing Commander and was awarded the DFC and Mentioned in Dispatches for his exploits as Hurricane and Spitfire pilot. Alan Atkinson was a merchant seaman who became a teacher after WWII and Ian Lunn was a Major in the Highland Regiment. John Holmes was a senior purchasing man at Hoover in London. Keith was a main board director of GKN. So, some heavy hitters on a personal basis, too, don't you think?

The British Motor Racing Marshals' Club came into being, officially, at a meeting on 16th June 1957 (we believe!) at the Queens Hotel in Birmingham.

There followed a series of meetings up and down the country to publicise the new Club and to invite people to join. Unfortunately, the costs of these meetings far exceeded the income from the 44 members attracted to join and the club was effectively broke! Another meeting was called in December 1957, at the Mollington Bannistre Hotel near Chester – something of a crisis meeting, I suspect – to reorganise Club finances.

Keith chaired a sub-committee to set up a series of local committees and the Club started to generate funds. In January 1958 they held a huge raffle, drawn by Raymond Baxter, the BBC's motor sports commentator, which seemed to set the Club on a much better financial footing. Raymond Baxter very soon afterwards became the Club's first President.

The main thrust to get the Club properly established and recognised seemed to start when John Ashton took over the reins as Chairman of Council. In 1959, Council consisted of Raymond Baxter President, Graham Peacock Vice President, Alan Atkinson Vice Chairman, Eddie Cornwall Secretary, Keith Douglas, Robert Bromley, Brian Fox, Mike Cunliffe and Denis Broadhurst of VSCC. Jim Kennard was Secretary of Northern Region, Vic Bonds in the Midlands and Doug Standley in the South.

However, there was soon to be another financial crisis. Northern Region had bought an ambulance in the Club's name, without Council authority and, more important, without the funds to support the purchase. The Club was once again, broke! Keith by then was Vice Chairman and he and Chairman John Ashton had a meeting in John's car in the market place in Stoke-on-Trent to try to find a way out of the Club's latest financial disaster.

The situation looked bleak. Club funds would nowhere near meet the bill for the ambulance. The Club was worse than broke – guarantees from all members could be called in. What was to be done? John Ashton then had a brainwave. The Club had recently commissioned a new Club car badge, the stock value of which roughly equated to what was owed for the ambulance. John offered to buy up all the badges and to take repayment of his very generous offer as and when badges were sold on an individual basis. Who knows what might have happened to the Marshals' Club if it had not been for this very generous offer. John Ashton most certainly saved the day.

In my time on Council, there have been a couple of further financial crises but none like the one just described and, truly, we owe a great debt of gratitude to John Ashton for his outstanding generosity.

From a formation point of view, the Club was now up and running, despite the financial disasters. Ford sponsored the book, 'How to Run a Motor Race' in 1964, compiled by Marshals' Club members. By 1966 Keith Douglas had become Chairman of Council. Raymond Baxter was still President and John Webb of Brands Hatch had become a Vice President. Roy Mitton had taken over as Chairman in Midlands Region, Garth Nichols in North East, Ken Gibson North and Vic Sparkes South.

Moving forward from that, South Midlands Region was set up in the late 1960's, Northern Ireland Region began as a sub-region of Midlands Region but became independent in 1980, at the same time as the British Rally Marshals' Club was formed as a subsidiary of BMRMC.

Keith's subcommittee clearly worked very hard during 1958. Midlands became the first region to have its own committee, ably assisted by Keith himself, Dick Twist and Brian Fox, whom Keith recruited from SUNBAC, where he had been helping to run SUNBAC's Solihull centre. Northern Region started under Graham Peacock as chairman. A new region started in the South, which Vic Sparkes later chaired. The Club was on its way, it seemed.

From those early days the Marshals' Club went on to gain great respect from everyone in the sport. Keith was responsible for a great deal of this improved recognition. He never ever stopped supporting the Club. In his role as commentator at Silverstone, he never missed an opportunity to plug the marshals. (Son Russell, also a regular race commentator, maintains this fine tradition!)

Marshals were still not well represented in the corridors of power, though. Here again it was Keith to the rescue. Keith was an initial Director of the newly formed RACMSA Board, became Chairman of Race Committee and held many other posts in motor sport's hierarchy. He used this influence well to arrange much wider recognition of marshals. First step was representation on Race Committee, closely followed by Rallies Committee and soon marshals were represented on every committee they possibly could be – all down to Keith's efforts. He was truly the best friend the Marshals' Club could ever have had!

The Marshals' Club's ascendancy continued until the early 1990's. Membership peaked at around 2,800 and from insurance declarations of days marshalled, it seemed Marshals' Club members put in some 80% of all days marshalled. This was certainly true of race marshalling but the figures were never quite so clear on rally marshalling. First, we were never sure we got a full return of rally days marshalled and, of course, there are a great number of rally marshals who turn out once or twice a year only, for their own single club event or on the Rally of Great Britain. Nevertheless, I think we could rightfully claim that the great majority of time controls were manned by members of the British Rally Marshals' Club or those who had been trained by BRMC.

From then on, however, marshalling numbers dropped all round. Our own membership dropped to a low of 1,400 before starting to climb back in recent years as our efforts to recruit increased. We cannot see the numbers ever getting back to where they were at the peak and as this chapter is being prepared, the Marshals' Club study paper on Alternative Marshalling methods forms the basis of discussion by an MSA Special Commission attempting to find a way to make better use of the reduced number of marshals available to us, without compromising safety.

Reasons for this drop off in numbers are many and varied. Many are outside our control; weekend shopping, plus other sporting activities, such as major league football, now taking place on both Saturday and Sunday probably provide the single biggest reason for the decrease. Many people find themselves having to work longer hours in their jobs.

Cost comes into the equation, too. Petrol stopped being a cheap commodity many years ago and marshals, who are not paid for their services, simply found they could no longer afford to do the number of meetings they once did. It seems the case that once the number of meetings drop off for an individual marshal, the interest drops off as well and frequently the marshal decides to stop altogether.

Within the sport, too many in authority paid lip service over the years in their apparent appreciation of all the marshal does for the sport. Many feel the governing body, the MSA, has been too reluctant to enforce the need for basic track side facilities for marshals. Similarly, they have been slow to encourage let alone enforce timetables that take sufficient account of the number of hours marshals have to be on duty, often needlessly. Some race organising clubs continue too long with unpopular, poorly supported championship rounds that bore everyone involved and marshals 'vote with their feet' at such meetings when they are repeated.

The Marshals' Club continues to lobby for improved consideration and respect for marshals, not always with the best of results and often at considerable harm to its reputation with some in positions of power within our sport. This is grossly unfair; the Marshals' Club deserves better and will continue its efforts to win over its critics.

Fred was one of the early members of the South Midlands Region when it was set up as a separate region from the old Southern Region. He lived around Stony Stratford and was a regular marshal at Silverstone.

My favourite story of Fred is when he was flagging at Woodcote In on the old Silverstone Club circuit. At that time, the pit lane entry ran right under the flag point and drivers would very often cut in, right to the wall almost, when racing.

Fred felt that one of the drivers during a session had not being paying sufficient attention to his yellow flag signals. He gesticulated at the errant driver a couple of times but there was no improvement in his behaviour. So, when same driver came into the pit lane at the end of the session, Fred let his crash helmet have it with the flag pole!!

After that, there are some discrepancies as to what happened next. Some say the driver lodged a complaint against Fred but was told where to go by the Senior Race Officials. Fred did receive advice not to do it again! Whatever the case, the story soon went the rounds and drivers were much better behaved for a while afterwards!

The British Motor Racing Marshals' Club – Acceptance

Some of the "political" views against the formation of the Marshals' Club were hard to believe. Others were understandable but none the less flawed.

The main criticism at the time was that the Club would become a marshals' union, ready to down flags and stop racing whenever things did not suit them. In the industrial climate at the time, this was maybe understandable, but also reflected something of a 'them and us' attitude that existed in motor sport at the time. As mentioned in a later chapter, senior officials of the time were generally drawn from the local gentry. Marshals were seen as 'other ranks' and were often dealt with a little too dismissively by those who ran our sport.

Despite the very impressive backgrounds of the steering committee that formed the Marshals' Club, antipathy to the Club proved to be a very difficult barrier to break down. Even in the early 1970's when I became involved, there were many who still saw us as a union. I further believe that lack of proper consideration for and consultation with marshals over the years is a principal factor in the current shortage of marshals throughout the country. Perhaps we should have been more of a union on occasion!

Be that as it may, the politics of motor sport frowned upon the Marshals' Club as it was being set up.

The RAC seemed reluctant to register the Club. Many within the RAC openly condemned the Club as a marshals' union and could see no place for it in motor sport. When *'How to Run a Motor Race'* was published, the same people asked, "What does the Marshals' Club know about running a motor race?" Well, it seemed we knew quite a lot. That publication and others to follow on Training and Grading, found their way around the world and became the race organisers' 'bible' in many instances. *BMRMC Training and Grading notes* became known in the USA, Australia, New Zealand, throughout Europe, Israel, Scandinavia, Hong Kong, China, Middle East and at one stage had been translated into sixteen different languages.

However, all that was in the future. At the time of formation, the Marshals' Club had few friends 'at Court'. John Watt, one of our longest serving members, recalls that Marshals' Club members were encouraged to add BMRMC after their name when signing on to marshal. This had two major effects; in the very early days of the Marshals' Club, some organisers objected to this and any marshal who dared to do so would be taken aside and lectured on what seemed to the organisers to be 'union activity'. John goes on to say that, because of this, many marshals at first refused to join and those that did join often did so surreptitiously!

In later times, recognition as a member of the Marshals' Club often brought appointment to a more senior task as, by then, Marshals' Club members were thought to be the experts, trained in every discipline. Tony Pernyes of South Mids region remembers turning up for his very first marshalling experience at a hill climb near Brighton, to be told that, "Ah, you are the chaps from the BMRMC, the experts; will you run the finish line for us?". Tony and his chums found this a daunting prospect but they seemed to cope fine. I remember from my own early days, turning up to do start line at Mallory Park, only to be instantly promoted to Observer at Centre Gerards and having to cope with an unconscious driver, with no first aid help since they were all busy with serious injury incidents elsewhere. Nothing like starting at the deep end, is there?

Despite all this recognition from those at the sharp end of motor sport – and ask any rescued driver how he/she feels about the *'Angels in Orange'* – some political undertones still exist in the lack of real consideration for marshals from those at the top of our sport. Do they still fear we might indulge in union activities? The smaller organising clubs, generally run by those who are enthusiasts first, profit-driven second, have shown what real consideration means to marshals. They are rewarded by excellent marshalling attendances at their meetings, while many major events are poorly manned as marshals show their distaste for unnecessarily long timetables, long often boring periods of practice for relatively short races, unexplained and seemingly unnecessary gaps in the timetable and a general lack of consideration for marshals' welfare.

Clearly, there is still some work to be done. The Marshals' Club, as the only apolitical voice, is still best-placed to represent marshals' interests in a totally non-political and constructive fashion.

The problem is that we all too often lack an effective voice within the 'corridors of power' at the MSA. Keith Douglas, as Founder Director of the MSA Board and principal founder of the BMRMC, provided us with a voice at high level for many years but following his retirement in 2002 and subsequent sad death in 2005, we became a little rudderless at high level within the MSA. All too often our views were not heard when marshalling issues were being discussed and it was always an uphill fight to get anything changed once Press Releases and the like had gone out. Hence many marshals were left with the belief that the marshals had no effective voice within the sport.

It is this more than anything else that drives trained, experienced marshals from our sport, of that there is no doubt. Many of our marshals come from fairly senior management positions in industry and are used to being consulted on management issues and to consulting with their own staff when issues come up from the shop floor, as it were. The days of 'mushroom management' are long gone in any company that wishes to get the best out of those they employ. Many marshals find it mildly insulting that their genuine complaints and suggestions are so often ignored by the organising authority.

Right up until his death, Keith Douglas tried his damnedest to get us new recognition at some higher level within the sport's hierarchy. Sadly nothing came of his endeavours. The Marshals' Club made a very well received presentation to Motor Sports Council in February 2006 and were offered, we thought, a seat on MSC, where we were told motor sports policy was discussed and agreed. Sadly, this too fell by the way-side, thwarted by our detractors within the sport's hierarchy.

With so many other weekend activities now available to everyone, we must work harder to communicate with and involve marshals in all that we do. There was a time that marshalling with a bunch of mates on post was an enjoyable way of spending a weekend. With current numbers, marshals are very often on their own on post, trying to do the jobs of several. This does not need to happen for too many weekends before the marshal says 'sod it' and votes with his feet.

The Marshals' Club feels it can and wants to be part of the solution. We cannot play a part in sorting out marshalling issues if we are not consulted by those who set the rules. I believe this is an issue that is set to "run and run"; I just hope we can continue to recruit those to our side who will keep on with the struggle for proper recognition by those who run our sport. And we must not let the politics and bureaucracy beat us!

A Pit Marshal's Memories

by Mike Abbott

Though I didn't know it at the time, the BMRMC was formed in the same year that I started marshalling. The probable reason why I knew little or nothing of the Club's existence or aims in its early days was because I only spent a relatively short time on the bank as a Course Marshal, mainly for the few events that the British Racing Drivers' Club (BRDC) ran in those days – the International Trophy, the Grand Prix (which alternated with Aintree) and the British Empire Trophy/Championship Finals. Thus I was never a member of Phil Morom's E S (Emergency Services) team, which almost certainly accounted for the fact that no approach was made to me to 'join the Club' until some years later.

Two other factors probably contributed to that situation. Firstly, my invitations to marshal at BRDC meetings – when it was considered a great privilege to be an official of, arguably, the most prestigious Club in the world – came about as a result of "chatting up" one of the ladies in Race Admin (later to become Eric Browning's wife – he was then Chief Observer, if I remember correctly). Secondly, in 1958, I moved into the 'pit area' (as the rear of the pits was then termed) and, in 1959, into the pits themselves under Peter Clark (one time *Le Mans* HRG works driver, twice winner of the *Coupe du Roi* at the Spa 24 hour race and who also drove a Jaguar XK and a works supported Aston Martin DB2 at *Le Mans*. Later he became the first Chairman of Silverstone Circuits Ltd. following the formation of that company and, for many years until his death seven years ago, a vice-president of the BRDC).

In the case of Pit Marshals (and, from recollection of names listed in programmes, almost certainly among Flag Marshals and Observers), it is probably true to say that, in the '50s/early '60s, a large proportion of those marshalling at BRDC meetings were either ex-drivers or BRDC members (or both). One such Pit Marshal was Edgar Kehoe who, when 'nearer ninety than eighty' (as he put it), would still drive from Hampshire to Silverstone or Donington for a BRDC meeting (as a spectator rather than to marshal!). On one such occasion, at Donington, Neville Hay (also, for a period, a Pit Marshal and now a well-known commentator and producer of motor sport videos) and I had lunch with Edgar. He became a BRDC member in 1930 and only died a little over three years ago. Another Pit Marshal and senior official was one L. Barrington-Upton (and to pre-empt the question: the father of the Club's current National Membership Secretary, Sue Whitlock). Among the flag marshals around that time (mid to late '50s) were Don Truman (the same!), Viscount Chetwynd (who he?) and the Earl of Denbigh (against whom I raced some while later) and among the observers were such 'notables' as Mort Morris Goodall, Major Tony Rolt (when not driving Jaguars around Le Mans), Philip Fotheringham-Parker, Lord Selsdon, Lord Strathcarron, Col. Mike Head (father of Patrick H., I believe) – and the aforesaid Edgar Kehoe. One who was often a steward or a judge was Captain George Eyston, the previous holder of a number of land speed records (who, on one occasion and in the absence of an appropriate armband, I attempted to eject from the pits – regrettably I didn't recognise him!), along with the Earl Howe, the Hon. Gerald Lascelles, the Marquis of Camden and other titled gentry. Even the scrutineers (at a single meeting) boasted no less than four army majors and a wing commander. Last, but certainly not least, the lovely little Liz Zettl, who started in the Race Office in 1949; Liz achieved a milestone in her life in September 2007 when she celebrated her 90th birthday – and she still does occasional duty keeping the race log in Race Telephones!!

At that time (and for some years after), Pit Marshals were classed (like Paddock and Startline marshals) as off-circuit – as opposed to on the bank, I suppose. As a result, our contact with Phil's E S personnel (and thereby the BMRMC) was minimal. As a further, and potentially more serious, consequence (as will be seen) we received no training whatsoever other than 'on the job' instruction from Peter Clark and his two Assistant Chief Pits with regard to the running of the pits, written reporting of pit stops and enforcement of the regulations (such as there were in those days) – and crowd control!!

In retrospect, it is all the more remarkable that we received no training to enable us to cope with incidents – whether serious or minor – when one considers that the pits, and all the many personnel who invariably gained access thereto, were completely unprotected from the competing cars which, in the case of Silverstone, were exiting the old (chicaneless) Woodcote Corner at or very near to their maximum speed. The fact that we were classed as off-circuit was a complete nonsense – we were very much more on the circuit, literally, than any Course Marshal! Moreover, at no time were we ever given any form of fire training or instruction in the use of fire bottles (I can't recall whether the items in question were even provided). Bearing in mind the use of milk churns for fuel storage in the pits, the manner in which cars were refuelled and their greater propensity to catch fire – to say nothing of the tendency for team personnel (and hangers-on) to smoke – this omission is all the more surprising.

Interestingly, even at major Silverstone meetings such as the G P and the International Trophy, relatively few Pit Marshals were considered necessary – albeit the pit lane was then less than half its present length (ending at the pedestrian bridge – still occasionally referred to as "Motor" bridge by those who were around in those days). Indeed, on occasions, we were allowed a break and I would usually wander down to the inside of Copse Corner's breeze-block wall to view proceedings. On one such occasion (in 1958, shortly before Peter Collins was killed at the old Nürburgring), Collins went off on the outside of Copse and, in the process of rejoining, caused Ron Flockhart to go off rather more comprehensively in his BRM. On my return to the pits shortly afterwards, I overheard Flockhart being berated by Raymond Mayes for 'bending' the BRM and, perhaps unwisely, chipped in with my view as to who was to blame (budding Observer, I was not); the upshot was that I was obliged to accompany Mayes and Flockhart to the Clerk of the Course – John Eason Gibson (father of Neil Eason Gibson), no less – to relate my version of events. Though this was my first experience of being grilled by a Clerk of the Course, as it transpired it was far from being the last!

On another such occasion, I was pressed into service by the sole flag marshal (located in those days on the inside of Copse) when an urgent need to wave a white flag arose – due to the decision to deploy the biggest 'wrecker' I've ever seen at a motor racing circuit to remove Sir Gawaine Baillie's Jaguar, which had embedded its sheared rear leaf-spring in the grass on the exit of the corner. The 'target' of my first-ever flagging performance was the leader of the saloon car event, one M Hawthorn, who, in the immediately preceding laps, had become aware of the stranded Jaguar but not of the considerably greater danger now posed by the 'wrecker'. My abiding memory of the incident was of Hawthorn – on seeing either 'my' white or the 'wrecker' (or both) – turning his Jaguar almost completely sideways in order to slow it sufficiently. At which point, he was headed directly towards me (or so it appeared) and, to my everlasting shame, I 'did a runner', though with flag still held high!

Both of those Copse incidents perhaps demonstrate the rather less formal approach to marshalling which existed then compared with the present day. Whilst undermanning nowadays necessitates a degree of multi-tasking, I cannot envisage a young (and, for all practical purposes, totally untrained) marshal acting, without any prior notice or instruction, as a Flag Marshal or Observer at a major international event.

In that period, as illustrated above, many of the BRDC's officials were titled or had some other 'handle' to their name (usually a military rank) and, particularly in the case of observers, were noted for 'setting up shop' at their appointed posts with liberal supplies of liquid refreshment – not, so far as I was aware, of the bottled water variety! I had little doubt that a similar 'policy' was prevalent among those in more senior positions behind the scenes. In fact, much later Pierre Aumonier (for many years Club Secretary of the BRDC and international race official) confirmed that this was indeed the case, together with the clear inference that Gerald Lascelles was, not surprisingly, one of the parties usually involved!

As an overall consequence, the 'troops' were similarly not averse to spending off-duty periods in the paddock bar – indeed it was not unusual for one's Chief to 'do the honours' at lunchtime. Whether this applied to a similar extent with Phil M's personnel, I know not – but, on the reasonable assumption that it did, even if to a somewhat lesser extent, it again clearly demonstrates the vastly different approach to marshalling that existed in the early days of the Club.

To say that it was condoned by the Clerk would, perhaps, be to overstate the case. Indeed, on one memorable occasion, John Eason spotted a pint of beer on the pit wall and instructed me to remove it forthwith – he didn't ask whose it was and I certainly didn't volunteer the information. Suffice to say that I removed it to a place of safety!

As a final insight into that 'relaxed' attitude, at one time the Paddock Bar demanded a deposit on their glass pint pots (2/- as I recall), whereas in the BRDC members' marquee there was no such requirement – perish the thought. A system was therefore devised whereby the first pint was purchased in the BRDC facility, the (unpaid) "deposit" on the BRDC glass was then redeemed in the Paddock Bar and the proceeds exchanged for further supplies in the BRDC tent – thus providing one with more or less free beer as and when one felt the need.

Though I cannot recall whether a 'subsistence' allowance was paid by other clubs, I do remember that the BRDC paid 2/6 (12½p) in the '50s / early '60s; this was effectively increased to 3/- with the introduction of Luncheon Vouchers for a short period (unofficially these could be converted into "beer vouchers" if one used the Paddock Bar / Restaurant) and then, in increments, to 5/-, 10/- and eventually – to great rejoicing – a one pound note.

To revert to more serious matters – the pits at Silverstone (and elsewhere) were, in effect, located at the side of the track, at the same level as the track and with no protection whatsoever for either stationary cars or, more importantly, for personnel – other than a yellow line painted on the track surface as a demarcation line!

Moreover, for some years, E S personnel were not generally positioned on the pits side of the circuit at Silverstone and it was therefore the responsibility of Pit Marshals to deal with incidents on that side of the track, including even initial checks on a driver's condition, 'killing' the electrics, the removal of debris from the track, etc. (at bigger meetings, paid professional firemen were based in the pits but their services – rarely, if ever, used – were limited to dealing with fires). In retrospect, it therefore seems all the more surprising that no formal training for pit-based personnel was ever carried out to the best of my knowledge.

As all too often seemed to be the case, it took a fatal accident to change all that – well, not quite all. Though the Silverstone pits and the pit lane itself were subsequently raised (to the level of the present signalling wall) and protected by steel railings, the only other apparent change was the positioning, albeit some while later, of E S personnel on the newly-built pit wall. However, so far as I am aware, despite the fatality, still no attempt was made to give any incident or medical training to Pit Marshals – presumably on the premise that, albeit belatedly, E S personnel were now on hand (though I don't recall them routinely being available at many of the lesser meetings). Also, their primary role was clearly in regard to on-track incidents, with little or no attention being given to the pits themselves.

I believe it's fair to say that so-called off-track personnel, such as myself, were never considered to be marshals who needed to be trained in the way that our on-track colleagues were; nor, by extension, was there any incentive to join the BMRMC (nor, indeed, any suggestion that it might be in anyone's interests that we should do so). Only much later – when endurance races such as the six-hour sports car events and European Touring Car Championship events started to be held at UK circuits – were there ever any graded BMRMC personnel in the pits; these were marshals who normally worked on the bank, but who elected to work in the pits because of the greater involvement that resulted from doing so at long-distance events. To demonstrate the significance of this lack of training, it is perhaps worth recounting the details of the tragic accident referred to previously, since the shortcomings resulting from this state of affairs will be all too evident.

During a 1963 G P support event, a Le Mans spec. works A-H Sprite got into a "tank-slapper" exiting Woodcote and, when the driver finally "lost" it, the car headed backwards at almost unabated speed towards the pit counter. A Scrutineer (Major Harry Cree) and I had been attending another car's pit stop and whilst, fortuitously, I had returned to the Control Pit (no pit office in those days) as quickly as possible to submit the pit report and was returning to my allocated pit, the scrutineer was still walking away from the pit in question; thus, whilst I was facing the oncoming cars when the driver lost control, he was not. As a result, I was able to dive over the pit counter at the moment the Sprite hit Harry Cree, slamming him against the pit counter and thence about 10-15 feet in the air. He (Cree) landed at my feet like a rag doll and the car bounced back on to the track. Partially due to my lack of experience, partially due to my complete absence of training and, probably, an element of shock, I froze. Fortunately, the more experienced Deputy Chief Pits grabbed me and told me to help him get the apparently unconscious driver out of the car. This we were eventually able to do – though how we did so, or how long it took, I have little idea. I subsequently learnt that the driver was actually severely concussed and only regained full consciousness some while later in the first aid tent; yes – a tent which in itself, provides a further insight into the very basic nature of circuits, well before the need to build comprehensively equipped medical centres became standard practice.

With hindsight, it's clear that the lack of protection for those working in the pits would, sooner or later, inevitably result in a very serious or fatal accident. During the course of many thousands of laps driven since the opening of the circuit in its configuration at that time, it was not uncommon for drivers to lose control exiting Woodcote – the famous newsreel shot of Mike Hawthorn's high speed gyrations on the grass opposite the pits is but one example. On another occasion, Peter Harper in a Sunbeam Rapier, having spun through 180 degrees, took the chequered flag whilst travelling at about 80-90 mph backwards! Also, around the same time, Innes Ireland had a lurid 360 degree spin at precisely the same point. Any one of those incidents (and doubtless others) could so easily have had a similar outcome. For the Sprite driver and the Scrutineer, it was their misfortune that, at the moment when control of the car was finally lost, it happened to be heading directly for the pits rather than down the straight or towards the bank opposite.

On the positive side, the accident resulted in the subsequent changes (both at Silverstone and elsewhere) which were, by then, long overdue.

The situation related above also highlights another very important difference between marshalling then and marshalling/dealing with such major incidents later. It was extremely rare for a race to be red flagged – and this was no exception. Though it would be unthinkable now, marshals were expected to deal with such incidents, protected only by a (single) waved yellow; I never forgave Mike Parkes (whose Ferrari was leading the race) for seemingly failing to slow one iota, as a result of which he and the rest of the field were passing either side of us at racing speed throughout our efforts to get the driver out of the car which, so far as I can recall, itself remained in the middle of the track for the remainder of the race – again something which could never happen nowadays.

The extent to which lack of training contributed to my actions that day is a matter for conjecture – suffice to say that, in the aftermath, I never thought I would marshal again. I have never been so frightened in my life. Maybe if both the Deputy Chief Pits and myself had been trained to deal with the situation, we would simply not have made any attempt to extricate the driver until the race had been stopped – as would certainly be the case today.

On another occasion, when flagging at Woodcote Approach (on the old Club Circuit), very early in a rain-sodden race an Aston Martin lost a wheel and came to rest on the apex and, with marshals unable to move it, it remained there for the duration of the race. No question of a red flag (and many years before the introduction of 'double yellows' or hazard boards – not that the latter would have been appropriate anyway); I was therefore obliged to wave a very wet (linen and therefore very heavy) yellow flag for the duration of the race. No great danger in this case (except perhaps for the drivers), but a sign of the huge difference in approach to situations of this type compared with the present day.

As a further commentary on the lack of training for marshals like myself, i.e. one not under Phil Morom's wing (or, perhaps, others who followed in his footsteps at other circuits), there were many occasions (in the '60s / early '70s, I think) when I would volunteer to marshal at "clubbies" (750 MC, Eight Clubs, etc.) at various circuits (mainly Brands Hatch, Thruxton and, of course, Silverstone) and would be told that I was to flag or observe at such and such a post. If one was fortunate, there would be someone on the post with the necessary expertise to ensure that one acted broadly in accordance with accepted practice. If not, it was a case of 'using your loaf', based on what one had seen others doing. I'm sure that there were many others like me who picked it up as we went along and, where necessary, had the error of our ways drawn to our attention by the Observer (or whoever). As an example, I recall flagging at Woodcote Gap and, in an attempt to show that I was on the ball, I displayed a waved yellow when a competitor was sideways on the grass and in imminent danger of losing it completely – in fact, more by luck than judgement, he didn't lose it and I got a mild 'rollicking' for acting on the assumption that he would!

I drew the line – wisely, I think – when asked to be the Observer at Brands Hatch's Paddock Hill Bend. I knew its reputation and, more importantly, I lacked any real idea as to what was expected of an observer. Nevertheless, if I hadn't refused to do it .... Again it comes back to the almost total absence of training for people like myself – I don't think the Training and Grading Scheme had yet come into being at that time but, even if it had, I like many others wouldn't have benefited from it because we weren't BMRMC members and no one had suggested or advocated that we should be. Perhaps that doesn't say a lot for the Club's recruiting policy in those days?

Eventually, in the mid '70s, Pierre Aumonier (then, I think, usually Secretary of the Meeting for BRDC events) and Peter Corrie (who had replaced Peter Clark as BRDC's Chief Pits by then and for whom I had been Assistant Chief for several years) became BMRMC members and prevailed upon me to do likewise. However, so far as I can recall, this made little material difference, since no training was on offer for 'specialist' personnel, nor did the grading scheme embrace such personnel that I was given a gold badge probably reflected the fact I had been an Assistant or Deputy Chief for some years – or, more realistically, the fact that no suitable alternative was available at that time!

Eventually, the grading scheme was expanded to include the various specialist disciplines. A little earlier, I had been appointed Chief Pits for the BRDC and, as a direct consequence, also for FIA / RAC MSA events at Silverstone and, in some cases, Donington. These two factors had a significant impact on the Club's role vis-à-vis pit marshals and, indeed, specialist marshals generally.

Unfortunately the introduction of Specialist gradings proved, initially at least, to be a double-edged sword. On the one hand it provided a structured grading system for pits, startline, paddock/assembly area, race administration and other specialist personnel; this was a very welcome, if somewhat overdue, step. However, its implementation was fraught with difficulties and problems, mainly caused by the differing approaches of the Club's Regional Committees when they deliberated on the initial grades to be allocated to those with varying levels of experience and ability.

When, in the fullness of time, these problems were resolved, the separate grading systems appeared to be infinitely preferable to that which existed for some years after the Club's introduction of the original 'one fits all' system. The ability, introduced more recently, to progress up both 'ladders' concurrently (rather than the previous, somewhat restrictive, approach) was, in my view, a very sensible move. Among other factors, it helped to diminish (though not completely eradicate) the 'them and us' philosophy which, regrettably, still prevails in certain quarters at some circuits more than at others!

To revert to the earlier days of the Club's existence and, in particular, to the unwelcome involvement ("interference" would perhaps be a better word) on the part of the RAC/RAC MSA in well-established practices; in the '60s (when the RAC took over, from the BRDC and the BARC, responsibility for running the G P) until the early '80s, for Grands Prix all regular senior officials were replaced by RAC personnel. Few (if any) of whom had the necessary expertise or experience to do the jobs, which, I believe, they took over by virtue of who they knew rather than what they knew. As a result, those usually in control (and those next in line) were demoted. This caused a degree of ill-feeling, not least because it was quite apparent (to those affected) that their 'Chiefs' were only able to appear to be in control due to the co-operation and guidance of those whom they had supplanted. Moreover, the marshals (particularly in the relatively close-knit environment of the pits, paddock, startline, etc.) found themselves under the control of someone they neither knew nor trusted and who, quite clearly, had little idea of what they were doing. Indeed, in some cases, even the less experienced marshals knew more about the job than their superiors and resented being told to do things which were contrary to normal practice and, in certain cases, could be considered to impinge upon their safety.

Two prime examples of the consequences of this situation are worth quoting – one occurred at Brands Hatch and one at Silverstone. I wasn't involved in the former (it is well documented anyway), due to the fact that, a year or so earlier, I had handed back my armband and walked out as a direct result of the factors mentioned above and was therefore not invited again until 1976! I was, however, directly involved in the latter. The Brands incident at the 1974 G P (which eventually involved a full-blown CSI [or FISA ?] enquiry in Paris) would appear to have been caused by the RAC-appointed Chief Pits' failure to realise that a driver might have to 'pit' in the closing stages of the race and the resultant need to maintain control of the pit lane to cover this eventuality. The competitor in question was Lauda in the Ferrari which, having "pitted" on the penultimate lap, was (to quote a *Motoring News* report) "forced to abandon his car in the pit lane as the exit road was completely blocked by hangers-on." The Paris enquiry awarded him the points for 5th place, notwithstanding the fact that he was a lap behind the winner and wasn't officially classified as a finisher).

The Silverstone incident involved both the pits and the startline marshals, both of which were under the 'control' of RAC appointees. A potentially highly dangerous situation arose for everyone on the grid (including marshals, of which I was one) due to the apparent failure of either of the said 'worthies' to appreciate the 'mechanics' of the situation. Those who did realise the potential for a major incident, and who would have taken steps to prevent the situation even arising, had been dispatched to the startline in anticipation of the need to clear the usual milling mass of people from the grid.

The situation arose well before the more recent procedure whereby cars could do one or more reconnaissance laps (using the pit lane rather than crossing the grid). However, on this occasion, it had been decided (and all concerned had been notified) that cars would do two 'green flag' laps (or the contemporary equivalent of 'green flag' laps) before taking up their grid slot. What neither of the "temporary acting" Chief Pits nor the ditto Chief Startline seem to have appreciated was that not all cars would necessarily leave the pit lane immediately the exit opened. As a result, several left after the leading cars had completed their first lap and been shown the chequered flag. As the later ones were, it would seem, not made aware that they now had only one lap available to them, they came through Abbey and approached Woodcote (and the rear of the grid) at 'full chat' on the mistaken assumption that this was the first of their two laps (no team radios then, of course). To appreciate the full implications of the situation, one has to bear in mind that, at that time, the 'complex' didn't exist – it was a flat out 'blind' from Abbey / Farm into Woodcote.

Fortuitously, unlike those with a misplaced opinion of their own infallibility, marshals at Farm (and doubtless also Abbey) immediately appreciated the potential for a very major incident indeed (I seem to recall that the track was damp, hence presumably the two laps). In consequence, they 'banged out' almost every available flag (some wholly appropriate, others perhaps not quite so) in their efforts to ensure that the drivers realised that something was very wrong and, more importantly, would back off. To their eternal credit (I'll never know who they were), those marshals averted what could have been a major disaster – particularly bearing in mind that not only marshals but also press, sponsors and a whole host of 'hangers-on' could have been involved. My abiding memories of the incident were; firstly, the realisation of what could (and probably would) happen if no one had warned the drivers; secondly, my inability to do anything whatsoever to avert it; thirdly, the sound of the approaching cars at racing speed; fourthly, a strong inclination to do a runner (again!) in the direction of the bank; and fifthly (and most importantly), the almost immediate reaction of the marshals on the post(s) preceding the back of the grid – the sight of virtually every available flag being waved furiously was something which I'll not forget.

In the days when radios were virtually non-existent and telephone communication at most (if not all) circuits was via ex-W D equipment, there was perhaps a greater need than now for marshals to react under their own initiative (as in the above example). The fact that nowadays, notably at FIA-run events, there is frequently a requirement to await instructions / permission / authorisation before one acts is probably one of the less obvious changes which have taken place over the years.

On a vaguely related train of thought, perhaps a selection of lesser events / happenings from days gone by, which probably couldn't happen in present day motor sport, would be of passing interest:

During the snowstorm which occurred at an International Trophy in the early '70s (the one which caused Ronnie Petersen to go off at Copse), following the stopping of the race, when one could barely see the grandstands from the pits, a line of three or four spectators, complete with rucksacks, appeared marching down the middle of the pit straight, for all the world looking as if they were heading for an Alpine ski slope. They were roundly cheered from the grandstand.

At the six-hour relay race at Thruxton, the only time that it was held there, one of the senior officials, driving his Rolls-Royce via the grass infield, arrived at posts on a number of occasions, during practice and the race itself, bearing either supplies of beer or 'girlie' magazines for the marshals. At one stage, I held up my pint of beer as Gerry Marshall passed – on the following couple of laps, he swerved towards the post (on which I was the observer) with his arm out of the window with a view to taking possession of my ill-gotten beverage.

On which subject, as implied earlier, in the '50s / early '60s, marshals at Silverstone were allowed (or, at least, no one stopped them) to purchase drinks in the BRDC tent; what a contrast with today's 'no pass back' (F1 Paddock type) electronic entry system to the BRDC facilities.

At a time when the wearing of overalls was not the 'norm', I got to know one of the Castrol marketing people and managed to negotiate the supply of a quantity of their orange tabards to make Pit Marshals more visible (and hopefully therefore less prone to being 'collected' by a competitor). However, I was not allowed to issue them because, at the time, Esso had the sole rights to advertise their products at the circuit (Silverstone). Whilst it was accepted that isolated marshals would not be precluded from wearing one, inundating the pit lane with the Castrol variety was felt to be an entirely different matter. In more recent times, when the issue and wearing of sponsors' sew-on logos on marshals' overalls became prevalent, it was necessary to ask those wearing such items to tape them over when an event was being televised, due to the tendency for TV cameras to zoom in on pit stops and thereby marshals in the immediate vicinity.

Before the use of security personnel, there used to be a police presence in the pit / paddock area at Silverstone at major events. On one occasion, a group of well-inebriated gentlemen repeatedly gained access to the pit lane and constituted a very real danger to themselves and others. When all efforts to remove them failed, the Clerk, Tony Salmon, asked the police the deal with the situation. They (the police) got the biggest cheer of the day from the grandstands as they hauled one of them across the circuit with his toes dragging across the tarmac. Tony later told me the sequel – having deposited the offenders by their car, they waited until they drove off and radioed their colleagues at the main gate, who had them arrested for 'drunk in charge' as they pulled out on to the public highway the Dadford Road.

Much has been said (and written) about the marshals' campsite facility in recent times – in the '50s, those wishing to 'camp' overnight were housed in Nissen huts (on the other side of the Dadford Road) which used to be the WAAF quarters when Silverstone was an operational airfield. Regrettably the previous occupants had, wisely in the circumstances, long since departed.

A slightly unusual and perhaps unique role was played by marshals when HRH The Duke of Edinburgh formally opened the new Silverstone pit lane on one of its several reincarnations. Our duty was to form a box around HRH, accompanied by Gerald Lascelles, as he progressed down the pit lane, to ensure that the press and sundry others were kept at a suitable distance from the royal party. Marshals were not issued with firearms – unlike Prince Philip's personal protection personnel, who clearly were.

On a related subject, when Mark Thatcher was competing in one of BMW's Touring Cars, there was apparently a fear that he might be in danger of being kidnapped – it was at the time of heightened security due to events in the Middle East (Iran, if I remember correctly). At Donington, I was warned that a 'number of gentlemen' would be present in the pit lane (and elsewhere, as it transpired) throughout proceedings, that neither I nor any of my personnel were to question their presence and that we were not to approach them or speak to them. In other words, we were to treat the situation as though they weren't there. Though 'they' had attempted to dress in garb appropriate to their location, in reality they stuck out like sore thumbs – the fact that they were clearly carrying firearms didn't help their attempts to merge with the scenery either. Despite the explicit instructions which I had been given, the senior man (of five, I believe) immediately approached me, introduced himself and asked that I and the marshals responsible for Thatcher's pit give him guidance as to where he and his colleagues should position themselves so as not to constitute a danger to themselves or anyone else. So much for the misguided attempts to ensure their anonymity.

On the subject of Donington security of a different kind; I was once bodily removed by two 'heavies' from in front of a works-entered Mercedes (which I was monitoring for an alleged infringement of the regulations). When I demanded an explanation for their actions, I was told that it was done in the interests of my own safety, as the car in question was about to depart the pits – they hadn't the intelligence to realise that even the mighty Mercedes team had yet to devise a means whereby a car could accelerate away from the pit whilst on jacks and without wheels.

On occasions, observers' reports have caused embarrassment (usually when the content didn't correspond with the known facts), but two pit reports, submitted at international events, and, as such, part of the official record, could have been construed as slightly 'problematic'. The first, at a F.3000 event, stated simply:

Adjusted front suspension – with a hammer.

The second, in rather more questionable taste, was submitted during a round of the European Touring Car Championship and related to an Alfa Romeo which refused to restart after a pit stop; in their efforts to identify the problem, the team had removed a spark plug and turned the engine over on the starter – at which point a jet of water emanated from the plug hole. The report, submitted by a marshal who has since gone on to a rather more senior role in motor sport, read:

Retired – engine comprehensively f***ed.

However, the marshal in question didn't use asterisks – and he even prevailed upon the Italian team manager to sign it. Moreover, since, by so doing, the team thereby confirmed the car's official retirement, it had to be submitted as it stood.

Another pit report is perhaps indicative of the differing approach adopted in earlier times. When one of his cars coasted into the pits with a dead engine, the report was submitted to Colin Chapman for signature (a requirement no longer applicable at F1 events). He refused to sign it until the reason for retirement was re-stated to read simply: "oil leak". As first submitted, it read (rather more accurately!): "broken con rod – hole in block". Strictly speaking, both were correct but the desire to disguise (from the press at least) the failure of the Ford-supplied engine was apparently considered paramount.

A number of examples of marshals (most, if not all, BMRMC members) getting themselves into trouble – mainly through their own stupidity but, in one case, due to a singularly unfortunate coincidence – might not come amiss:

At a Brands Hatch G P, Startline Marshals were provided, by the event's sponsors, with Gitanes/Galloises jackets. A number of them decided to wear their smart attire at the following year's (Silverstone) G P – their appearance on umpteen TV screens thus attired didn't go down too well (to put it very mildly) with the sponsors of the latter event, John

Player! I believe that, as a result, the Chief in question (the holder of a BMRMC gold badge) never again performed that role – and certainly not at a GP.

Another marshal, better known at the time as a noted painter of motor sport scenes, appeared at a J P S sponsored Brands Hatch G P wearing (as was not unusual) ex-driver's overalls; problem was that, on the front and back, the word "MARLBORO" appeared in 4in. high letters. He refused to accept that it might be a good idea to remove (or cover up) the offending word.

At one time, marshals' instructions almost invariably included the words "no marshal shall carry a camera" or words to that effect. This didn't deter two gentlemen (both BMRMC course / fire graded members, it has to be said). One – at Silverstone – thought that videoing the start of the Grand Prix parade lap from the signalling wall would be a good idea, notwithstanding the fact that he was in full view of Bernie E's bus, and that anyone (media or otherwise) was required to have a FOCA sticker on his/her video camera (for which, presumably, a charge was levied). When I hurriedly reported the matter to the Chief Observer, Don Lawrence, both he and Jim Keegan (no doubt because the marshal was Brands-based) arrived within a very short space of time, removed the marshal's passes and, very unceremoniously, the marshal himself.

The other E S marshal was not content with taking the odd picture surreptitiously but insisted on sticking the lens a few inches from the driver's face; in this case Piquet at Brands Hatch. The offender was duly relieved of his passes and duties by Jim Keegan again, apparently spent some while drowning his sorrows and then managed to regain access to the pits – by now comprehensively p***ed. His final act was to threaten to 'thump' John Newman (the same!) who he believed (wrongly) had reported him for his earlier behaviour.

Another incident at Brands Hatch, involved a pit marshal (now the holder of a well-deserved gold badge) who, at my behest, on Bernie E.'s instructions, removed the FOCA pass being worn by someone who was clearly not entitled to be wearing it – it was Danny Sullivan's and he (Sullivan) was, at that precise moment, circulating fairly quickly in a Tyrrell. Only after I had returned it to Mr E., did it emerge that the illicit wearer of the pass was a senior executive of Fiat (UK) – which didn't worry Bernie one bit. But it did worry the marshal – he had joined Fiat

(UK) only a short while before the event in a managerial position and feared the possible repercussions if the connection was realised by the person concerned.

On the subject of Bernard Charles Ecclestone, Esq., it's probably fair to say that most marshals, both in the UK and elsewhere, don't have a particularly high regard for this gentleman, due to the widely held perception that he considers us to be a necessary evil, rather than an essential part of motor sport at every level.

He is also certainly seen as unapproachable, humourless and totally disinterested in the activities of the volunteer marshalling force – until, that is, something goes spectacularly wrong in full view of a world-wide television audience.

At the risk of incurring the wrath of my fellow marshals, I have to say that, in reality, many of those perceptions are somewhat wide of the mark. Indeed those same marshals might, quite understandably, question my justification for putting forward such a controversial point of view.

In fact, I've known Bernie E. for some years (since the late 1970s) and it is probable that I'm the only marshal (as opposed to, say, MSA or BRDC/SCL executives) who has had irregular meetings, discussions and correspondence with him over an extended period. Indeed, it seems likely that few, if any, other working (i.e. actively marshalling) members of the Club will have ever met the man in question – albeit our present Chairman did so, briefly, fairly recently.

As a result, a number of facets of BCE may well come as a surprise to many marshals and, bearing in mind his huge influence on the sport over much of the fifty years covered by this history, a few examples of his real as opposed to reported or perceived attitude may be of interest:

Probably the most telling example of his concern for the safety of marshals arose when the then FIA President, J-M Ballestre, decreed as was his custom that pit marshals should be positioned throughout practice, qualifying and the race, in the 'tramlines' between the working lane and the outside lane. Presumably in the interests of the 'spectacle', they were required to display a yellow flag as 'their' car departed from its pit garage and, much more significantly, were to face inwards rather than in the direction of oncoming cars – and this before pit lane speed limits were introduced!

Clearly this was potentially highly dangerous for the marshals concerned and, as a result, I made repeated representations to both the Race Director and the Clerk of the Course, with a view to having the President's demands rescinded. Since both were, in effect, employees of J-M B, unsurprisingly neither was prepared to accede to my pleas.

Coincidentally, I had to see BCE on another matter and as a last resort, took the opportunity to mention my predicament to him. I still have a very clear recollection of his immediate, unequivocal response: "It's nothing whatsoever to do with Jean-Marie; the safety of marshals under your control is your responsibility; you should act as you think fit and you will have my full support" problem solved. By chance – or perhaps not (!) – it may also have enabled BCE to 'score points' at the expense of his then rival for overall supremacy; nevertheless, it was clear that his concern in regard to marshals' safety was genuine.

As some Incident Officers and Observers may recall, some years ago arrangements were made for them to visit the pits prior to GPs to check on the location of cut-off switches for the electrics, the means by which F1 steering wheels could be removed, etc., so that they would be in a better position to deal quickly and effectively with major incidents. This was prompted by a comment to me by an Observer regarding the lack of information on the subject at that time. In turn, I mentioned the problem to Mr E., who immediately instructed one of his personnel to make arrangements with one of the leading teams (Williams, as it later transpired) for those concerned to be given access to their pit to receive suitable instruction for this purpose and for other teams to co-operate in the interests of all concerned.

As an aside, contrary to popular belief, so far as I am aware, BCE himself was not averse to marshals being given access to the F1 pit lane at appropriate times. Where responsibility for the embargo on doing so lies is a matter for conjecture. However, there is little doubt that, subsequently, the above arrangements were curtailed as a direct (and highly regrettable) result of one of the (RAC)MSA appointees apparent inability to appreciate the point of the exercise – probably because he himself was not the instigator!

On another occasion before the 'Paddock Club' came into existence, the personnel of one of the leading teams refused to be at the circuit in time to open their garages for the benefit of those who had paid to participate in the early morning pit lane 'walkabouts'. Though their stance was perhaps understandable, bearing in mind the times thereof, when I told BCE that this was, inevitably, causing the marshals a great deal of unnecessary 'aggro', he immediately dispatched one of his personnel to "deal" with the matter. Again – problem solved, thanks to BCE's unhesitating response.

A further example of his attitude when team personnel (in this case the team principal) were 'uncooperative' occurred in the aftermath of a F3000 event, when it was run as a stand-alone event a month or so prior to the GP. This was a rather more serious matter because the team principal in question had been abusive to three separate experienced marshals, me being the third.

The dispute arose as a result of the team principal's contention that we had no authority whatsoever over the use of FOCA passes. Two youngsters, no more than about 8-10 years old, were wearing team guest passes and were larking about in the pit lane during practice for a support event. Following my involvement, the team principal was hauled, almost literally, before the Clerk and 'told his fortune' – which should have been the end of the matter.

However, at the subsequent G P, I sought clarification of the situation vis-à-vis FOCA passes for future reference. Mr E. asked what prompted my query. Having answered that question, he then asked who the culprit was. Perhaps ill-advisedly, I declined to answer the second question on the grounds that the matter had been dealt with by the Clerk of the Course at the earlier event. After twice refusing to answer his question, it seemed unwise, to put it mildly, not to accede to a third – rather more compelling – request for the details.

Having thus established the identity of the individual concerned, Bernie turned to his senior 'enforcer' and instructed him to "remove all the team's guest passes forthwith". This incidentally, in the presence of Silverstone's Circuit Director. Though I've no idea what subsequently transpired, it is reasonable to assume that the removal of those passes (which, by inference, included sponsors' passes) may not have been entirely unconnected with the fact that the team in question was conspicuous by its absence the following year.

Again this demonstrates that Ecclestone does respect marshals rather more than is perhaps generally assumed. Clearly he did not act as he did for effect – he doesn't need to – but rather to show that he is not prepared to tolerate unacceptable behaviour towards volunteer personnel, irrespective of the status of the perpetrator.

And, almost certainly contrary to popular belief, Bernie does have a sense of humour. This was clearly demonstrated when, as a parting comment shortly prior to the start of a British G P and in the knowledge that the weather forecast was 'iffy', I asked whether he thought it was going to rain. His response was to point skywards, remark that he was generally believed to possess God-given powers and ask me on which particular lap I would like it to rain! My response was "lap 68 please" (it being a 67 lap race!), to which he promised to "exert the necessary influence". In fact it didn't rain on "lap 68", though it did during the Touring Car event which, in those days, followed the G P. So perhaps …

Finally, as soon as he became aware of my enforced 'retirement' as Chief Pits for the GP in the aftermath of the Schumacher 'ignoring-the-black-flag' incident which, in fact, had little to do with me, he wrote assuring me that he would make arrangements to ensure that I would still be able to visit the pits. True to his word which is a facet of his character accepted as a fact by almost everyone, I believe, for a number of years he provided me with a 'go anywhere' pass. Indeed, the following year, I was the slightly embarrassed possessor of pass no. VSG 5 which, as I subsequently discovered, was "Very Special Guest 5".

As with the Ballestre affair, I don't doubt that there was more to that final gesture than met the eye (as is almost certainly the case in many of BCE's actions. In this case, the dual purpose was almost certainly to demonstrate clearly to the 'blue-blazered' fraternity at the MSA that he was well aware of the true circumstances of my 'retirement' – though I have to admit that I had earlier taken the precaution of making sure that he was!!

Nevertheless, it was a further indication that Bernie Ecclestone does appreciate our efforts – even if he doesn't often acknowledge the fact openly. Doubtless, like everything else he does, he has his reasons; upon which I would not presume to speculate!

Finally, two or three "happenings" in the late '50s / early '60s which might help to provide a "flavour" of the times – notwithstanding the fact that they are not directly related to my (or anyone else's) marshalling activities and certainly have no specific connection with the BMRMC's early days:

John Bolster was perhaps the originator of the pit road 'walkabout'. Supposedly in his role as journalist and commentator, from fairly early in proceedings he would progress from pit to pit taking liquid refreshment; gin, pink or otherwise, was almost certainly the main ingredient), stocks of which were invariably held 'on the premises', before the days of sumptuous hospitality facilities. By mid-morning, it was usually clear that Mr Bolster felt that his idiosyncratic approach to public relations had borne fruit.

The same gentleman, at close of play, would almost invariably adjourn to the paddock beer tent to 'hold court' and discuss the events of the day. His audience used to comprise a cross section of the general public, the odd support-event driver, quite a number of mechanics and, unsurprisingly, a number of marshals. As mentioned earlier, there was normally a police presence at such meetings and Bolster's habit, whenever a pair of them came in sight, was to lead a rousing (and usually drunken) chorus of 'All Coppers Are Bastards'. Neither he nor anyone else was ever arrested (ASBOs hadn't entered the English language then) so far as I'm aware – probably because 'plod' was usually outnumbered about 75 : 1.

On one occasion, a fellow marshal and myself were able to put our somewhat limited expertise to good use – albeit some distance from the circuit. Returning down the A5 after a practice day, we came across the Austin A35 entered for Graham Hill by Speedwell Engineering, of which he was a director. It was being driven back to its base in north London for some overnight work by Len Adams; also a director of Speedwell and a fairly accomplished driver – when was the last time a car entered for an international event driven to and from the circuit, I wonder? It transpired that the car had sheared the left stub axle as it entered Hockcliffe shortly before we arrived on the scene I'll always remember Adams' unprintable remarks regarding the likely consequences had the breakage occurred as Hill was coming through Woodcote the following morning. Incredibly, almost the next vehicle to come into sight was a Godfrey Davis flatbed recovery truck which, it transpired after it had been flagged down, was headed for London. Between the four of us; Adams, the truck driver and two of Silverstone's finest, we managed to get the A35 on to the flatbed and thereby on to the grid the following day. The sequel to this was that my colleague was offered, and took a job at Speedwell shortly afterwards and, a little later, I was allowed to drive one of their highly-tuned, and very rorty A35s round Hendon and Golders Green for half an hour or so – in full "boy-racer" mode, I have to say.

When the F1 paddock and paddock restaurant/bar were open to all-comers, I was enjoying an early breakfast when someone (also with a 'full-English' on a tray) asked if I minded if he joined me. I didn't mind at all and we had a very pleasant chat whilst eating our respective breakfasts; The 'someone' was Jo Siffert. It would be somewhat difficult for a present-day junior say, Course Marshal to even see one of today's F1 drivers at close quarters (except on television), let alone have a quarter of an hour's chat with him over breakfast.

Lastly, an example of marshalling at a G P, also before the fortress-like F1 Paddock. En route to Silverstone, a big-end on my car sounded decidedly 'iffy' and it was suggested that I sought the advice of Castrol who were located in the paddock. To cut a long story short, they told me to bring the car round, whereupon the Competition Manager instructed his lads to drain the sump and refill it with the heaviest duty oil available which, he felt, would get me home if driven circumspectly. It did, albeit with regular stops to allow the engine to cool down – the old A5 then, as now, had a very reasonable selection of hostelries!

Two incidents at Donington also warrant a mention – one because it concerns a driver who never required the services of BMRMC members he won his only British Grand Prix the year before the formation of the Club. The other because the complete opposite could be said to apply (he's now our Chairman).

Twenty-three years after that British G P win, Fangio, then in his 68th year) was prevailed upon to drive a pre-war W125 Mercedes round Donington. As the late Keith Douglas noted in a regional newsletter; in response to an article which I had written for an earlier edition, "lesser drivers would have done several familiarisation laps" and "Fangio's best time was five seconds quicker than Neil Corner's" (the car's owner. Indeed, within two laps Fangio had, "really wound the

Merc up" and was, I believe, circulating in a time very close to the then lap record – this in a car which he had never driven before and at a circuit he had never seen before. As he was exiting the corner immediately before the pits with armfuls of opposite lock, together with one or two other marshals, I was standing close to a number of then current F1 drivers who were similarly watching proceedings. Alan Jones, not one noted for praising his fellow men, turned to the others (James Hunt and John Watson with the telling remark, "we've still got a hell of a lot to learn". Though I saw Fangio's win at Silverstone, as a spectator, it is unfortunately probable that few, if any, currently active members were marshalling on that day. There is, however, one known – and notable – exception; a gentleman by the name of Don Truman – who else? But, to be strictly accurate, Don didn't marshal on the day Fangio won, though he did have a pretty good excuse for not doing so – he was competing in the F3 (500 c.c.) support event!! Nevertheless, at the next major Silverstone event the International Trophy on 14th September the following year, Don was 'driving' a flag. That was also to be my first event as a marshal – and, like Messrs Jones, Hunt and Watson, I had 'still got a hell of a lot to learn!' For those wondering why the International Trophy was, uniquely, in September, the Suez crisis the previous year was to blame).

My final recollection must be reserved for the Club's current Chairman – when he was employed in a rather less exalted role (in charge of the weighing team for the European Grand Prix at Donington in 1993. It's also a further sad reflection on the activities of Donington's 'heavies' at such events. When Ron Dennis attempted to go to the podium to receive the Constructor's Trophy, for Senna's winning McLaren, he was precluded from doing so by the 'chief heavy' – who, in his position of authority, had decided that only the drivers finishing 1st, 2nd and 3rd, together with those presenting the 'tinware', were to be allowed access thereto. Enter C. Hobson, Esq. as 'chief negotiator'. Since, as it happened, the somewhat fraught negotiations took place on the periphery of the live TV coverage, it was fortuitous that Chris was able to defuse the situation successfully and very quickly – otherwise ...

Yet another role for a member of the British Motor Racing Marshals' Club – even if perhaps not envisaged by its founding fathers.

One Marshal's Memories

by Ken Cowley

It seems an awful lot of years since I marshalled regularly with Ken Cowley at Silverstone and Donington. However, Ken was one of the first to reply when I asked for contributions to *50 Years of Marshalling*. Ken was also one of the very early members of the Marshals' Club and his memories, reproduced *verbatim* below cover some very important events and times for the Club.

Ken writes:

My interest in motor sport goes back to the late forties and early fifties while I was still at school. Motorcycles were my first love and with several scrambles courses within walking distance of my home, I was well catered for. There were also road races at Osmaston and Alton Towers, as well as reliability trials held by local clubs. The first motor race I attended was the British Grand Prix at Silverstone in 1952 when, if I recall correctly, Alberto Ascari won the race. After a three-year spell in the Royal Air Force, followed by a few years following motorcycle scrambling which was all the rage at the time, being televised on each Sunday afternoon during the winter months, I started spectating at a few car meetings at Mallory Park and Silverstone.

It was at a Sprint meeting at Mallory Park in late 1967, organised jointly by the MiniSeven Club and the British Motor Racing Marshals' Club, that I came into contact with two officials who suggested I might like to become a race marshal. Neither the possibility nor the appeal of this had occurred to me before but after some thought it wasn't long before my application for membership of the British Motor Racing Marshals' Club was in the post.

I soon became a member of the North Region of the Club and in March 1968 I attended my first training day at Silverstone, where I was introduced to Phil Morom and the Emergency Services Team. Little did I realise that the following weekend I would be on the bank at Maggotts for the Daily Express International Trophy Race for Formula 1 cars. I don't remember who I spent the day with on that occasion but I do remember Denny Hulme spun his McLaren in front of us. This was the first of many hundreds of incidents I was to witness or get involved with over the next twenty or so years.

The Silverstone Emergency Services Team, manned by members of BMRMC, was formed to provide an efficient fire fighting and incident handling team at a time when the sport was beset with a number of serious fiery incidents. The object was to provide this service at all Silverstone events, great and small. In the early days, about fifteen of us would assemble by the guardroom near the main entrance to the circuit, at the crack of dawn, to be allocated our position for the day. We usually worked in pairs, one wearing the fire entry suit and the other one handling the fire extinguisher. Some members drove the circuit ambulances and later the Land Rover fire tenders.

I remember marshalling a Dunlop Tyre Testing day on the Wednesday before the 1969 Grand Prix. There were only about half a dozen of us that day, so we had a corner each. I drew Becketts and was given a set of flags, two fire extinguishers, a bucket of cement, a brush, a shovel and a fire blanket. Which do I pick up first, I thought! However, I managed to find a piece of pipe which I fixed in the bank at a suitable angle, to enable me to display the yellow flag should I be called upon to leg it towards Chapel with an extinguisher! Luckily, apart from a few twitchy moments, the day was uneventful. I did, however, have the good fortune to see the Cosworth four-wheel drive car turn a wheel.

One unusual event I recall was the Guild of Motoring Writers' Test Day. This is where journalists get to drive the latest models prior to the Motor Show. It was one of those occasions where, as the day wore on and the stock of spirits in the bar became more and more depleted, the squeal of tyres out on the circuit become more and more pronounced! I remember seeing two well known scribes wearing deerstalker hats thundering through Copse in a Morgan Plus Eight, sideways. Anxious moments for a novice marshal!

I was to learn a lot in the early days and at Oulton Park I did various jobs, including pits, start line while my activities with the Silverstone ES Team occupied a large slice of my spare time. To arrive at Silverstone for 07.30 hrs I had to leave my Derbyshire home before 5.00 a.m. and very often did not return until about 8.30 in the evening. Travelling by road was enjoyable in those days, with little traffic about in the early hours. However, the going was rather slow in an Austin 1100 and the M1 had not been completed, coming only as far as Crick. It was not unusual to visit Aintree, Silverstone and do an Autocross meeting all in the same Bank Holiday weekend. Travelling was not quite so expensive in those days, with change from £1 for four gallons of petrol and travel for the whole weekend could be less than £3.

In 1969 I had marshalled in the pits for the RAC Tourist Trophy race for sports cars and whilst I thoroughly enjoyed this aspect of the sport, I always preferred to be out on the circuit where the real action is. As a Track or Fire Marshal it was often necessary to work on the track. Jobs like treating an oil slick with cement dust or retrieving a discarded exhaust pipe (always while wearing strong leather gloves, of course!) were always carried out in complete confidence, relying upon cover from the Flag Marshals and the Observer on the bank with his Acme Thunderer (whistle!). Races were very rarely stopped in those days and the safety car had yet to be invented. Push starting a Vintage racing car off the start line was also a hazardous exercise but I quickly learned never to choose the exhaust side of the car!

Towards the end of 1969 I had my first opportunity to try my hand at Flag Marshalling. This job requires serous concentration and is one for the dedicated enthusiast, as knowledge of the cars and drivers is a definite help. In later years I was to enjoy the long distance endurance races for sports cars and the 750 Motor Club's Birkett Six-Hour Relay, as these were a Flag Marshals' dream, with a wide variety of cars and much overtaking. Ten-lap sprints, although often with action a plenty, rarely produced the same unexpected results.

I continued to marshal regularly at Oulton Park, Silverstone, Mallory and Cadwell Park, with the odd Autocross thrown in to ease the monotony. In 1972 I was invited by Gary Davis to join a party of several BMRMC members on a trip to the *Le Mans* 24-Hour race. The object of this mission was to signal during practice and race for Jo Bonnier's team of two Lola T280 cars sponsored by Swiss Cheese. This was an opportunity not to be missed and I jumped at the chance.

We were located in the pits at Mulsanne Corner with telephone contact with the Team Manager in the main pits. This was quite an interesting exercise but sadly ended badly. The first car retired about midnight, with brake failure, and the second one when Jo Bonnier left the road just before Indianapolis Corner and came to rest among the trees. It was a disastrous end to an exciting week. The race was won by Graham Hill and Henri Pescarolo in a Matra.

Early in 1973 the then Chairman of North Region of BMRMC, Alan Gayes, suggested I might like to take on the job of Newsletter Editor for the Region. (*That's how I got roped in as well, Ken! – G.C.*) After some thought I decided to have a go at this important job and soon found myself burning the midnight oil to get newsletters out to the region's ninety or so members each month. I was elected to the regional committee and enjoyed myself going to the meetings and club nights at Hale Barns, Burtonwood and Alsager.

However, by 1976, with this and all my marshalling it was beginning to get too much. Both my parents became seriously ill and clearly this was my main priority. Reluctantly, I resigned from the committee and gave up the position of Newsletter Editor. I had made many friends and contacts in the sport and gained an insight into what made things tick – and the tremendous amount of work put in by enthusiastic volunteers to allow meetings to run smoothly.

The 1973 Grand Prix is one everyone remembers, where Jody Scheckter ran wide on the outside of Woodcote, then spun back across the track skittling half the field. I was at Abbey that day and had to deal with another nasty accident where three drivers were injured in the morning's saloon car race. It was a very busy day for marshals and this is not unusual, especially when the weather is bad. I can recall many das when cars have skated off in the wet into the catch fencing or into the gravel traps all around the circuit.

I remember once having to sweep snow off the track at Lodge Corner at Oulton Park before practice for a Formula 5000 race could begin and I also seem to recall sweeping the track between Maggotts and Becketts at Silverstone before the last race of the day, when a sudden snow storm swept in. That night I battled through snow on the M1 and finally abandoned my car and walked the last mile home because the snow was over a foot deep by then. The days were long and sometimes hard in atrocious weather but always in high spirits with friendly colleagues; the effort was worthwhile for anyone interested in the sport.

In 1976 I made my one and only trip to Brands Hatch for the GP and travelled on the Thursday evening with the intention of camping until Monday. At about midnight we had an almighty thunderstorm and the campsite in the paddock was awash. We did not get much sleep that night but thankfully the following day was very hot, so things soon dried out.

At the 1975 British Grand Prix at Silverstone I was the Incident Officer on the outside of Woodcote corner, adjacent to the starting grid. This was a position I was to occupy on many occasions during the next few years and the experience of being so close to the start of a big race really has to be experienced to be properly appreciated. However, spectating it is not! Being a marshal means you are there to help ensure that the meeting runs safely and efficiently.

Donington circuit reopened in 1977 and being less than twenty miles from my home meant I would be spending many hours at this track in the future. The increasing number of circuits and race meetings was making increased demands for experienced marshals and although the membership of the Marshals' Club had increased dramatically during the seventies, the demand always seemed to be greater than the supply. For my part, I concentrated on Silverstone and Donington, with the occasional visit to Mallory Park, but I sadly I had to give Oulton Park a miss.

About this time, I transferred my membership to the Midland Region of BMRMC, to keep abreast of what was happening in the region and so that I could support the functions at Donington, which had become very much my local circuit. In 1978, the USAC Indy Cars came to the UK for races at Brands Hatch and Silverstone. I marshalled the two days scheduled for this event at Silverstone as Incident Officer at Woodcote. Alas, the weather was not co-operative and rain prevented the race from taking place until the following day when I was committed to a race meeting at Donington.

At this meeting, marshals were invited to drive their road cars around the circuit to help with drying the track. Jackie Stewart was out as well, showing various VIP's the circuit. He was driving at fairly sedate pace and many marshals took the opportunity to overtake – to boast forever afterwards about "overtaking Jackie Stewart into Copse, Stowe, Woodcote or whatever "!! – G.C.

In 1983 I decided to curtail my activities further. The situation was not improving and I needed to spend more time at home. I had been marshalling for sixteen years with the Silverstone Emergency Services Team and I was not getting any younger! So, my future was to be at Donington with the occasional foray to Mallory Park. I spent most of my time flag marshalling at all types of meeting, including truck racing which became popular during the eighties. I did as many meetings as I could fit in until 1989.

In the early eighties, I had been having some problems with my eyesight but this had always been corrected with the aid of glasses. However, at a meeting at Donington in early 1989, I realised something was seriously wrong. The consultant I saw told me I was suffering from Macular Degeneration (loss of central vision). The situation would get worse and there was no known cure. I realised I had no choice but to throw in the towel; my marshalling days were over.

I had been a regular marshal for over twenty years and spent over 500 days trackside. I know this is by no means a record but I had enjoyed every minute of it – the speed, the noise, the excitement, even the weather and the long days. I had seen the introduction of wings on the cars, the four-wheel drive and the turbo era and had witnessed some epic drives, by both the stars and club drivers. I had marshalled at car, motorcycle, truck and kart races and had assisted at Sprint, Autocross, Drag and driving test meetings, as well as races.

Over the years I have seen many changes. Earth banks and ditches which used to surround the circuits have been replaced by crash barriers, Armco and tyre walls. Rows of catch fencing appeared on corners but were later replaced by gravel traps and wider run-off areas. Corners have been reprofiled; chicanes introduced and in some cases track layouts have been changed considerably. Flag signals have changed and the safety car has become an important element of the race. The cars are more sophisticated and cornering speeds have increased enormously. The emphasis of all these changes has been to improve safety for spectators, drivers and marshals.

I have made many friends around the circuits and, in their company, enjoyed many anxious and exciting moments. The Howmet TX and Lotus gas turbine cars and the Cosworth Four-Wheel Drive car all appeared at meetings where I was marshalling and I shall never forget the wonderful sound of the Matra V12 Formula 1 car.

The Marshals' Club has served me well.

Now, apart from the occasional outing in my brother's V-Twin JAP-engined Morgan three-wheeler to a VSCC Sprint at Curborough or local club runs and an occasional visit to the Donington Museum, I am a true armchair enthusiast – but, of course, I have my memories.

Author's note:

Ken, thanks for sharing your memories with us. Our marshalling experience covered just about the same period. Thankfully, I still have my sight but spending half the year abroad, as I now do, cuts into my marshalling time. Like you, I don't get around much any more on the marshalling scene but, also like you, I have so many good memories, especially of those early days, when the camaraderie between drivers and marshals was much better and we could mix with the best of them, even at big meetings like the Grand Prix, etc. One of June's Doghouse ladies, a Formula One wife, who remembers those early days too, said to us recently that she believes we had the best of motor racing then!

Another Marshal's Memories

by Chris Hobson

Hello to the BMRMC

It was 1968 and I had recently moved up to Leeds. I saw an advert for the Leeds Motor Show and decided to pay a visit. There, among the new cars and commercial stands was a caravan, with a pile of straw bales and a mannequin holding a yellow flag. "Interested in Motorsport? Come and talk to us" read the banner. I was, so I did. Over half an hour later, after listening to Les Bentley and Paul Marsh espouse the virtues of the club, I emerged from the caravan, having paid my membership fee to the British Motor Racing Marshals Club, and having volunteered for my first meeting – the world record speed event at Elvington airfield.

I arrived at Elvington very early – in fact Kathryn (my fiancée at that time) and I were the first marshals there, so we sat in our mini and waited. Eventually along came more marshals who introduced themselves – a very friendly bunch and I was sent by the Clerk of the Course, Garth Nicols (then regional chairman) to sit in my car, with a field telephone three quarters of the way down the runway with the briefing "Watch the cars and report anything that you think is wrong".

Time passed, cars thundered down the runway and Kathryn and I enjoyed ourselves. Then I spotted some people on the far side of the runway in a prohibited area. Cranking the handle on the field telephone I reported them to Garth. "Get the b****s out of there then" was the reply. Kath got out of the car, and, after asking permission to cross the runway I set off in the mini. Halfway across the runway I looked to my left – to see a 1908 Metalurgique (24 litres, 2 tons, 104mph and cable brakes on the rear wheels only) hurtling down towards me. We passed within five feet of each other. I stopped, threw up, chased off the spectators then returned to race control a quivering wreck.

Suitably consoled by Paul Marsh, with an apology from Garth, I returned to my marshalling duties. Thirty-nine years later I am still marshalling, I am happy to say. Older, wiser, and rather less prone to leap into action before summing up the full situation – but still as much in love with motorsport as in 1968.

Lord of the Flies

The first few meetings of any new season at Silverstone were blighted for Observers who found the enclosed Observers' boxes at Copse, Becketts and Stowe alive with blue bottle flies crawling out of the woodwork, after a winter's hibernation. As we entered the boxes for the first time, a few would crawl out from around the windows where they had been hibernating. Then a few more, then even more, until the place was literally crawling with half asleep blue bottles. It only took a bit of sunshine and leaving the door open for a bit of fresh air for the damn things to start flying around the box. By lunchtime we often had to vacate the box, as these half-dopy blue bottles dive-bombed us and anything we tried to eat.

On one occasion, when the two cans of fly spray we always tried to bring with us had run out, we rang Race Control for some help from circuit staff. Sadly, we found a particularly bumptious Clerk who told us, basically, to stop bothering him, he had too much else to do. Next time the Course Car appeared, my fellow Observer, Bob Sketchley, presented the Deputy Clerk of the Course with a paper parcel of flies he had gathered up, with the message, "If the Clerk is too busy to come to the flies, here are some to take to him!"

Very soon afterwards, Silverstone stalwart, Les Dickens, appeared with a selection of fly sprays, with which he very quickly dealt with our problem. Thereafter, Les made sure the boxes were thoroughly sprayed before the opening meeting.

The Early Days of BMRMC

by Tony Hodgetts

In the summer of 1957, while I was still working my way through National Service in the RAF, I noticed a very handsome badge on the front of Alfred Galuszka's Bugatti when preparing to set off on a treasure hunt one fine evening. This turned out to be the emblem of a newly formed club for marshals, of which Alfred was a founder member. As this was what I wanted to do when my time was once again my own, I made further enquiries and Alfred undertook to get me an application form and to propose me for membership. The 'pink and white' soon arrived, and I returned them at once – address "Officers' Mess, RAF Rufforth"; experience "very minor, plenty of spectating at all sorts of events, but very keen to learn". The forms came back with a letter explaining that the club was for experienced marshals, and they were "not accepting novices for training – please apply again when you have more experience".

In October '57 my National Service was completed and I was free to get on with life. I had joined the BARC at the same time as I had applied to BMRMC, and through the winter I began competing in road rallies, and marshalled on our part of the 1958 RAC Rally (held in those days in February), until the racing season started at Easter. My first serious race meeting was at Full Sutton, and as my rally navigator was already an experienced Flag Marshal, I was put with him to learn the trade. There were very few of us in those days, and a post with two marshals was well manned! So I found myself under instruction with a yellow flag and a job to do. Being thrown in at the deep end made me work to learn, and I went to as many events as possible, willing to do any job that brought me experience. If I went to a BRSCC race meeting at Full Sutton I would be flagging, if I went to Oulton Park I would probably be a Spectator Marshal, I acted as a Clerk of the Course on a couple of road rallies, as a Paddock Marshal at Catterick, and in between was competing in rallies, autocross, sprints and driving tests, and acting as a mechanic for an F3 team with a Cooper 500cc racing car. At that time there was no system of grading the ability of volunteers; if the organisers knew you, you would be in a responsible position, if they did not you would probably be patrolling a stretch of rope to stop spectators sitting at the side of the track with their feet on the tarmac at the exit of Old Hall. Don't think I am joking, I've had it to do, and they were often unwilling to move!

At the end of the season, I filled in the application forms once again and submitted them, with more than forty events for approval, and I was accepted into the BMRMC. Innocently, I put on the form that I could type and was willing to do a bit of secretarial work if required; in a matter of days I was approached by Jim Kennard, the Northern Region secretary, to see if I would take on the task of recruiting and organising a team of marshals for the area, and after a bit of deliberation the 'North Eastern Splinter Group' came into being as an offshoot of the Northern Region. There was a very small number of existing members in the area, so to begin with I began recruiting Airedale and Pennine MC members, with whom I was spending a lot of competing and social time. I quickly gathered about twenty new members who, like me, were willing to go almost anywhere and do almost anything, and we began to get the Marshals' Club known to anyone who needed staffing for a motor sport event. John de Lacy Taylor, Ron Hudson and Brian Derbyshire formed the nucleus of the committee, and the basis of a team who were rapidly learning the necessary skills as I had done in the previous season. We were much indebted to Peter Alcock of the BRSCC Northern Centre, who needed marshals for race meetings and gave our volunteers the chance to learn their skills and get 'field promotion' to fill gaps, which brought them added responsibility at a speed that would not be approved of in 2005.

We went to Full Sutton, Rufforth, Linton on Ouse, and occasionally to Silverstone (for the MMEC's midsummer meeting). We stood out all night on road rallies, and manned a control on the 1959 RAC Rally.

We timed driving tests, scrambled up banks on trials, both sporting and production, ran paddocks, swept tracks, and even staffed the Rufforth test for the Lorry-Driver of the Year competition.

Dr. Lewis Jamieson recruited several members for events further north, Garth Nicholls moved from Northern Region on a change of job, and landed straight into the committee without a noticeable pause, Harry Tinkler came in via Croft, and Alwyn Pritchard and John Ison joined to do rallies and soon found themselves doing everything else. We staffed a very early Kart meeting at Bradford Greyhound Stadium, which produced hazards that definitely would not be acceptable in 2005 (dog poo makes the run-off areas very slippery as well as smelly), and recruited the Clerk of the Course, Brian Pearson. David Easthope did every conceivable event, and on a couple of occasions two at once, though he gave that trick up after being delayed by a Stewards' enquiry at Oulton Park and only got to his time control in Kirby Malzeard two minutes before the first competitor arrived. Gordon Heighway joined from the A & P, bringing in a batch of new enthusiasts from Huddersfield, including Peter Newby, Ronnie Varley (who later became a successful rally navigator with George Hill), Henry Crowther (who later raced Jaguars in Classic events) and a young David Gledhill. John Taylor recruited a round dozen Bingley Young Conservatives of both sexes in one evening, which livened up the club nights quite considerably.

By this time the Council decided that we were big enough to be a Region in our own right, we were elevated in status, and I was appointed first Chairman and invited to attend a Council meeting in Solihull. John Ashton was in the chair, Vic Bond was secretary, and the council included Keith Douglas, Alan Atkinson, John Holmes, and Brian Fox. John Ashton was quiet, courteous and intelligent, a very good C.O. and a very charming man. Keith and Brian in particular were very helpful to the 'new boy'. That first meeting was very interesting, as the council was deep in the preparation of the first edition of 'How to run a Race Meeting', and masses of contributed data was arriving. I remember Vic holding up a huge wad of paper and asking if anyone knew the author, Dr. Lewis Jamieson. I knew Lewis, and gave a brief outline of all the things that he did, whereupon Vic said that he'd read through the submission, and had been staggered by the amount of detail – "He even tells us the size of envelope the Post Office prefers!" Lewis's contribution went straight in to the approved draft. I later met the club's President, Raymond Baxter, who was a pleasure to meet, and just as erudite and urbane as he appeared on television.

One matter that was exercising the minds of the council at that time was the creation of the marshals' insurance scheme. Sadly in July 1961, I was much involved in the first serious claim, when Cliff Shaw from our region was killed at Linton on Ouse. As the Observer on the post I had to attend the inquest, and afterwards Garth and I discussed ways in which we could improve safety, and agreed that if Flag Marshals stood face-to-face, rather than back-to-back as was the current practice, the reaction to an impending accident would be safer and more rapid. I had quite strong views on this, as at my very first race meeting as a Flag Marshal I had a narrow escape when my partner fled from an approaching spinning Porsche (Jim Clark) and forgot to warn me, and I only realised how close he had been when John apologised from his position of safety and I turned to see the tracks in the snow (yes, Full Sutton 1958 had snow!) finishing a yard from my back. We made a proposition, which was discussed for a while, and eventually, thanks to some powerful persuasion from Garth, the rule was changed.

In 1962, with the demands of an increasing family requiring attention, I handed the Chairmanship of the North-Eastern Region over to Garth, whose energy and communication skills had much to do with the development of the region and the club as a whole, as he went on to hold national office.

Looking back, when the BMRMC started, marshalling was parochial. If you went to help at a circuit where you were not known, you would be doing something menial until the organisers got to know you, which could take some time if they only ran one race per annum, and Fred Bloggs had always been the Flag Marshal on post X even though he was colour blind and short-sighted. I know that one particular Chief Marshal regarded our list of volunteers with details of their skills as a gift from heaven! Before long, we were able to offer assistance at circuits where we were not known, but our qualifications were. We trained all our members, both for the job they were doing now and the jobs they might be expected to do – above and below their current level, and knew that whatever they were given to do they would not let us or the organisers down.

In the fifties, safety was a matter of personal concern, and you were present 'at your own risk'. If you were a Flag Marshal, you had a straw bale, which was more to tell you where to stand than a means of protection. If you flagged at Cascades at Oulton Park, your first job on arrival at the post was to clear out the hole into which you would dive if a car spun towards you! I've had a Mini-Cooper across my back as I dived for cover. If there was oil on the course, you grabbed your bag and dashed out. If you'd been trained, you applied the cement facing the oncoming cars (no, not everyone thought that was obvious), and if you were lucky your Observer had a whistle to warn you of oncoming competitors. If, that is, you had an Observer. I've run a post all alone with a set of flags, a telephone, a pad, a fire extinguisher, and a broom and cement. At most circuits the spectators were a few yards from the track, behind a rope slung on stakes 'pommed' into the ground, relying on the good old British trait of doing what you were told by the person in charge – which did not always work. Fire extinguishers were untested, and medical attendance would be the local St. John's Ambulance. As far as marshals were concerned, you lived on your wits and your ability to run when you saw trouble approaching!

Of course, it wasn't all downside, and in any case (we, most of whom had lived through a war and were accustomed to doing what we were told) did not really regard the hazards as a burden. There were definitely compensations, particularly the fact that we were going motor racing from the inside, without having the money to actually do it. In the fifties, it wasn't sponsor's money, it had to be real hard earned cash, so the difference mattered. We were getting a close-up of the action, and working with our heroes close up. And our heroes were, in many cases friendly and approachable, appreciating our efforts. I wonder whether young Mr. Turner remembers four of us lifting up a DKW in the woods near Ingleton while two others changed its front wheel on the 1959 RAC Rally – he was certainly very happy at the time! Jim Clark was always friendly and approachable, Innes Ireland would stop after the flag and call his thanks for a good bit of flagging, and Graham Hill always had a friendly word for a Flag Marshal stumping back through the paddock in the rain. After the 1958 British Grand Prix, I hauled the equipment for our 500cc race into our allocated pit and found it had been Ferrari's for the GP, and there, sitting chatting on the counter were Mike Hawthorn and Peter Collins. Pete had just won the GP, and yet they stayed and chatted to us for twenty minutes, until our race started and they ambled off for a beer, bidding us good luck. I've mentioned three World Champions there; I don't think the current holder is in the same mould, nor some of his predecessors.

How to Become a Marshal

My introduction to marshalling was probably similar to many, starting with initial interest as a 12/13 year old, cycling to the airport that adjoined Turnberry Golf Course in Scotland to see amateur racing there. I seem to remember about two race meetings there and then no more.

It was not until I came to London in 1958 to join the Metropolitan Police that I went motor racing again. I was stationed at Scotland Yard (when it was still by the Thames) and there met June, who was to become my wife. She had attended the inaugural British Grand Prix as an infant and her family were avid racegoers. Many a weekend thereafter we got up at some unseemly hour to be at the starting gate at Goodwood or Silverstone, to join the rush to get as near the ropes as we could at our chosen corner, Woodcote at Goodwood, Club at Silverstone. In the early days we used to be able to drive our cars right up to the ropes at Club.

Married in 1962, we settled in Towcester – which gave all our friends from the London area a staging post when heading for Silverstone. We were regular attendees at Silverstone until our children came along. Once, with June quite obviously pregnant, we hitch-hiked into Silverstone for one British Grand Prix when our bus from Northampton got tied up in the miles of traffic heading for Silverstone. Our son now reckons he attended his first Grand Prix at the age of minus three months!

A new job took us to Salisbury in 1966 and Thruxton became our nearest circuit. However, we chose to buy a house in a village surrounded by motor racing people. Our next door neighbour, Martin Goodall, was head technical honcho at Downton Engineering, who turned my Morris 1100cc into a fairly swift 1300cc, with oil and petrol consumption to match! Our children were taught by Mini-ace Richard Longman's Mum. Abbott racing was nearby and there were four or five other racers in the immediate vicinity. With a tow-bar on my car, I was occasionally drafted in at the last minute, to tow a race car trailer to Thruxton, which was fine by us as it meant we got in free to watch some excellent motor racing. The Spring F2 meeting was the highlight of our year and if Jackie Stewart did not appear we supported Jochen Rindt instead.

Another career move brought us back to the Silverstone area in 1971/72 and now with a decent salary and company car to ease our motoring costs, plans to go racing myself were resurrected. June bought me a set of lessons at the Jim Russell Racing Drivers' School. While these showed me to be reasonably competent, it seemed that my plans to become the next Jackie Stewart might be hampered by a certain lack of talent! We certainly lacked the cash and, just as June and I had "more or less agreed" to buy a racing Escort, educating our two children became an issue; education won!

So, I became a marshal! I jumped over the fence at one Bank Holiday meeting at Silverstone to ask the Flag Marshals how they got their jobs. I was advised to call in at the Marshals' Club hut behind the Woodcote grandstands and speak to Phil Morom. Those of you who remember Phil will know that was it, my fate was sealed! Phil was such an enthusiast for all things marshalling and put across the joys of being a marshal so well, that I signed up straight away.

I was assigned to South Mids region under the tender care of then Chairman Pat Todd and spent much of my time being trained by that other Phil, Phil Huffer. After the first social event I attended, Pat Todd had me as Newsletter Editor!

Gary Davis took over as Chairman a couple of years later and it was he, in conjunction with then President, Jack Lambert, who first proposed what was to become the Marshals' Club Training and Grading Scheme. As first proposed, I was not an avid supporter; I thought it was far too rigid a scheme to impose upon volunteers. In part, my fears were justified and the Scheme eventually introduced, under the tutelage of Dave Scott, was a bit more 'marshal-friendly' and became probably the best recruiting tool the Club ever had. Marshals wanted to be trained and many joined our Club solely for the training we offered. There was, though, still a degree of unnecessary rigidity which John Felix (Midlands Chairman) and I tried to change but it was several years on before further softening occurred. (There is a separate chapter on training that comments on our loss when our Training and Grading Scheme was nationalised.)

Gary's reign as Chairman did not last too long, as his job took him off to Italy. Everyone else took one pace smartly backwards and I found myself Chairman of South Mids. I have to say I found this a very interesting period in my marshalling career. South Mids was the biggest region at the time and, in many ways, the most innovative – or at least tried to be. In preparation for Council meetings I often spoke to Phil Morom, to seek his advice on matters where I lacked experience, enjoyed good support on most issues from Mike Blakey, as Silverstone Emergency Services Co-ordinator, and John Felix as Midlands Chairman. John and I, by that time, represented over 60% of total membership but getting agreement to our ideas was never easy. Never mind, many of the ideas came to pass at later dates and the two regions, South Midlands and Midlands, can claim credit for many of the innovations that took place at that time. I stood down as Chairman and member of Council to start my new business in 1978.

My disappearance from Council lasted less than two years! Ray Darvill, National PRO at the time, whose Milton Keynes Motor Racing Show contributed substantially to Club funds, asked me to explain to him where all this funding appeared to have gone from Club accounts. There was nothing sinister to report; only that we had been caught out big time on Personal Accident Insurance cover for marshals. We had been caught out by that old insurance adage, "you are comprehensively insured until you actually claim"!! No one was to blame within the Club but the truth was we were technically insolvent. I agreed to help out for no more than eighteen months – and here I sit almost thirty years later still nagging everyone to be careful with Club cash!!

Amidst all this, we managed to spend many weekends marshalling. Friday night was often hitch up night; on went the caravan to the back of the car and off we headed for Snetterton, Oulton or even to 'old' Croft just before it closed. For bigger meetings at Silverstone and Brands Hatch, the marshals' caravan site was the place to be. Our kids all played together, the men stood around, very often with a beer in hand, sorting out the problems in the world of motor sport and the ladies gossiped!

In those early days, we were able to wander through the pits in the evenings, even for F1 and other major meetings. We would chat to the mechanics and to drivers who often stayed on as company for the mechanics who seemed to work all the hours god sent on occasion. It was a great atmosphere, sadly missed now as the creep of greater commercialism in Motorsport created divisions that were never there before and, frankly, seemed to cause no difficulty at the time!

I officiated at twenty-seven British Grands Prix, before people like me who had become Clerks, were discouraged from backtracking to Observer for the Grand Prix meetings. I resented this at the time but GP meetings were several times over-subscribed at that time and some way had to be found to limit numbers. The change also allowed some newer marshals in and that can only be a good thing for the longer term.

During this period, too, I was quite flattered to be one of six Observers to be appointed Safety Observer for the British Grand Prix, following the hullabaloo that followed James Hunt's win then disqualification at Brands Hatch in 1976.

Although I am rarely on the bank these days, trackside marshalling has not changed a great deal. We still moan about poor facilities on circuit – but we keep turning up for race meetings, albeit in reduced numbers! We turn out in all weathers and it often seems as if the worse the weather the greater the humour on post! Marshals' humour is a bit cryptic, at best, but when it rains the humour becomes ever more 'dry'!

The European Grand Prix at Donington, where we saw that magnificent first lap by Ayrton Senna, was perhaps my wettest marshalling weekend ever. I would strip to the skin in the caravan awning each night (you do not have to imagine the sight), change into dry clothes and hope that my wet weather gear would be dry enough to put on next morning. The caravan sunk about six inches into the mud over the weekend and we got away on the day after the Grand Prix thanks only to Steve Angel who borrowed one of the snatch tractors to tow us all out of the mud onto the road. Nevertheless, my main memories of that weekend were that truly stupendous first lap by Ayrton Senna and the humour on post all weekend as we coped with the weather. That's marshalling!

The detail of how I became a marshal may differ but I know that many others came to marshalling by pretty well the same route. It starts with an interest in the sport, often the realisation that talent or cash prohibits becoming a competitor and then, usually, a meeting with someone who is a marshal, who extols the virtues of this fine profession! Thereafter, it is down to the people we meet, in my view. Marshals come from such a wide cross section of the community, it is virtually impossible not to find a group of people you can get on with. There are some very, very talented people in marshalling, something I think many 'in authority' fail to recognise.

Personally, I have had a brilliant time as a marshal and while I now do mainly Clerking, I still think of myself as a marshal. I have met some wonderful people, made firm friends of many and have much to be grateful for to the Marshals' Club. Although I have belonged to other Clubs from time to time, the Marshals' Club has been my principal interest. The Club has provided me with some super opportunities to marshal abroad, gave me welcome relief at weekends when my fledgling manufacturing business was not going so well and even now, I spend a great deal of my time on Marshals' Club business. I do not find this any hardship, merely repayment for the enjoyment both June and I have had over thirty five years as members of the best Club in motorsport.

I did manage to get some racing in, too, with the Silverstone Racing School and Jim Russell. I did reasonably well with both and the bug *almost* bit! By the time I started to race regularly – at 45 years of age, the same age film star Paul Newman got started – I had the money but not the time. BlowMocan, my company, was growing like a weed and demanded an awful lot of my time. When, eight years later we sold BlowMocan, I had both the money and the time. By then, maturity was clearly settling in, however much delayed this was, and I felt disinclined to spend the money I had worked so hard to earn on anything so frivolous and incredibly expensive as motor racing! So, back to being a marshal!!

Motor Racing Hierarchy

Motor racing's chain of command, its hierarchy, derives directly from horse racing; hence Race Stewards, Clerk of the Course, etc. In the early days, even the bowler hats worn by the horse racing officials filtered through to motor racing – as seen again, more recently, at the Goodwood Revival Meeting in September each year.

Inevitably, this meant, too, that many of the top positions of authority in motor racing went to the local landed gentry. One of our members reports from an early Silverstone meeting that the flag marshals' roll included one Viscount, one Earl, two Lords, one full colonel, one major, one captain from the military and several drivers of note, who were between race engagements. Elsewhere in the organisation was another Earl, one Marquis and several Honourables! The Scrutineering team boasted no less than four army majors and a wing commander; heady stuff, indeed!

This pattern continued into the early 1950's and a few drivers would go marshalling if not racing – including the late, great Duncan Hamilton, who when officiating would appear with a hamper of exquisite food and 'fortified' liquid refreshment! A few of our early marshals recall enjoying a friendly tipple with Duncan at the trackside while the race went on. Indeed, when I started marshalling in the early 1970's there was one start line crew who looked after the inner man with portable barbecue and a 'sufficiency' of red wine! Another Doctor at Oulton who chose to go out on the circuit could always be relied upon for a nicely chilled gin and tonic, once 11.00 hrs came!

As motor racing grew, however, I don't suppose there were enough Viscounts, Earls and Lords to go around and more ordinary people became involved! There was, initially, still an element of who you know rather than what you knew about marshalling and, of course, there was no training. If you knew roughly which end of the flag to hold and didn't mind standing on a straw bale while two-ton cars whizzed by your feet you became a Flag Marshal. If you looked strong enough to handle a fire extinguisher or pull a fire cart, you became a Fire Marshal.

As motor racing became more professional, this did not quite cut the mustard and largely, this is what led Jack Bannister, John Ashton, Keith Douglas and their merry bunch of men to set up the British Motor Racing Marshals' Club in 1957. The aim was quite simply to better organise and train those marshals who were already there and to attract a good few more to the ranks, to meet the demands of an ever-growing race meeting calendar. This was an almost immediate success, despite misgivings from some at the RAC and the odd circuit owner that the Marshals' Club would become some sort of trade union for marshals. This never became the case and many of those who harboured doubts became firm supporters of the Club

More professionalism, still from a strictly volunteer force, came with the formation of the Emergency Services Team at Silverstone in 1967. This was the brainchild of Phil Morom, aided and abetted by his great friend Jimmy Brown. Together they pursued the idea of a highly trained team of fire and incident marshals, more or less dedicated to Silverstone events. Again, there were those 'in authority' who had doubts and Phil's teachings of how to space marshals and fire extinguishers around the circuit were somewhat at odds with teaching from professional equipment suppliers at the time. Silverstone decided to stick with Phil Morom's pattern and I have no doubt many drivers have reason to be grateful for this decision. Sadly, neither method works all that well today, through lack of marshals on the bank and we need another Phil Morom to come along to show us how best to cope with this new set of circumstances.

Similar BMRMC ES Teams appeared at Donington and Cadwell Park (all still running successfully) and in mildly modified forms at other circuits where the BMRMC influence was not so well established. Watching these teams in training and in action on the circuit, as an

Observer or Clerk, I believe they have played a very major part in the increased safety of competitors around our circuits. Their very prompt, initial response has surely saved innumerable lives since 1967.

The hierarchy changed, too. Silverstone, in the shape of the already oft-times mentioned Jimmy Brown, gave the Marshals' Club its own race day each year at the circuit, totally free of charge. This was something Jimmy and Keith Douglas put together, to allow our members – trained marshals – the opportunity to learn and practise Senior Official and Clerking duties. The result is that the vast majority of Senior Clerks and Race Directors in the UK now come from a marshalling background. This has been a major change from 'who you know' to 'what you know' and is reflected well in a UK judicial system that ranks amongst the best in the World. MSA Clerks' and Stewards' seminars have become ever more professional and in most classes of racing in the UK now, the Clerks' decision on judicial matters is pretty well accepted as fair and reasonable. Appeals to MSA Tribunals from motor race events are now few and far between.

Personally, I am not so sure that the present pattern of appointing separate Clerks for individual race series makes best use of the number of officials we have. I have been part of this and have operated as Series Clerk for overseas rounds but I am unconvinced that every series needs its own Clerk. At many major meetings there can be as many as eight or ten Clerks or Deputy Clerks – and not enough Observers to man all posts on the circuit!

I have queried this with all the organising clubs and they say the practice better guarantees consistency of judgement at all rounds of whatever series or championship is involved. Is this always true, I wonder, or could there be a corresponding tendency for favouritism and/or prejudice to creep in with the same Clerk always appointed to sit in judgement? As Sir Terry Wogan might say, "Is it me?" Maybe I am the only one out of step but it still seems to me to be an unnecessarily expensive use of the Clerking resource, when everyone should be trying to keep costs to a minimum if we are not to make the sport too expensive for the competitors who inevitably foot the bill.

In my early days of Clerking with John Felix at HSCC, we covered the continuity/consistency aspect with a simple alphabetically indexed book, in which we recorded any warnings or 'advice' given to drivers over the season. Steve Lydon, then Competitions Manager for HSCC, kept each book going for several seasons and this proved invaluable when dealing with future indiscretions.

It also meant we took one Clerk and one or two Deputies to all meetings, however many separate series or championships were being run. It also considerably reduced the cost of the meeting and is still the procedure adopted by most of the smaller organising clubs today – who often spend the money they save on better benefits for the marshals!

All that said, my limited experience of Clerking abroad and now seeing how the system works in the USA, leaves me with the very distinct impression that, overall, we do things rather well in the UK. As already mentioned, the MSA training sessions for Clerks and Stewards are invaluable and still not all that common in other countries. Since the change to having the Clerk as the first line of disciplinary action, the UK judicial system works well. The current hierarchal structure seems about right and the MSA judicial system is probably the fairest in the world – due no doubt to the number of lawyers in 'high places' within Motors Sports House!

Consideration and Respect

Just as Health and Safety ('Elf 'n' Safety!) have become the two most feared words in industry, consideration and respect became the two most common words in the Marshals' dictionary, when talking of why they do what the do. Consideration and respect is all that marshals have ever wanted in return for their services.

By and large, this was always available in big dollops from competitors, especially those who had been taken ever so carefully from wrecked cars by the 'Angels in Orange' – or, of course, the 'Angels in Black' at Silverstone. *(Author's Note: Silverstone Emergency Services Team selection of stylish black overalls came in for criticism when introduced but I cannot imagine any of the drivers they rescued complained!)* Consideration and respect was always there from the organising clubs, the smaller ones especially, who always treated their marshals as part of the family. It was readily available, too, from the major circuit owners of the day, Jimmy Brown at Silverstone and John and Angela Webb at Brands Hatch Circuits.

In the days of Jimmy Brown and the Webbs, they were always approachable. More important, they *ruled* their domains and if your case was well made, things happened. For instance, marshals who wanted to camp out for major weekend meetings, camped with spectators. All very fine but spectators often wanted to party into the early hours. Marshals needed to be on duty as dawn broke. The two did not mix very well. A quick word with Jimmy and marshals were inside the circuit at Silverstone. The MSA Race Committee undertook to arrange the same at Brands Hatch. When that failed, a quick phone call to Angela Webb and we were in there, too!

Sadly, marshals in recent years have had to exit their circuit camp sites. At Silverstone this happened during Octagon's rule, aided we are told by an edict from the GP organising body to get those scruffy caravans out of sight. This included BRDC members' and their caravans too, who had to move to a partly hidden site behind the farm.

Marshals understand and appreciate the economies of motorsport. They see that if space within the circuit is at a premium and the circuit owner can rent land previously used for marshals' camping, marshals' camping might become a casualty. However, what happens to consideration in these circumstances? What recognition is there for the fact that marshals contribute some £2,500,000 to motorsport each season in free labour?

To put that figure into perspective, the marshals' contribution represents around one third of the MSA's annual operating budget, i.e. the money the MSA raises from those who pay to participate in motorsport. It is calculated at minimum working wage; many marshals earn many times that rate! It makes marshals the single biggest contributor to motorsport in the UK. Yet still, to many in the sport, marshals are seen as a necessary (or even unnecessary!) evil!

Following the nearest thing there has ever been to a mass walk out at the British GP in 2001 over a withdrawn camp site, camping facilities were restored at Silverstone. The facility is still outside the main circuit but there is what seems to be a very functional sub-committee of circuit and marshal members who have steadily improved the facilities provided for marshals.

However good this sounds, it is still true that facilities provided for marshals steadily deteriorated over several years, almost in inverse proportion to the amount of 'big money' coming into the sport at that time.

The Blue Book lays down certain minimum standards for marshalling facilities on circuit. Somewhere for observers to write reports, in the dry, and for marshals' spare clothing to be stored, again in the dry. Until recently, very few circuits in the UK met all the required standards and there are still some where almost none of the required facilities exist. Yet circuit licences are still issued!

None of this is new. Our own, Marshals' Club newsletters of 1963 and 1965 asked why it was that there were still many *unsafe* marshals' posts around, yet track licences were still issued.

When the Grand Prix Drivers' Association started to take a closer interest in circuit safety in the late 1960's/early 1970's the Association, President Jackie Stewart in particular, was heavily criticised in certain sections of the Press. While doing a newsletter interview with Jackie Stewart in 1973, I asked if the GPDA could also look at the location and safety of marshals' posts when inspecting tracks. He immediately put me in touch with the newly appointed GPDA President, Denny Hulme.

When we met at Silverstone a little later, Denny explained that the GPDA came in to being, largely so that drivers could get the same sort of consideration that marshals now sought for themselves. Prior to the GPDA, drivers had to fight for entrance tickets for their families. One Formula One wife told us that the first covered transporter for Lotus was used to smuggle in wives and families to major race meetings! The ladies had to ensure that their colourful frocks did not show through the knot holes in the plywood sides! Denny assured us he would be including the location and safety of marshals' posts in all future circuit inspections. Clearly this would have limited effect in the UK, with only two circuits involved, but the very fact the GPDA was taking an interest helped our case.

What was to be done, you might ask? Keith Douglas issued a 'Green Paper' on motor sport in 1989. His committee of helpers was like an 'honour role' of all interested parties. The paper highlighted all the then current dilemmas with motorsport and made suggestions where future problems could be avoided and improvements made. The paper was well received in all quarters but in the years following there was little evidence of any real affirmative action on the points raised and suggestions made.

Keith tried again in 1998 with his *People in Motor Sport* paper, aided and abetted at various times by our own Chris Hobson and Dave Darley, both very skilled presenters. I was on the consultation committee for that paper and I was distinctly impressed at the level of networking Keith had put in with TV companies, industry bodies and the like, to obtain their commitment to support the ideas the PIMS paper propounded.

This paper, too, was received well on the face of things but many 'in authority' scoffed at its 'unachievable/undeliverable aspirations'. Again, rather than give PIMS a chance to prove its aspirations might well be deliverable, the paper was quietly filed away.

The Marshals' Club had another 'stab at it' with a paper first issued in September 2000, presented to the MSA, the circuit owners (AMRCO) and via the Association of British Motor Racing Clubs, to all organising clubs. This time there was some progress, helped in no small way by the arrival of Volunteers in Motorsport, a government-funded initiative on marshals' activities. The initial ViM questionnaire came up with the very same issues that had been a major part of the various BMMC papers.

The main issues identified were:

- Perceived lack of real consideration and respect for marshals at policy making level within the hierarchy of the sport

- Unrealistic timetables that pay scant regard to marshals' need for comfort and refreshment breaks

- Poorly supported races that persist despite Championship Control Panels

- Consistently poor trackside facilities for marshals, openly in breach of Blue Book guidelines, while circuit licences are continually renewed

- Reduced or no contribution to marshals' costs of attendance

- All of which leave the marshal feeling generally undervalued

When I started to write this book, in 2005/6, it would be true to say that progress on these issues was slow. Thankfully, the situation has improved steadily and measurably during 2007 and 2008. Many circuits have introduced or substantially improved marshals' track side shelters. Timetables have improved and the MSA only recently issued a note to all organising clubs, reminding them that marshals' time on post should be regulated and that proper relief breaks must be allowed for in all race day programmes. The qualification level of number of entrants for Championship events has increased twice in recent years. The average numbers per race have increased (according to records) but no one can guarantee the racing will always be interesting, especially the odd race which the competitors choose not to attend, something that drives us all mad at times!

There is the odd circuit which has done little or nothing to improve the marshal's lot, the odd race organiser who pays too little attention to the time marshals are on duty. It would be nice to name and shame but I would not want to risk being sued and getting the same judge who decided the Mosley case! However, the marshals know where these situations exist and with the cost of marshalling ever on the increase, marshals are becoming incredibly picky where they marshal. Said circuits, said organising clubs are now finding it increasingly difficult to find enough marshals to safely man meetings.

On the other hand, marshal attendance at other venues, where marshals' welfare is better considered, is on the up over the past two seasons. It is yet to be seen what effect there will be on marshalling numbers following the worldwide financial crisis that hit us all in Autumn 2008. On the American scene, the biggest player, NASCAR, has taken draconian action to try to stem the tide of team withdrawals, as sponsorship dries up and the three major car manufacturers in the USA bolt for cover of a government bail out. Some major club meetings have seen entries at little more than half what they were twelve months before.

Granted, the American financial scene tends to be more immediate than ours but it is hard to believe that the situation will not be somewhat similar here, as the full impact of the 2008 financial crisis is felt here, too. We will have to wait and see.

However, after a long period of inaction it is good to report some of the highlights of 2007 and 2008, where the marshalling scene has improved, thanks to ongoing support from the smaller organising clubs, new recognition by some circuit owners that marshalling facilities on-track can be improved for little or no extra cost if included in normal day-to-day maintenance schedules and improved recognition by all in the sport that marshals do matter!

Marshals' Club Funding

As long-time (Scottish!) Treasurer of the Marshals' Club, I am sure you would expect me to make some mention of how we have funded our activities over the years.

I was Chairman of South Midlands region for some years but resigned that position and left Council in 1977/78 to get my fledgling business off the ground. Less than two years later, Ray Darvill, our then PRO asked me to help him understand where the money he had raised for Club funds from his very successful Milton Keynes Motor Racing Show had gone to. He could not see it in the accounts and I offered to investigate. As often seems to happen in the Marshals' Club, pop your head above the parapet and you get a job to do! I was very quickly the new National Treasurer!

Ray's premonition was right. Club finances were in pretty poor shape, due principally to an unprecedented rise in Personal Accident Insurance costs and to the growing costs of the new Training and Grading Scheme. The Personal Accident insurance increase was totally unexpected, caught everyone by surprise but Tony Pernyes, the outgoing Treasurer, had already put a recovery plan in place.

However, the costs associated with marshals' training were escalating at a prodigious rate and were eating into Club resources. It was not proving easy to deal with and 'the authorities' were showing scant interest in our Training and Grading Scheme, let alone offer any help with funding. In fact, the recovery of training costs became one of the most frustrating aspects of Marshals' Club finances and – thanks to the intervention of a perverse VAT ruling – remains so today!

I have covered elsewhere the initiative that led to formation of a formal training and grading of marshals and how important and effective this proved to be; it was however proving costly. Some sponsorship had been obtained for some of the early publications but the Club itself had to bear the cost of training exercises, except for some help with facilities and extinguishers from regular Club benefactor, Jimmy Brown at Silverstone Circuits. I felt then – and now – that it simply was not right that marshals, who gave their time freely to the sport, should be expected to also finance their own training.

I contacted Keith Douglas, as I did so often over the years, and he arranged a hearing with the Motor Sports Training Trust, a charity operating within the RACMSA that had funds available for deserving causes. We were able to convince Derek Ongaro of the Trustees that marshals' training was just such a cause and we were awarded partial repayment of our costs.

That was fine, for a while. However, the Training and Grading Scheme quickly grew in popularity. The Scheme attracted new members to the Club and we soon found ourselves training marshals from other clubs as well. We were even entertaining visitors from other governing bodies in Europe, at the request of the RACMSA – but at our expense! All this was an additional cost that simply could not be met from Club funds and Keith arranged another approach to the Training Trust, who granted us further funds. We eventually persuaded the Trust to refund all our training costs, other than our own admin costs which, as you might imagine, was a great help to our finances overall. Unfortunately, it was taking up to two years for the refunds to arrive with us and our cash flow suffered. So, yet another presentation, via the Race Committee, and thanks to the support from the circuit owners (Hamish Brown of Silverstone and Nicola Foulston from Brands Hatch) we were soon being paid much more promptly. We were doing well!

Several clubs had by now adopted somewhat similar training and grading schemes, often run by Marshals' Club trainers and instructors. The MSA then decided they wanted a National Training and Grading Scheme and – with some reservations on the effects – we 'gifted' them our scheme. Indeed, Dave Pierre, who was then our National Grading Officer, pretty well ran it for the first year, while the MSA struggled to get to grips with the administration of the new Scheme.

Sadly, our reservations soon proved correct. The Marshals' Club lost some of its previous uniqueness and many of those members who had joined principally to benefit from our training and grading scheme could now obtain the same training elsewhere and decided not to renew their membership of the BMRMC. Worse still, the refund arrangements we had with the Training Trust, were now extended to the other clubs, all of whom took an income from the sport. Despite the fact we take no income from the sport – rather we subsidised it at that time to the extent of £2M to £2.5M per season with the free labour we provided – we were cut severely short in refund in the first year of the new arrangements.

The refund shortfall in that first year was £9,000, not far short of half our total subscription income – subscriptions that come from those very same marshals who give up so much of their time to the sport free of charge.

It was time to consult with Keith again! He arranged a series of presentations to John Quenby, then Chief Executive of the MSA, the financial panel of the MSA and Keith himself did a fair degree of lobbying within the corridors of power at Motorsports House! Net result was partial recovery of our loss but this was merely the start of an ongoing, yearly battle to be properly recompensed for our training activities. The new attitude from those organising the refunds was that "the MSA does not exist to subsidise marshals' training costs for the Marshals' Club", an attitude you can well imagine I found and still find totally misplaced!

During the next ten years we spent, on average, 60% of our subscription income on training exercises, many at the request of the MSA in further flung regions of the UK, where costs were disproportionately higher – and were then criticised for a higher than average training cost per head! During that same period we were short-changed by almost £20,000 and it was not until 2005 that, finally, it was agreed we should be reimbursed in full, following unequivocal support for this to happen from the circuit owners and the major organising clubs.

Just to add to the frustration, though, we now had a perverse ruling on VAT that meant we lost, in effect, 15% of all refunds received from the Trust!

Elsewhere, it never ceases to amaze me how innovative folks have been to bring funds into the Club or to save costs. The two largest contributors over the years were Ray Darvill's Milton Keynes Motor Racing Show and our annual race meeting at Silverstone, gifted to us by the oft-mentioned Club benefactor, Jimmy Brown of Silverstone Circuits.

Ray's Motor Racing Shows in the late 1970's produced some £7,000 over the three years it ran and our race meeting at Silverstone could produce a profit of as much as £6,000 when it came under the commercial tutelage of Val Adaway. Sadly, we lost the Racing Car Show when principal sponsor, Victor Gauntlet of Pace Petroleum and Aston Martin, had to cut back on business expenditure during one of the lows in the economy. We lost the race day at Silverstone when Jimmy Brown died and son Hamish left the circuit after a relatively short time in charge. Hamish was later involved in the development of a race circuit in Russia and went on from there to the superb new circuit in Dubai and has contributed to this book with memories of his Dad and marshalling in general.

Robert Fearnall of Donington then stepped up to the plate with a generous annual donation in return for the help provided by the BMMC Donington E S Team. Other organising clubs chipped in, too. SUNBAC paid for the annual update of our training notes for several years, 750MC, AMOC and MGCC provided funds for training occasionally, too. Lately, we have had regular, generous donations from Top Hat Racing. Over the years, we have had numerous donations from a wide variety of donors, including, sadly, collections from friends of drivers who have died and numerous bequests from time to time. If I attempt to list them all I will inevitably miss someone. May I leave it, therefore, that we are eternally grateful for all these donations.

We try to find a suitable, special use for all such donations. Our accounts are now organised in such a way that normal subscription income is set to cover day-to-day running costs of the Club, allowing donations received to be spent on special projects. These mainly involve training but in recent years, with a fast diminishing number of marshals available to the sport, we have increasingly used this 'extra' cash to fund more active recruitment of new members, thankfully with some increased numbers to show for our efforts.

Cost saving is the other side of the profitability coin and here again some of our regions have been exemplary in how frugal they can be with Club cash – always designed to appeal to a Scottish Treasurer's heart! Many members and/or their companies supported the Club by not charging services they provided. I hesitate to think how much my own company spent on Marshals' Club 'sponsorship' over the years. When Ken James was National Secretary, he often did more copies on our machine than we did in a week! Even Ray Allen, the insurance broker who rescued us from the situation that cost us so much just as I took over, regularly donates the major part of his commission on our business as a discount on our Personal Accident insurance.

We have all those people within the Club who have organised race, rally or sprint events to the advantage of Club funds; all those who have organised social events, 24-hour Scalextrix racing, raffles, tombolas, etc. Again if I attempt a list I will miss someone. I try always to thank those involved at the time. Thanks again to those I have thanked before, grateful thanks to anyone I missed!

It is important perhaps to distinguish between the different areas of marshals' funding we principally refer to.

First, there is what we might call the infrastructure cost. This is the cost of setting up and maintaining the Marshals' Club and all the necessary expenditure this incurs. Principally, this is the cost of providing trackside insurance for members, the cost of newsletter to keep marshals informed and the everyday cost of maintaining membership lists and income and expenditure accounts (and necessary audit of same!). All of this is met from normal subscription income.

Then there is the cost of continually updating training notes and procedures, the cost of organising training days and the like. This is generally our single biggest cost and is met largely from funds given by the MSA Training Trust.

What is not covered within the foregoing descriptions is the cost of recruiting new members and the sort of publicity/advertising we might need to do to improve our performance in this area. Volunteers in Motorsport, with fairly generous government funding available, showed us what could be done in this respect – and also how much it can cost!

Separate from all of this is the individual welfare of the marshals who regularly turn out, in all weathers, to allow motor sport to take place. Each marshal has to provide his or her own wet weather gear, protective overalls, travels to the event at his or her own not-inconsiderable cost (with petrol now approaching £6 per gallon!) and stands trackside, often for many hours on end, during which time they will have to provide their own food and drink. Some clubs provide a token contribution towards this total expense, many do not.

Several clubs have schemes where drivers can make a voluntary contribution as they sign on. This goes towards the welfare of marshals who attend that club's events. Many of the clubs have been particularly inventive in how this money is passed on to the marshals and those clubs see their meetings regularly staffed to a level other clubs can only dream about! We can but hope that those clubs who are not so dedicated to looking after their marshals take the hint and improve!

Aside from this, there is still the infrastructure cost, largely met from marshals' own subscriptions, and the ongoing cost of trying to recruit ever more members to our cause.

We have proposed many times over the years that there should be a small 'tax' on race entries to pay for the recruitment, retention and training of marshals. The MSA have always resisted this suggestion and so, too, did the major organising clubs, fearing it would simply become another sum of money disappearing into MSA coffers. Following a Marshals' Club presentation to the Circuit Owners in May 2004, we did win approval for the idea, only for special government funding to appear, which for reason of how the grant had been justified, had to be spent on a new study of marshalling needs and a complete review of recruitment and training. We in the Marshals' Club felt much of this was a rather unnecessary repeat of the study we had already made of the marshalling dilemma in 2000 but, equally, we understood why things had to be done this way to continue to justify the available funding.

Volunteers in Motorsport was a catchy title and with funding readily available made swift progress. The Marshals' Club offered and gave its full support to the effort. Marshals' Club members formed the great majority of panel members and were pleased to see in 2006 the adoption of many changes to the training and grading scheme they had been proposing for some time.

At the time of writing, continuation of this government funding is in some doubt. The MSA have pledged to maintain the initiative for at least a year after government funding ceases. Thereafter, we may well have to look again at a small levy on competition entry fees, ring-fenced for use in the better recruitment, retention and training of marshals. Not unnaturally we hope the Marshals' Club will be allowed a major role in this activity, reflecting its efforts and successes over the past fifty years – and for the next fifty years if we are allowed to do so!

What we would like to see happen, too, is that we might better attract some of the sport's major sponsors to help with marshalling costs. The RAC offered marshals' overalls at British Grand Prix meetings a few years back and recently swapped some of these for new at a BTCC meeting. Mike Newton, a regular sports car entrant and competitor based in the Oulton Park region, allows one of his companies, Remguard Ltd, to provide a generous subsidy for marshalling overalls supplied via the BMMC. AWS, the overalls supplier, offers a discount and provides an excellent service to our marshals when ordering.

We need more of this and to a large extent what we might achieve is down to just how much effort we put in to attract motor sport sponsors to our side. In the past, some of our successful appeals have been turned away because of advertising conflicts, where the supplier not unnaturally would like to see some recognition of the company's input but this clashes with other advertising at circuits. Clearly we need some improved concessions from circuits where this might be the case.

Also, we need better support from some of the motor sport 'comics' when we make an appeal for sponsors' help. *Motorsport News* has recently been very generous in the coverage of marshalling issues it allows and one of their editors, Matt James, seems especially in tune with what marshals think, say and do and how important marshals are to the future of motor sport. It has proved very difficult over the years to excite the same interest from other motorsports journals.

Above all, we as the Marshals' Club must increase our output of publicity articles, to better establish our place in the sport and make all participants more aware of exactly what it is we do and the circumstances in which we do it.

THOSE DAYS when finding sufficient marshals was the great headache of a small race-promoting club must almost have disappeared. Since its conception in the winter of 1956/57, the British Motor Racing Marshals' Club has gone from strength to strength. During the last summer, it claims to have supplied 1,400 officials at eighty-seven different race meetings. I have no idea how many members this club now has, but it looks as if some of them spend very full weekends during the season.

THE AUTOCAR, 25 DECEMBER 1959

Marshalling

I HAVE just read Peter Fulke-Greville's excellent article on Motor Race Marshalling and I think I must give an extra blast to the trumpet for that much-maligned body of men—the Observers.

I do not think Peter gives them their full credit, as without first-class observers, the flag marshals, fire marshals, first-aid men, etc., will not do their job properly.

It is my opinion that the motor-racing public do not realize the responsibility that the observer has to bear, and that he is directly responsible for *everything* that happens in his section which, incidentally, ranges from half-way to the preceding corner to half-way to the following corner.

For the benefit of budding marshals I would also like to mention that an observer is a man who can do every type of marshalling job with equal facility and knowledge.

To close, although I have been frequently told that "my journey was unnecessary", I never expected to see it in print, and can only sign myself

DON TRUMAN.

WALSALL, STAFFS.

AUTOSPORT, JANUARY 12, 1962

Observers

FURTHER to Don Truman's letter in 12th January issue and his remarks about Observers—I would venture further and suggest that there are still many organizing clubs who do not appreciate the importance of efficient observing. All too often one encounters individuals undertaking responsible marshalling duties that they are not suited for. It is not fair to his fellow officials, the competitors, or to the man himself to delegate the responsibility of observing to a person who hasn't either the temperament or the experience to handle the job. We repeatedly urge our members never to accept duties that they do not feel competent to handle.

By organizing theoretical training in centres throughout the country during the closed season and countless hours' actual circuit work each summer the British Motor Racing Marshals Club seeks to raise the standard of its members' marshalling to the highest possible level. It does, however, take many years of even this intensive work to turn a marshal into an Observer. A greater awareness of this fact is needed by all concerned.

ROBERT BROMLEY, *Press Officer*.

BRITISH MOTOR RACING MARSHALS CLUB.

AUTOSPORT, JANUARY 26, 1962

EDITORIAL

VINTAGE AND VARIETY

THE big crowds which flocked to last Saturday's Aston Martin O.C. Martini Trophy meeting certainly had full value. Few will forget the sight and sound of the Hon. Pat Lindsay thundering round with 24 litres of Napier Railton, and securing second place to John Taylor's modern Cooper-Ford, in a field which included Marsh's 2.5-litre B.R.M., Summers's Cooper-Chevrolet, Eyre's Cooper-Buick, a couple of E.R.A.s, Burton's fast Bentley, Charnock's powerful Alvis and many others. It was indeed a pity that most of the meeting was run in a rainstorm, but nevertheless, everyone seemed to stay till the end, and they were rewarded with a perfect display of fast driving under the worst possible conditions by Mike Parkes (GTO Ferrari), to win the Martini Trophy. A very pleasant touch was to be found in the well-produced programme, in which tribute was paid to the 300 or so marshals and officials who gave their services without payment to ensure the success of the meeting. AUTOSPORT endorses everything that was said concerning these enthusiastic ladies and gentlemen, and would also add its congratulations on the efficiency of that excellent organization, the British Motor Racing Marshals Club. Since its inception, it has gone from strength to strength, and it cannot be denied that the influence of its members has contributed in no small measure to the organization of motor race meetings in this country, which has earned admiration from every other nation. Saloon car enthusiasts were catered for at Brands Hatch, where dreadful weather was also experienced for *The Motor* Six-Hour Race.

AUTOSPORT, JULY 12, 1963

MARSHALS to the rescue: The battered car of an unfortunate competitor is dragged to a position of safety.

Another racing
season is coming
along: in anticipation
P. FULKE-GREVILLE
discusses

MOTOR
RACE
MARSHALLING

WITH the motor racing season almost upon us, there will, no doubt, be quite a few newcomers, intent upon entering motor racing activities as officials, such as course marshals, flag and fire marshals, observers, or the many varied official duties that go into organizing a meeting and ensuring that it runs smoothly for all concerned, from the competitors down to the spectators.

In most cases officials are drawn from either the membership of the motoring club putting on the meeting, or by an invitation from the promoters. In cases when the enthusiast is not a member of a motoring club, he or she can, by contacting the organizers, have his or her name put down for invitations to events for which they may be requiring additional officials.

For the enthusiast who is a novice to motor racing, it is well worth while joining an officially recognized motoring club, or the British Motor Racing Marshals' Club, and so, by attending their

regular monthly social meetings, gain the vital knowledge—and love of the sport—that is the basic essential of all motor racing officials.

I would like to draw attention to a few pointers concerning motor racing officials' duties, mainly concerning the enthusiast who has not previously officiated at motor racing events. It is hoped that those officials who have been working for the sport over the past seasons are by now fully conversant with the full aspect of officiating, but there does still exist a lack of training of officials in some of the motoring clubs: there is far more in it than just going to a meeting and being a course, flag or fire marshal! All motor racing meetings are run under the International Sporting Code of the C.S.I. and, in Great Britain, under the General Competition Rules of the R.A.C.

As a guide, normally a race meeting is made up of the following officials:—
1. The stewards of the meeting.
2. *"The Clerk of the Course"*, who,

being the main representative of the promoting club, is chiefly responsible for the smoothness, success, or the failure of a meeting.

3. *"Race Control"*, which is the operational H.Q. for the chief organizing officials of the meeting, from which the minute-by-minute organizing of the meeting is carried out, including competitors, emergency services, timekeepers, etc. Under the jurisdiction of Race Control come the timekeepers, *public safety*, which is controlled by the course marshals, under a chief course marshal and the police, who work in co-operation with the course marshals.

4. *"The Emergency Services"*, which comprise the medical officials, such as doctors, first aid personnel and ambulances.

5. *"Fire Marshals"*, who, acting under a chief fire marshal, are stationed with the necessary equipment at vulnerable points where hazards are known to be likely to occur. Theirs is a highly skilled job.

6. *"Breakdown Services"*, which comprises of breakdown vehicles, and their crews, who ensure that, if possible, a circuit is cleared of any racing cars that have "fallen by the way".

The Competitors, directly under the jurisdiction of Race Control, are attended to by the following officials, whose job it is to see their needs are attended to, a degree of discipline is maintained, and to assist the competitors in having a successful meeting.

1. *"The Scrutineers"*, whose job it is to check on every car before it enters on to the circuit, to ensure that everything is as it should be, that the car complies with regulations as laid down, and that it is in such a condition that it is in no way likely to be a danger to either the driver, or other competitors, on the circuit.

Other officials in the paddock and pits are made up from:—
2. *"Paddock Marshals"*, who are there to see that unauthorized cars do not take up vital room, and so hinder the competitors, as well as many other tedious

jobs of generally policing the area—but in the main to see that competitors present themselves at their periods of practice, and to get them organized prior to going on to the circuit.

3. *"The Pit Marshals"*, under the control of a chief marshal, cover multiple jobs including being thoroughly familiar with the area, of fire protection equipment positions, keeping unauthorized people out of the area; if possible to keep the chief pit marshal informed of all pit stops, and the recording of times of cars in and out of pits. The chief marshal, in all matters concerning the pits, consults with the clerk of the course.

4. *"Starter"*, whose job of work is only too obvious. In his hands two flags only are used, the Union Jack (in this country) for starting a race, and the chequered flag for the finish.

Last and not least are the observers, who are the eyes of the circuit, and the flag marshals.

"The Observers" are directly under the jurisdiction of the clerk of the course. The sector in which they are placed, and which comes under their control, includes the flag marshal or marshals for that area, a fire marshal, and in some cases first aid personnel. They ensure that duties by the officials are duly carried out in a competent manner; they also report any incident connected with the competitors in writing to the clerk of the course.

"The Flag Marshals", upon whose shoulders lies the responsibility not only of being fully conversant with the various flags, but also having a keen sense of pending trouble, being able almost to anticipate it before it happens, and, above all, having quick reactions. The flag marshal is equipped with the following flags which, in his anticipation of the situation, he waves in the face of the oncoming competitors, and thus conveys information to drivers.

Yellow Flag (held motionless) indicates danger, take care.

Yellow Flag (waved) indicates great danger and be prepared to stop.

Blue Flag (held motionless) indicates that a competitor is following another competitor very closely.

Blue Flag (waved), another competitor is about to or trying to pass you.

Yellow Flag with Vertical Red Stripes. Indicates that there is oil on the circuit and care should be taken.

White Flag. Used by the clerk of the course on his patrol round circuit between events and also indicates ambulance or breakdown vehicle on circuit.

Black Flag, with competitor's number, indicates to the competitor to draw in at the pits.

To become a flag marshal it is essential to have a quick eye, a keen sense of pending troubles, and "knowing form" and the techniques of the various drivers and cars. Too many flag marshals do, unfortunately, carry out indiscriminate flag waving, especially where the blue flag is concerned. As a result, to the drivers, it becomes a case of "crying wolf", and they ignore it. Thus the marshal must make sure the incident calls for the correct type of flag and correct indication given with it. He must not wait until the competitor is upon him—the driver must be given ample warning, and that is where being able to judge distances requires a keen eye.

Finally, as I intended this article for the newcomers (and I hope I have shown just a few of the pointers in the make up of a race meeting), I would strongly recommend that they start off as course marshals in order that they can see what's going on around them, and above all become familiar with motor racing and the circuits in general. After all, it is best to crawl before you try to walk, and so start right from the bottom. A course marshal's job is no less important than any of the others—it is a highly responsible job, and one in which I consider every novice and some other grades of officials should both start off, and have a "tour" of.

With a view to assisting newcomers I should like to draw to their attention a few pointers as to what may be expected of them in the course of their duties. As novices, most will commence as course marshals, whence the initial experience as an official is gained.

The essentials at any motor race meeting are the competitors and officials, particularly bearing in mind that races are organized for the benefit of competitors, spectators, the Press, and lastly, the officials!

The first and most important qualification of any official is a deep love of the sport. It is most essential to remember that an official's brassard is not meant to grant the wearer the privilege of a grandstand view at the expense of others whose duties are such that they see very little of the day's events.

On the day of the meeting, having suitably clothed himself to meet the eventualities of our British weather, a marshal should collect his armband and instructions as to what his duties are from his chief course marshal, and proceed without question to the position allocated to him, wherever it may be.

The duties of the course marshal, which mainly ensure public safety around and on the circuit, are as follows:—

1. They should report at the time specified in their instructions.

2. They should have read their instructions and understood them.

3. Having "signed in" they should report to their chief marshal for allocation of their course position, taking up such position at least 20 minutes before practice, or racing, commences.

4. They should station themselves between the spectators and the circuit, but also in a position of safety to themselves!

5. They should see that spectators do not encroach beyond the limits of the public enclosures, with an eye especially on young children.

6. Make sure that "home-made grandstands" do not obstruct the view of other spectators.

7. Marshals should not collect in groups, nor stand with their backs to oncoming cars—it could be fatal.

8. They should become acquainted with the location of all facilities, such as first aid, fire equipment, police, toilets and telephones, near to their station.

9. They must not, as officials, take photographs while on duty.

10. No dogs, whether on leashes or not, are allowed within the race circuit areas.

11. They should report any incident or difficulties to their chief marshal and not leave their post unless relieved or granted permission.

12. They should at all times be civil and helpful when dealing with competitors and the public alike, above all being certain of their facts before making a statement.

DRIVER O.K.? A group of officials round a shunt.

13. Finally, they must see that the track is clear of any debris, and, above all, see that no one crosses the track whilst racing is in progress—the only exception is in the event of a "prang", when a doctor or first aid men may do so, *only* when safe to do so.

The marshal's full co-operation will be appreciated by the officiating club, and will assist in making the day's racing run smoothly. Everyone will then enjoy the meeting without too much regimentation.

PETER FULKE-GREVILLE

deals with the Individual Functions of

Motor Racing Officials

FIRE
MARSHALS

*

*AT THE READY:
A fire extinguisher
on hand just in case
this pranged Austin-
Healey 100S decided
to ignite.*

*

Up to date I have covered the duties of the Observers and the Flag Marshals and I now propose to bring to light some of the duties and hazards of the Fire Marshals at race meetings. Their job requires technical knowledge, especially of the types of fire appliances that they have to handle. Two circuits are never the same, in the manner of equipment put at their disposal.

Having duly received their instructions, and having reported at the circuit at the specified time, they will sign on and then report to their Chief Fire Marshal, who, if they have not already collected their armbands on signing on, will issue them, and will allocate the positions they are to take up. Some promoting clubs, however, allocate the positions on the instructions sent out to the officials.

The Fire Marshal will see that he is suitably dressed for the day, and it is always best to go prepared for all eventualities of our weather, but he is advised not to wear anything too heavy or too bulky, as he might find it encumbering if he has to start dashing around with a heavy extinguisher in his hands. Above all, he should fit himself out with a really tough pair of boots or shoes—gumboots are not recommended, as if there is oil on the circuit, or spilled petrol, he will find his feet sliding all over the place.

Having reported to his Chief Marshal, he will, if he has not already done so, collect the following equipment for his post: fire extinguishers, buckets of cement powder, shovels, brooms, asbestos or suitably impregnated fire blankets, and a grappling hook, if supplied. It is the usual practice at most circuits for these items to be already placed in position prior to the officials arriving, but it is up to the Observer, under whose jurisdiction the Fire Marshal comes, to check with him and ensure that all necessary

equipment is to hand before either practising or racing commences.

The first thing that the Fire Marshal must do is check his equipment, then check the fire extinguishers put at his disposal and read their instructions very carefully. As far as checking the workability of the equipment, the units are usually pre-checked, but if he is able to do so, all well and good!

At all circuits it will be found that there are in attendance official fire-fighting officials, and usually the Fire Marshals have had experience in fire-fighting themselves. Anyone contemplating taking up fire marshalling should arrange to undergo a series of lectures and courses, which can be had through the recognized fire-fighting services in the country. As it is a highly technical and dangerous occupation, especially when one realizes that a driver's life may be at stake—as well as their own—they must understand their job thoroughly.

The Fire Marshals should know, if possible, the layout of the different types of cars they are likely to meet at the circuit, especially bearing in mind if the car is front- or rear-engined, where the petrol tank is situated—or the petrol cock, if so fitted in the fuel system—and a host of other necessary technical information which will assist them when fighting a fire or when taking preventive action following a crash.

In the event of a crash, on the directions of the Observer, they will convey to the scene such equipment as is deemed necessary, and they must bear in mind that their first duty is to see that the driver is got out of the car. Having done this, they will then attend to putting out the fire with the equipment at their disposal. Or they must see that necessary action is taken to ensure that fire does not break out in the crashed car, and having ensured that this has been seen to, should the car be still on

the circuit, they will then, with the help of others, move the car off the circuit. The driver, having been got out and clear of the car, will be attended to by the doctor in the area and the St. John Ambulance men. It is always advisable to wear asbestos gloves, as it will save having one's hands burnt should one have to drag a driver from his burning car or handle hot metal following a fire.

There are numerous methods of attacking a fire and I feel that these technical points are best left to the technical experts to explain more fully, but for guidance, the types of fire extinguishers one is likely to come across are as follows (each has its individual merits): foam extinguishers—which are widely used at most race circuits, in combating petrol and oil fires; dry powder—which over the past few seasons has started to become more and more popular. The benefits of this type of extinguisher are to give a protective blanket in front of the operator to allow him to get closer to the fire—but he has to be careful of "flash-back". Foam gives a much more positive blanketing of the fire; and then there is the C.T.C. extinguisher, which has been used over the past years in fire-fighting.

When handling a foam extinguisher great care must be taken to see that it is not knocked over, as it may discharge its contents and leave a slippery sludge, which, if this happened during a race, may go on to the track and cause a serious hazard to the competitors. So, as with all types of appliances, be careful in the way you handle them, and when tackling a fire hazard be certain that your handling of your equipment is correctly done.

In the event of oil on the track, on seeing the oil flag displayed by the Flag Marshal and having received instructions from the Observer in charge that it is in order for the Fire Marshal to enter the circuit, he will attempt to subdue the oil by the use of the cement powder he has at hand. He will spread the powder over the oil and preferably lay it a few feet from where the oil patch commences. The powder is then brushed into the oil, while passing cars will carry any surplus cement on to the oil patch, if it still remains.

Fire Marshals are not only placed around the circuit, but are stationed in such areas as there are likely to be fire hazards, and this includes the pit and paddock areas, as, with cars starting and refuelling, the risk is very high. It is worth while mentioning that the chief Pit Marshal and his officials should be well acquainted with the positions and the handling of all equipment in the area.

You will have seen from previous articles that I have dealt with Observers, Flag Marshals and Fire Marshals, and it is hoped that, with the condensed information given, it will enable those newcomers to motor racing officiating to understand what is expected of them, should they find themselves in any of the positions described.

The next officials that I wish to deal with are the Paddock Marshals who, on the day of either practising or racing, certainly have their hands full in dealing with the arrival of competitors and other officials alike.

Having received their instructions, they will thoroughly read and understand them. They will report at the time stipulated and, having signed on, they will then report to their Chief Paddock Marshal who, if they have not previously received their arm band, will hand this to them. Usually, the Chief Paddock Marshal, having assembled his officials, will run over the instructions for the day and allocate his officials positions.

Armed with pencils and a pad, they will then synchronize their watches, and will collect the necessary programme.

The Paddock Marshal should have a keen sense of organization and should be in a position to be able to lay the Paddock out in an orderly manner so that the competitors will be able to go to their preallocated positions without any fuss and bother.

The Paddock officials work closely with race control in such a way that, should a competitor be a non-starter, they will immediately inform them so. The officials will also pass on to race control any such information that may be of interest, not forgetting that the Press are to be included in information being issued. Before making any statement it is advisable to see either the Chief Paddock Marshal or the Clerk of the Course, if he is nearby.

It is essential to see that cars entering the Paddock area do not hinder the movement of the competitors. Transporters must be parked in such a position as not to block the entrance or exits of the Paddock area. All cars entering Paddock must bear an official sticker and persons entering must have official passes.

The Paddock Marshals must be thoroughly conversant with the layout of the Paddock area and, if possible, they should let the competitors have a plan of the Paddock and the starting grid for the events in which they may be competing.

It will be found that on the day of the race there are usually stocks of petrol and possibly a tanker in the Paddock and it is most essential that the Paddock Marshal makes himself familiar with the whereabouts of fire-fighting equipment. Above all, he must ensure that there is NO SMOKING in the vicinity of any such fuel stores for rather obvious reasons!

For those who have officiated in the Paddock area before, it will be appreciated that many spectators roam around and it is therefore most important to see that they do not interfere with the competitors' cars, equipment, or anything lying around. At all times the Paddock Marshals should be as helpful as they

Individual Functions of Motor Racing Officials

PADDOCK MARSHALS

By PETER FULKE-GREVILLE

can with the competitors, but at the same time must be firm in the issuing of any instructions.

Prior to a race, a "good" Paddock Marshal will assemble the competitors in advance in the Paddock, in grid order. Most circuits have their own ideas of the marshalling area for cars prior to going on to the grid but one of the best examples of this is found at Mallory Park where they have a separate and closed-in marshalling area for competitors due to go on to the grid. This area is prohibited to all except those officials, competitors and their staff who are actually connected with the event.

One important matter should be raised. NO DOGS must be allowed into the Paddock area and if they are found, they must be removed at once. It is likely to cause not only the animal mental suffering with the roar of exhausts, but if one did get on to the circuit it could cause a serious accident.

Should a car during a race have to withdraw and come into the Paddock, it is always advisable to contact Race Control and inform them. This information will then be given to the lap scorers and timekeepers.

Finally, remember that at the end of the day's racing the Paddock Marshals' job is not over until the Paddock is cleared. They must ensure that all those leaving get away in an orderly manner.

BRUCE McLAREN WINS N.Z.R.D. CHAMPIONSHIP

BRUCE McLAREN won the New Zealand Racing Drivers' Championship for his performances in the Tommy Atkins 2.7 Cooper during the "Down Under" season in January. McLaren was highest-placed New Zealander at Ardmore, Levin, Wigram and Teretonga—where he won. Three points behind McLaren was Pat Hoare, who won the Dunedin Road Race in his 3-litre V12 Dino Ferrari. Young Jimmy Palmer was third in his ex-works Lotus 20 now fitted with a 1,475 c.c. Cosworth-Ford motor, and fourth was the "Driver to Europe" last season, Angus Hyslop, in his 2.5 Cooper. Both McLaren and Hyslop missed the final two championship races.

The Sports Car Championship was won by Barry Cottle's 1,100 c.c. Lola, second was Doug Lawrence's 1,500 c.c. Climax-engined Lola, and third was Rod Coppins' huge Corvette-powered Tec Mec converted to a sports car by fitting the body from the ex-Louis Rosier 4.5 Ferrari sports-racer.

Ray Archibald won the saloon championship with his 3.8 Jaguar. Ray Macdonald's Zephyr was second and McLaren (Cooper-Mini), third.

MOSS ON A PANEL

THE Incorporated Advertising Managers' Association, in conjunction with the Dunlop Rubber Co., Ltd., presented "Advertising Success", at the Royal Overseas League, on 4th April. Introductions were made by Stuart Janes, F.I.A.M.A., and Dick Jeffrey, Dunlop Racing Manager, spoke on "How motor racing helps the motorist". He was followed by George Freeman, who spoke on the advertising of Dunlop racing successes, and presented films showing the remarkable organization which goes into the making of the ultra-successful "same-day" TV commercials.

Stirling Moss, Dick Jeffrey and George Freeman then formed a question panel under the chairmanship of the Editor of AUTOSPORT. Many searching questions were asked, mainly directed at Moss, who answered all of them in scintillating manner. He revealed considerable knowledge of tyres in general, and gave nothing but praise for the D12 or "rain covers", saying that they are now equally effective in the dry.

Leslie Smith, Dunlop's advertising chief, later gave a dinner-party to those concerned in what the I.A.M.A. say was the most illuminating and successful event of its kind so far arranged.

Now that the racing season has started, many newcomers will be officiating for the first time and I would recommend them to read my first article on motor race marshalling. I now propose to bring to light some of the expectations of what a pit marshal's job entails.

As with other officials, the pit marshal, having received and understood his instructions, and having signed-on at the circuit, will collect his arm-band and report to his chief pit marshal who is usually situated in the pit area.

The chief pit marshal briefs the pit marshals and, if this has not already been done, he will allocate them positions. They will then synchronize their watches, collect their programmes and proceed to their positions. On taking up their positions, they will familiarize themselves with the fire equipment to hand and see that it is correctly positioned.

The pit marshals must check on the possibility of fuel stores in their area and they must ensure that nobody smokes. Even though fire marshals may be to hand, the pit marshal must know how to operate the fire equipment, just in case the fire marshals may be dealing with another fire hazard.

As in most prohibited areas, one will always find unauthorized persons appearing on the scene and the pit marshals must ensure that they are kept out of the area. This rule also applies to other officials, other than chief marshals, whose duties are not in the pit area. Overcrowding of the pit area can cause chaos and may hinder others who have an important job to do.

This also applies to the mechanics, and the pit marshal must take steps to see that only the authorized number of mechanics per car are in the area. Any mechanics or other officials using the pit area as a grandstand must be politely asked to leave. At all times be courteous and firm in your handling of all con-

The Author having time off for a noggin.

Individual Functions of Motor Racing Officials

PIT MARSHALS

BY PETER FULKE-GREVILLE

cerned as, should there be an accident involving those in the pit area and unauthorized persons are on hand, the pit marshal in that particular area will be held responsible. If any difficulties arise, the thing to do is to contact your chief pit mashal, the chief marshal or the clerk of the course depending on who is available.

It is important to see that no dogs come into the area and do not carry a camera as this is one of the golden rules for officials!

The pit marshal must see that people do not sit on top of the pit counter—and it is especially dangerous to have one's legs dangling over the side as, should a car pull in rather suddenly, some unwanted and unnecessary surgery might take place! The front of the pits should be kept absolutely clear of all persons excepting the pit marshals, fire marshals, course marshals and any other person who is officially allowed into the area. Also allowed into the area are the official photographers. However, if one is not satisfied that any person is an official photographer, it is advisable to ask him to show his official pass or press card.

The pit marshals must not congregate in groups or stand with their backs to oncoming cars, and they must keep in contact with those officials in adjoining pits. During the racing, they report on the reasons of pit stops—and, if possible, in which lap the stop was made. In the event of a car being unable to continue in a race, the pit marshal should see that facilities are available for the car to be pushed back into the paddock—without using the circuit—and help should be given to the competitor and his mechanics.

Prior to the practice or the race, the pit marshal's job is very hazardous as he will find all sorts of people flocking into his area, especially after the starting flag has dropped, and it is most essential that he sees the area in front of the pits is cleared immediately.

As a pit marshal's hours of duty may be very extended, and knowing the unpredictable British weather, he must come prepared for all eventualities. Be armed against the weather, therefore, and bring plenty of food!

Easter Preview—*continued*

additional races, bringing the total up to 12, have therefore been arranged.

The main event is for Pre-War Racing Cars and in the true B.R.S.C.C. tradition, an excellent representative entry has been received for this race. Dudley Gahagan, Syd Day and Peter Waller are down to drive E.R.A.s, Scuderia Rossa have entered a 4½-litre Invicta, an Alfa Romeo and a 6C Maserati, Dan Margulies will drive his 3-litre 8CM Maserati, Bergel a Type 35 Bugatti, Tozer an Amilcar and there is also the ex-Cuff Miller Lago-Talbot and the ex-Guy Gale 4-litre Lago-Darracq.

There are three saloon car events for up to 850 c.c., 1,000 c.c. and over 1,000 c.c. cars. The "big" race sees Peter Sachs's massive Chevrolet opposed by the 3.4 Jaguars of Peter Woodroffe and Dimitrios Hadoulis, Doc Merfield's Classic-engined Anglia, no fewer than three Tornado Talismans to be driven by Bill Woodhouse, Colin Hextall and Roy North, and others.

The unlimited sports car race for the Grovewood Trophy sees Roy Pierpoint and Douglas Graham (Lotus Fifteens) oppose Ian Raby's 1½-litre Climax-propelled Merlyn sports car and a host of "1100s".

There are two heats and a final for Formula Junior cars. The Belgian driver, Al Stappers, is appearing with a M¹rk 3A Gemini, Ken Simmons has an A.exis and Ian Raby his familiar Merlyn. They will have plenty of compe-

tition from John Mew, Len Gibbs, Martin Gould, Marcus Niven and John Fenning (Lotuses), Teddy Pilette (Lola) and the American, Roy Pike, who will handle an Ausper. Cars entered for the various G.T. races include Kenny Baker (Jaguar "E"), Elizabeth Jones (Austin-Healey 3000), Roy North (TR3), Ken Mackenzie (Turner-Climax), Gordon

Jones (Marcos-Climax) and six Elites including one to be driven by AUTOSPORT's Patrick McNally. A 1,500 c.c. G.T. Maserati is also promised.

Midland enthusiasts will not miss the Nottingham Sports Car Club's National British meeting at Mallory Park which starts at 1.30 p.m. There are races for *Formule Libre*, Formula Junior, G.T. cars and Minis. An excellent entry has been received which includes Jack Fairman (Cooper-Maserati), Tim Parnell (Lotus - F1), Jimmy Blumer (Cooper Monaco), Chris Summers (Cooper-Chevrolet and T.V.R.), Chris Ashmore (Cooper F1 and Elva Junior) and Brian

Hart (Lotus 20). All this sounds pretty exciting and if Jack Fairman and Tim Parnell race the way they did in last year's Whit Monday Mallory Park meeting the spectators should be more than satisfied.

The Middlesbrough and District Motor Club are also holding a race meeting at Thornaby, the South Wales Automobile Club have a Castel Farm hill-climb and the West Cornwall Motor Club their Trengwainton hill-climb. Castel Farm is 7½ miles north-west of Bridgend and Trengwainton 2½ miles north-east of Penzance. Also, the Cheltenham Motor Club have a sprint at Little Rissington Aerodrome, Gloucestershire.

The Pau Grand Prix, also on Easter Monday, sees most of the Continental Grand Prix drivers in action and even a few entries from Britain have been received. Heading the list are two works Ferraris which will probably be driven by Ricardo Rodriguez and Lorenzo Bandini. Jim Clark and Peter Arundell will drive works Lotuses, Maurice Trintignant pilots the Rob Walker Lotus and Joseph Siffert and Nino Vaccarella will also drive Cheshunt machines. Jo Bonnier will drive the ex-works Porsche of the Scuderia S.S.S. Repubblica Venezia. Ian Burgess a Cooper, John Campbell-Jones an Emeryson and Jack Brabham also has an entry. Tony Marsh and Jack Lewis must be considered strong contenders with their V8 B.R.M.s.

Wherever you live, there should be some form of motoring sport going on.

Individual Functions of
Motor Racing Officials

THE STARTER
AND
GRID MARSHALS
BY PETER FULKE-GREVILLE

STARTER

THE starter, as other officials, having received, read and understood his instructions, will report at the time stipulated, sign on and report to the clerk of the course and the chief timekeeper with whom he works very closely. After having had his conference with the above and having collected his official starter's armband, he will collect the two flags needed to carry out his job. They are the Union Jack, which is used in this country for starting, and the chequered flag, which is used for the winner and the finish of the race. They are the only flags which he handles.

He will not, of course, forget to synchronize his watch as the time of the start of a race is in his hands.

The position of the starter is to be found in front of the starting grid—sometimes on the left and sometimes on the right, depending on the circuit.

When the competitors take their places on the starting grid, the starter will display the required warning signals in advance of the start of the race. These are usually in the form of numbered boards denoting the count-down, say, from five minutes to one minute before the start, and they are usually accompanied by a siren warning. The count-down signals must also be shown to the public who, after all, like to know what is going on. The grid should be cleared of all people—officials, mechanics, etc.—by the one-minute-to-start signal.

When the starter is in position, he must ensure that ALL personnel other than, of course, drivers are clear of the

starting grid before he starts the race. When he is quite satisfied, he will raise the flag for the start and approximately five seconds afterwards he will smartly drop it. And the competitors roar away!

It must be remembered that as soon as the starter raises the flag, the competitors are "under starter's orders" until he has dropped the flag. Any driver not coming under starter's orders is considered a non-starter.

GRID MARSHALS

GRID marshals have a responsible job to carry out and they must see that when the competitors enter the circuit to take up their grid positions, it is done so without any fuss or bother. They will obviously find that there may have to be some shuffling to get the right grid positions, especially should a competitor be late in coming out of the paddock or marshalling area.

Having marshalled the competitors on to the starting grid, they will ensure that no unauthorized person enters the area. This is a very difficult job as so many people seem to find their way into the

area—including officials who should be on duty elsewhere! It is up to the grid marshals to see that these people are asked to leave as they will only hinder the operations on hand and could cause a race to start late.

It is therefore advisable to clear officials, mechanics, photographers and others from the grid as soon as possible —about three minutes before the "off"— and then the grid marshals will have to make sure that nobody tries to come back —especially over-enthusiastic official photographers.

Keep a weather eye open for any oil that may be dropped by the competitors' cars while they stand on the grid and, if any is seen, report it at once to the nearby fire marshal who will take the necessary action.

The grid marshal must be firm in any instructions that he gives, especially in the handling of competitors and mechanics, but at the same time he must be courteous as there is nothing worse than upsetting a driver before the race—it is his day, and it is he who is risking his neck, not you,

---

Ferrari Factory—*continued*

Ferrari now employs some 400 men who produce around 650 cars per year. This total is made up of three basic models, the 250GT Berlinetta, the Spyder California and the 2+2, the last-named being produced in the largest numbers. One Superamerica is built each month.

The first thing that strikes you is the utter cleanliness of the place. The buildings are light and airy too. Then there is the precision with which the parts are made. No Swiss watch is made more carefully.

In 1952 Ferrari set up his own foundry and today this produces over 100 parts for an engine alone, not to mention the gearbox housing and differential. This foundry makes the factory virtually self-sufficient and there are very, very few parts of the Ferrari that are not made on the premises.

Having been cast and polished until it has become the finished article, each part is then electronically crack-tested and if any flaw, no matter how tiny, shows up, then the part is thrown away.

Each engine is built up by two men, one an experienced mechanic, the other quite often a senior apprentice. Between

them they complete the engine in about eight hours, or one day's work. The completed unit weighs just under 400 lb.

It then goes to the test room where it is turned electrically for 10 hours during which time the engine speed is changed three times, approximately at three-hour intervals. At first it is run at 1,400 r.p.m., then 1,800, then 2,400, and finally it does perhaps one hour at 2,800 r.p.m. If it has survived that test it is then moved on to an ordinary bed where it turns under its own power for the first time, running for three hours at 3,500 r.p.m. and then another two hours at 5,000 r.p.m. The engine is then considered run-in, but before it is put in a chassis it undergoes further tests to check power curves, etc.

Each chassis is welded up on a jig at the beginning of the production line. The body, coming from either Pininfarina or Scaglietti, is then mated to it and the whole unit is put on to the raised line where the engine, transmission, wheels, etc., are added. (The bodies are, of course, fully trimmed on arrival at Maranello.) A couple of days later the finished car rolls slowly down the ramp and is taken out for a test run before being passed for release to the customer.

It is quite an experience to watch a Ferrari come to life, so to speak, and one cannot but delight in the precision and care that goes into the making of it. The mechanics are painstaking in their work and are proud craftsmen who enjoy their work (although when the bell for lunch sounds they drop everything, and in a second the place is deserted! In this respect they are no different from any other workers it seems).

A detailed schedule is kept of each man's work, and so, if any faulty part is found, it can be traced back to the mechanic who made it. This method ensures accuracy and saves a lot of time and money.

It is to be hoped that this article will give the reader a good indication of the care and thought that go into the making of a Ferrari. This, coupled with its racing heritage, its breeding, surely makes it one of the great motor cars of the world. Indeed, in the world of boxing it used to be said of Sugar Ray Robinson that, pound for pound, he was the greatest fighter of all time. There are many Ferrari owners who will tell you that, pound (lb.) for pound (£), the Ferrari is the greatest car of all time! One can but wonder.

COURSE MARSHALS

BY PETER FULKE-GREVILLE

THE largest body of officials to be found at any race meeting are the Course Marshals. Their main job is the policing of the circuit—an unthankful task at the best of times.

Due to the ever-increasing number of spectators that are attending race meetings it is becoming more and more obvious that really keen and first-class Course Marshals are needed. This does not mean that this job needs high skill, but it does entail having a keen eye and a persuasive but tolerant manner, as one is dealing with a large portion of the public and, at times, with other officials and competitors.

Having received their instructions from the promoting club, they will have thoroughly read them. They will report at the time stipulated and will sign in—this is very important as they will then be covered by insurance for the day's events. It is most essential to point out here that those having submitted their names for a meeting and having been accepted should turn up. If they are unable to do so they must let the promoters know so that they can rearrange their officials if necessary.

Having signed in, they will then col-lect their arm bands and programmes and should then report to their Chief Course Marshal who will then allocate them their positions around the course. The Course Marshals will proceed to their positions without any argument and will get there at least 20 minutes before the practising or racing commences. They should stand in a safe position between the public and the track—usually in front of the public safety fence.

A Course Marshal must not at any time carry a camera, for, as a responsible official, he cannot take photographs while on duty. He also has to make sure that home-made "grandstands" are not erected by the public, thereby obscuring the view of other spectators. Members of the public must not stand on top of rungs of the safety fences, nor must they throw anything onto the circuit as it might be of danger to competitors—and it is the Course Marshals' job to see that they do not do such things. Marshals must not collect in groups or stand with their backs to oncoming cars and they must make sure that no dogs enter the circuit; if one is seen the matter must be reported to the Chief Course Marshal at once.

A Course Marshal must prevent all unauthorized persons from entering his area—this includes marshals who should be on duty elsewhere and, of course, members of the public. If he has to vacate his position for any reason at all —and this includes accidents—he will first ensure that the officials on either side of him close in and fill the vacated position. He must remain on duty during the lunch break unless, of course, it has been arranged for somebody to relieve him of his duties for a while.

The Course Marshal should acquaint himself with the day's sporting programme in case he his asked any questions by spectators. He should also know positions of the telephones, toilets, first aid, etc., which might be near his station.

At all times he must see that the circuit near his position is kept clear of debris, and should he spot oil on the circuit he should immediately inform the nearest Observer who will then take care of the situation.

Finally, one must bear in mind that all jobs carried out by the officials are not done by regimentation, but by a keen band of enthusiasts who are prepared to devote as much time as they can in the carrying out of the duties allotted to them, no matter where they may be placed.

Our First Race Meeting?

I am thankful to Ken Wooldridge who sent me a package of newspaper clippings about the early days of organised marshalling, including a very helpful series of articles in *Autosport* by Peter Fulke-Greville who tried to enlighten the general public on what it was we marshals did. These are reproduced in the previous chapter.

Ken also sent me the programme from one of the very early BMRMC race meetings at Silverstone (possibly the first?) on 13th July 1968. The list of officials notes almost all the early club 'worthies' and the names will be familiar to longer-serving members of the Marshals' Club.

Stewards:	Paul Steiner *(later BARC Regional Chairman)*
	Alan Brittain *(a very early committee member)*
Clerk of the Course:	Norman Butterworth *(another very early committee member)*
Deputy C of C:	Tony Bird *(doyen of the Marshals' Club and Prince Michael of Kent Award winner)*
Chief Observer:	Harry Ketley *(major figure in Midlands marshalling for many years)*
Chief Marshal:	Brian Wright *(still around as sometimes MGCC official)*
Asst Chief Marshal:	Gary Davis *(listed as an original Director on Articles of Association, later South Mids Chairman and proposer of the Marshals' Club Training and Grading Scheme)*

Starter:	Garth Nicholls *(a very early member and Treasurer for many years)*
Chief Start Line:	Lewis B Wooster *(another famous name from the early days, celebrated in the Lew Wooster Memorial race)*
Commentators:	Keith Douglas *(Founder Member and constant supporter of all things marshalling)*
	Neville Hay *(race commentator for many, many years and founder of Hay Fisher TV Productions, responsible for much of the motor sport that appears on several of the digital channels)*
Secretary:	Barry Simons *(our first and very effective PRO, currently residing in the USA I believe)*
Chief Course:	George Smith *(went on to be Circuit Manager, then Development Director at Silverstone and later Building Director with Tom Walkinshaw at Arrows)*
Timekeepers:	Roy Oates and Mike Eyre *(who trained my wife in timekeeping)*
Race Recorder:	Col. Charles Barker *(prominent and well-liked member of South Mids)*
Press Officer:	Alan Gayes *(another prominent early member of BMRMC)*

From the list of drivers who supported our race meeting, I remember the following:

Brian Henton	In a Marcos, went on to a brief F1 career with Lotus, with his own team in a March 761, then on to Toleman, Arrows and Tyrrell.
Bill Cox	Went on to be prominent racer in big saloons, popular at the time
Nick Overall	In a Lotus 7, later Chairman of HSCC
Malcolm Jackson	In Lotus 7, became front-running Clubmans driver

Hugh Chamberlain	In U2 Clubman, long history as *Le Mans* Constructor/Entrant and still in LMS today
Peter Baldwin	In a Mini and still a very successful Mini racer today
Mick Hill	In an Anglia Jag, went on to many race wins with the Tricentrol Capri, still at Silverstone most weekends but as a spectator now, following heart replacement surgery some ten years ago
Marin Birrane	In a Ford Fairlane, went on to race an amazing assortment of machinery, including NASCAR in the USA; currently owns Mondello Circuit in Ireland and has revitalised Lola Cars in Huntingdon after baling it out of receivership a few years ago
Geoff Friswell	Former speedway star, front runner in F Atlantic until sponsor fled the country owing millions
Bernard Unett	Became prominent driver in early days of British Touring Cars
Richard Lloyd	Died with David Leslie in tragic plane crash in 2008 after career as prominent sports car builder and entrant
Brian Lambert	Son of BMRMC Chairman Jack Lambert, in an MGB he, his wife and son still race today
Bill Nicholson	In an MGB, gained reputation for being star tuner of MGB engines
John Gott	Very forward-thinking Chief Constable of Northamptonshire who sadly died of a heart attack at the wheel of one of his beloved 'big' Healeys in a race at Lydden
Reg Woodcock	Sadly remembered as the driver involved in the tragedy of our 21st Anniversary meeting but remained popular with marshals everywhere
John Narcisi	In a Lotus 20/22, went on to race F 5000 cars with HSCC, where he was Treasurer for a while

There are a whole host of other names I recognise but not well enough to comment on "where they are now". Tony Brooks turned up to drive demonstration laps in the GKN Vanwall car and Trevor Chinn of Lex Motors Limited (became chairman of a greatly enlarged Lex Group of companies until retirement only a few years ago and was my son's boss for some time) came along to promote the Variety Club of Great Britain.

The race meetings we went on to organise after this one, allowed us to train Clerks and other senior officials and in the later years became a valuable source of income for the Club.

That's What Friends Are For!

Flagging was always my favourite job around the circuits and my fondest memories come from that time. When I started my business in 1978, I stood down as Chairman of South Midland Region and thought of giving up altogether on marshalling. June talked me out of it, reminding me how relaxing and enjoyable I found my weekends flagging and just how many friends we had in motor sport. What good advice this proved to be!

Anyone who has ever started a business from scratch will know how traumatic the early years can be. We got into manufacturing, borrowed huge sums of money from Barclays but found initial sales very hard to come by. Our products were beamed at multi-national oil and chemical companies, major household chemical companies such as Lever Brothers and Proctor and Gamble. Getting in at the right level was the first hurdle we had to overcome, getting a decision the next and often longest stage. We were getting through our borrowed cash at a prodigious rate and there were two or three occasions when all seemed lost; Barclays' bailiffs were lurking nearby!

During all this time I spent as many weekends as I could with my usual flagging mates, who always managed to take my mind of business. It was only later, when our Company was doing well, that one of the crew told me they had come to an agreement during the early years of BlowMocan to steer me away from any mention of business. Clearly it was not going too well and they vowed not to allow me time on post to feel sorry for myself! It worked and I am forever grateful to them for their consideration.

The Drivers' Appreciation of Marshalling Issues

As marshals we have all, heard widely divergent views on competitors' understanding of how marshals work. When my wife, June, was Secretary of the Doghouse Club, she was amazed how many of the ladies and their Formula One driver husbands assumed marshals were paid for their services. Many others automatically assumed we got expenses and safety clothing supplied. This is true in many countries around the World but is very seldom the case in the UK.

Club level drivers are usually more knowledgeable on this score and much more appreciative of the marshals' efforts to keep them safe and make sure race meetings run reasonably efficiently. Any driver who has had to be rescued from a wrecked car quickly gains an immediate appreciation of 'the Angels in Orange'.

For a book on fifty years of marshalling I could think of no better idea than to go to the top for a view on drivers' appreciation of marshalling issues – I asked Sir Jackie Stewart! Jackie's instant response was that of course he would like to contribute, when we could meet? Getting together proved difficult; Jackie's travels around the World make my own journeys seem quite pedestrian. We eventually achieved our aim through a series of e-mails, prepared questionnaires and the valuable assistance of Sir Jackie's Diary Secretary, Susan Johnston. I had some contact with Ruth Kinnear, Jackie's Secretary for many years while he was in Switzerland and he does always seems to surround himself with nice people!

I first asked how conscious of marshals Jackie had been throughout his racing career. He says he was always conscious of marshals from very early on in his career but confesses that for much of his time he would not necessarily have known whether or not the track was manned to an adequate standard. He assumed, as do most drivers we speak to, that if the race meeting goes ahead someone on the organising side has made sure the track is properly manned.

This is, what the regulations call for of course, and drivers cannot be faulted for making this judgement over the years. However, current evidence is that drivers are becoming much more aware of present manning difficulties and are increasingly complaining about the lack of proper flag signals and the absence of Observers' reports of on-track incidents where driving behaviour is questioned.

Another reason for seeking Jackie's views was his one-man safety crusade during his racing career. He did not always get the best Press for his efforts but I suspect there are many drivers still walking around who might not have been, were it not for Jackie's efforts. In my own case, I fitted a set of safety belts to my first decent car, before seat belts became a legal requirement because we were starting to see seat belts on racing cars, another Stewart initiative.

He was quick, too, to introduce the Marshals' Club to the GPDA circuit inspection team in 1973 when we complained that circuit inspections then did not include any examination of the safety of marshals' posts. This particular aspect of circuit safety had concerned the Club for many years and it was a constant source of complaint that track licences were still issued where unsafe marshals' posts were in evidence. I do not recall any instant reaction but I am fairly certain that the fact we now had GPDA support helped our efforts to have post safety included in regular licensing visits.

Towards the end of Jackie's Formula One racing career, the Phil Morom inspired Emergency Services Team at Silverstone was achieving some eminence in the field of motor racing safety. It was ES Team initiative that led to regular visits to the racing pits to see where emergency switches were located, how drivers' helmets could be removed safely, the safe way to remove a driver from his safety harness when upended, etc. Jackie was aware of all this and of course, more recently he became involved with one of his race team sponsors in developing the extractable seat for single-seaters. This has proved a great boon to safe extraction of drivers and the concept is finding its way into other race cars as well.

If only for the deficiencies spotted at other circuits around the World, most drivers of Sir Jackie's era were aware of the better standards that prevailed in the UK. On balance that is probably still the case, although marshalling standards around the World have caught us up, in Australia and New Zealand in recent years especially. We in the Marshals' Club would like to think we had a little to do with that improvement, by the export of our Training and Grading notes to those countries over many years. There is now a regular interchange of information and, as marshalling numbers drop in the UK, we may well find ourselves in this country adopting some of the rescue vehicle practices we see in other countries. For instance, I was invited as guest official for a major historical race meeting in Daytona towards the end of 2006 and 2007, where I saw practices not at all unlike those contained within the Marshals' Club's paper on Alternative Marshalling Methods which became the basis of a special MSA Commission enquiry in November 2006.

The common feature in the countries I visit currently is the growing shortage of marshals everywhere and the average age continues to rise! We are not doing at all well, anywhere, in the recruitment of young people to marshalling. The MSA's Volunteers in Motorsport initiative is helping to address this issue but it does seem sometimes that society has moved on and marshalling has been left behind. Many say that Health and Safety have become "the two most dangerous words" in UK business life today. Now we have the Child Protection Act, which seems to presume we are all raging paedophiles by the new restrictions it places on the employment of anyone under 18 years of age out on the circuits. Couple all of this with how litigious we have become in the UK, especially where the rights of minors (anyone under 18!) are concerned and we might wonder if we will ever attract new blood to our section of the sport!

Drivers we have spoken to are rarely aware of these constrictions on what we do. They simply see much reduced numbers around the circuit and wonder why we cannot provide them with the on-circuit service we once did. We hope to attract their greater interest and support via drivers' participation within the MSA Commission on Alternative Marshalling Methods.

Jackie supports our view that the governing bodies of our sport, whether it be at National or FIA level, have a major part to play in dealing with marshalling issues. Alan Gow, appointed MSA Chairman in 2006, has been a welcome breath of fresh air in our own governing body. He has been a long-time supporter of marshalling matters within the management committee of the Association of British Motor Racing Clubs, on which we both sit, and it was he who initiated the MSA Commission on Alternative Marshalling referred to above.

Additionally, the year long survey of marshalling issues carried out by those conducting the Volunteers in Motorsport confirmed much of what we had been saying in our various reports since 2000. ViM has the full support of the MSA and quite generous funding from the Government, to carry out many of the improvements that we have been trying to implement but, of course, without the funds to do so. I am pleased to say that we get on well with those who run ViM and we see many of our ideas being implemented at a faster rate than we could have achieved on our own.

As far as I am aware the FIA is not greatly involved at this stage. This is a worry in some ways. Many countries seem to care less than we do about overall race safety. We see the same in many overseas rallies, where the crowds move to and fro as the cars go by. These countries seem to have a more benign legislature than we do in the UK but therein lies the problem! In the early 'Stewart years' marshalling abroad was often decidedly sub-standard compared to the UK. Are we to see that same set of circumstances repeat itself as we run out of marshals? We can but hope that the action we have already taken on alternative marshalling methods will allow us to still marshal UK circuits safely even with the reduced numbers of marshals most of us believe is the pattern for the future.

To end on a somewhat brighter note, Jackie was quite emphatic on what a fantastic activity marshalling is for those who are at all interested in motorsport. This is absolutely true and I think sometimes we, as marshals, tend to forget what attracted us to marshalling in the first place. The camaraderie is fantastic! I know more people from marshalling than I know from any other chapter of my life. I have had some great trips to other countries – the Philippines the furthest – to run motor race events; I have even shot, as a marshal, in a Jackie Stewart clay pigeon shooting event! It was all this that kept me marshalling when I all but left to start my manufacturing business in the mid-1970's and it is this same feeling of involvement and friendship that keeps me plugging away now.

This is the message we must emphasise when we are trying to recruit new members to our ranks and we should be grateful to Sir Jackie Stewart for the timely reminder and for his contribution to this book on fifty years of marshalling.

Press and Public Relations

Even in the very early days, the Marshals' Club saw the need for good public and Press relations and we usually had someone appointed to the position of PRO. As always, this was a volunteer, rarely anyone with any specialist knowledge and I suppose it is true to say we had mixed success over the years with how well we did in pushing our name forward. We suffered especially with an unexplained reluctance of the two main motor sports journals *Autosport* and *Motorsport News* to publish much of what we circulated in the way of Press Releases.

This changed in 2004/5 when our present PRO, Stephen Green, was a guest contributor to *Motorsport News*. We got good coverage then and there have been some excellent editorials since in that same publication. Matt James, in particular, seems to get to the heart of marshalling matters in his fairly frequent articles on the current marshalling dilemma, i.e. the shortage of marshals and the reasons why. Generally, though, the take up on our Press Releases can be pretty poor. For our part, the flow of Press Releases could be inconsistent at times and maybe we should have sought more professional help from time to time.

The PRO who made the greatest public impact during my years in the Club was without doubt Ray Darvill, who reigned as PRO from around 1975/6 until the early 1980's.

I was Chairman of South Mids Region when he joined the Club and I well remember our first meeting. Would we like him to arrange a trip around the Hesketh works, he asked? We were just getting over at that time the adverse effects of one 'chancer' in Midland Region, who had brought considerable discredit to the Club, going around to all and sundry within the sport, obtaining goods for raffles etc, some of which never saw the light of day within the Marshals' Club. Not unnaturally, we were a bit wary of this new guy promising so much, so soon!

Three weeks later it was all arranged! Lord Hesketh was there to greet us himself and food and drink had been laid on in abundance. There were no limits on numbers and many of us in South Mids remember this night as the best factory visit ever!

Ray went on to initiate and organise the Milton Keynes Motor Racing Show. For the first show, he was able to get sponsorship from the management committee of what was then a very new shopping centre. The management committee were keen to promote the centre and saw a motor racing show as an ideal promotional tool. The recently revived motor racing show in London had just ceased to be and at the time, the Milton Keynes Show was the only motor racing show in the country.

Support from drivers, teams and motor sport sponsors was not easy to come by but Ray worked tirelessly to get enough support to put on the first show, which was a great success. Drivers such as Walter Robertson, based in Edinburgh, made the trip south with his vehicle and became a staunch supporter of all things marshalling. Walter is now an International Clerk of the Course and still regularly supplies pies for the marshals at Knockhill.

The shopping centre management committee were keen to go ahead with a second show but were not able to help with funding. Undeterred, Ray went on the sponsorship trail! Victor Gauntlett of Pace Petroleum and Aston Martin stepped in to help. Victor was seen by many as the saviour of Aston Martin. He became joint owner and Executive Chairman in 1981 but following a period of uncertainty, he encouraged the shipping family, Livanos, to invest in his dream of a much revived Aston Martin Group. Pace Petroleum was sold to the Kuwaitis in 1983 to allow Victor to concentrate his efforts on Aston Martin. He greatly revitalised the Group, took Aston Martin back into sports car racing for some time and in a move that probably guaranteed Aston Martin's future, he backed it into the Ford Motor Company in 1987.

Coming right up to date, of course, Ford's problems worldwide led them to sell it on to David Richards in 2007. Richards' track record in motor sport is well known (look at how poorly BAR/Honda has performed since he left!) and if anyone can, I am sure he will maintain the history of Aston Martin, both in road cars and the already successful Aston Martin sports car racing teams.

However, all that is a bit of an aside in recognising the help Victor Gauntlett offered the Marshals' Club. Always favouring the underdog, Pace Petroleum sponsored Nigel Mansell – before he was famous! I do not think he saw any underdog in Ray but he did want to support the marshals and offered his full support for the second and third Milton Keynes Racing Car Shows.

The shows went on to make money for the Club and indeed, it was Ray's question on where all this money had gone that led to me taking an interest in the Club's accounts – and still here as Treasurer almost thirty years on!

Sadly, Ray is no longer with us. Both he and wife Gill died at tragically young ages. Gill died at age 42, following a protracted illness, just as only daughter Katie graduated from Art College. Ray then went on a bit of a fitness regime, did a couple of legs on one of the round the world sailing clippers and was preparing for the Fastnet race when he died at exercise in the gym. He was just 49 and had just completed all the preparations for Katie's wedding. Katie bravely went ahead with the wedding as planned but there were a few tears shed (my own included) when best friend Mac made his speech as Ray's stand in at the ceremony.

Ray was a one-off and a born organiser. When he became a little disenchanted with marshalling, following a rather pointless altercation with "officialdom" at one British Grand Prix, he became interested in canal boating. Before long, there was an exhibition of long boats in Milton Keynes and a considerable upsurge in local interest in canal boating. This was Ray at his best!

Similarly, when he suggested a boys' outing to *Le Mans*, we left him to organise it. This became an annual event, where Ray and I, plus a couple of friends would head out on the Wednesday, to secure the best pitch for our caravan and to get 'victualled' – a posh name for getting the beer in! My son and his friends would join us later in the week but it was always Ray who said, "Come on, let's go!"

Ray is sadly missed and when we meet with mutual friends it is amazing how many times we get to talk about Ray.

Remuneration

Remuneration or non-remuneration of marshals has been a topical subject since day one.

Let me say first that the very great – and I mean the very great – majority of marshals do not want to be paid. As mentioned earlier in this book, the marshal is first and foremost an enthusiast and argues that if we introduce pay scales to marshalling, we may (a) attract the 'wrong type' to marshalling and (b) most of the existing marshals would give up marshalling.

Does this make sense in current times, when many marshals are struggling to make ends meet? Apparently it does because this feeling has not changed much in the almost forty years I have been in and around marshalling. The very great majority are happy not to be paid, although a little better consideration from some in the sport would be nice and I have included a chapter on consideration earlier in this book.

Some have argued that paid marshals would be more professional. So far, there is no evidence to support this view. There are a few (probably very few) professional marshals in the sport, who manage to eke out a living from track day marshalling and the like. However, the amounts paid are very low and 'pin money' is attractive only to those who have perhaps other sources of income or are between jobs; it is unlikely to create many career openings! Many of those who do mid-week marshalling are already weekend marshals and the training they have enjoyed over the years, from the Marshals' Club and others, helps to up the standard of those attracted by the immediate rewards on offer.

On the one occasion in recent years when, *in extremis*, help was sought for a critical weekend meeting from the ranks of the mid-week 'professionals', the differences soon became obvious to all concerned. Track day marshalling is much more relaxed. The competitive element is not there as it is on race days and incidents are thankfully fewer. Neither is the timetable so critical and the red flag goes out for even the most minor on-track incident. The race meeting in question was a full-blown FIA event, where steep fines apply if FIA events do not start on time. We seemed to spend most of that weekend cajoling our paid helpers to move cars to places of safety while the track remained live so that practice/racing could continue and we could keep to timetable.

Even with the minimum numbers of marshals envisaged in the Marshals' Club proposals on Alternative Marshalling Methods, I doubt if the sport could ever afford to pay a living wage to all marshals. On *minimum* numbers, at current average earnings, the cost would be well in excess of £2,000,000 per annum, *before* any associated costs of employment were included. Add these costs and we would be looking at an increase of some 70/80% on the current cost of competition entry fees in this country. So, it is most unlikely that motor sport marshals will ever be paid. The sport cannot afford it.

One of our ex-Presidents said, on more than one occasion, that the marshals escape attention and proper consideration because they are *not* paid and that we may receive the attention we deserve only when and if we cost £50 a day and appear regularly on competition budgets. Mind you, that same ex-President is a Director of one of our major organising clubs which struggles to make profit on race days and may think rather differently when considering that Club's budgets! Although they look after their marshals quite well, they are not spending anything like £50 per day per marshal!

He may well have a point, though. I sit on the Management Committee of the Association of British Motor Racing Clubs, charged with looking to the future of club racing in the UK, and we spend a great deal of time talking about the ever-increasing cost of circuit hire, timekeeping, medical services, insurance, *per capita* fees, licensing – the whole nine yards as our American cousins would say. As we come to the end of these discussions, I often say, tongue-in-cheek, "Now we come to marshalling costs"! I do get some strange responses from time to time!!

Paid marshals are not the answer, for all the reasons already given. However, there is still a case to be made for better and more effective consideration for marshals by those in authority within our sport. The Marshals' Club still represents marshals who put in 70/80% of the overall marshalling effort in racing in the UK. We see it as our task to persuade the authorities and other major players in our sport to recognise and consider marshals' interests as well as many of the smaller organising clubs already do.

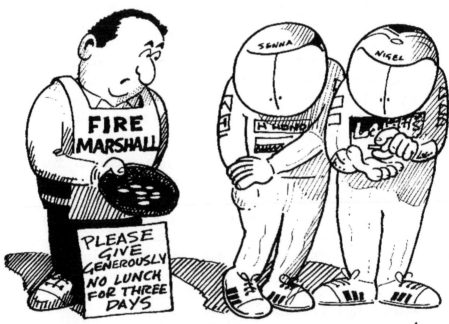

SPARE A THOUGHT FOR THE MARSHALL'S AT THE BRITISH GRAND PRIX, BECAUSE NOBODY ELSE WILL . . . . . . UNTIL THEY'RE NEEDED!

July 7 1992 **Formula 1 News**

As this book (finally!) went to press in the latter part of 2008, we were hit with the biggest financial crisis in living memory. Petrol reached almost £6 a gallon and was heading even higher until the financial world fell about our ears. Many, many marshals had to seriously curtail their activities right there and then. Many more told us that they would finish out the year, as they had committed to do certain events, but would have to consider some serious reduction in 2009, if not cease their activities altogether. Jon Cordery, chairman of the British Rally Marshals' Club, was quick to remind me that many rally marshals travel from one end of the country to another to officiate on rallies and petrol costs were affecting them particularly badly.

Alistair Garrett, one of our long time members in the North West, conducted a season long survey of marshals' benefits at circuits in his area. This confirmed, rather graphically, that it was the smaller organising clubs (and the amateur drivers who took part in their meetings) who were consistently the most generous in the perks they provided for marshals. In contrast, the 'professional' racing registers (BTCC, F3, GT and the like) rarely made any direct contribution to marshals' benefits. In part, this is due to how these racing registers are financed and entry fees are paid; in part it is due to their not having been asked to do so!

Well, we did ask! Sadly, our proposals for 'a-fiver-a-day' on competition entry fees, to provide roughly 'a-tenner-a-day' marshals' travel allowance found no favour at all amongst the "professional" ranks. So, it remains the case that it is the enthusiastic amateur driver who best supports our cause, while those who may well go on to the higher echelons of our sport do not. *C'est la vie!!*

Like Avis, we may have to try harder!

Silverstone Emergency Services

The Silverstone ES team was formed in late 1967 by Phil Morom (of what was then BMRMC) and Jimmy Brown of Silverstone's owners, BRDC – as Mike Blakey recalls here.

Jimmy was nominally Circuit Manager but always took a great interest in officials and marshals and was keen that the circuit support all clubs at Silverstone by providing a nucleus of trained marshals to supplement the clubs' own officials.

The first ES training took place in early 1968 and concentrated on fire and recovery. These two topics were important to the circuit for totally different reasons; safety and timing.

The death of Jo Siffert was still three years in the future and, more than any one other event, that focussed attention on all aspects of fire marshalling – training, positioning of equipment and marshals and the quality of the equipment itself. In 1968, the idea that a team should be available to concentrate on certain aspects of marshalling was new and its reception mixed amongst organising clubs. The numbers in the ES team was small, even on the Grand Prix circuit there would be only 15 – 18 marshals, so there was no feeling of clubs being overwhelmed, but some preferred to keep the status quo and saw the team as circuit interference in running their event.

Fortunately, a number of happenings brought about a more general acceptance. The formation of the team coincided with the start of one of the regular falls in marshalling numbers, so within two years, some of the team's biggest critics were grateful to accept well trained marshals to their events rather than seeing them as a necessary (or even unnecessary) evil. By 1972, team numbers regularly exceeded 40 and the relationship with some clubs had turned full circle as their own club marshals got fewer and the ES members were seen as a solution to shortages in all levels.

Communication within the team was really non existent for many years and even the advent of a mobile medical car (the 'Flying Doctor') which made a dramatic impact on the speed of medical support to a casualty relied on a well aimed rock! At major meetings, the control point for the team's recovery vehicle(s), medical car and a Northants fire engine was a hut under a very rickety scaffolding tower on Copse runway. The Chief Incident Officer and his deputy would be based up this tower observing half the circuit each and authorised to dispatch a vehicle as necessary. There was a telephone link from Race Control to the hut below the tower but it was considered the norm to send a vehicle to the inside of the nearest corner to await instructions or, in an emergency, to go to an incident. It should be remembered that almost any part of the circuit infield was accessible from the runways with few fences or gates as today.

To dispatch a vehicle, one of the tower's occupants would drop one of his collection of stones on to the roof of the hut and shout to the crew below the nature of the incident, what was needed and the type of vehicle to be sent. This primitive scheme worked amazingly well and incidents at Chapel and Copse Inside were reached long before anyone could get there from circuit posts. The advent of radio usage changed both the sophistication of communications and the accuracy of information and, obviously, spread to become a valuable supplement to the telephone systems in existence already.

Pete Clamp, who has just hung up his marshalling books after 43 years as a Fire Marshal, remembers this particular situation well. It was Pete Clamp and Phil Morom who, between them, devised the first circuit based emergency vehicle. Pete manoeuvred himself into a couple of fire station visits to see what equipment might best suit. Phil's metal-bashing business transformed a rather ancient Transit for circuit use and there we had a first.

Primitive as the system may seem, especially seen at this distance in time, it seems to have worked remarkably well. If driver John Hine is still around, he may well recall an occasion when his two-litre sports car 'crashed and burned' at Woodcote. From the tower, Phil Morom, launched an immediate hail of stones on Pete's 'hot tin roof' and away he went in the newly acquired rescue vehicle. He arrived at the scene along with the fire engine, by which time the car was well alight. One of the firemen, Ron, in a silver fire suit (remember those?) dived into the blaze and hauled John to safety.

While the improvement of safety standards lay at the heart of the team, the circuit had become concerned that late running meetings were becoming more frequent causing discontent among the circuit's neighbours who felt that 7.30 on a Saturday evening should be a quiet time. As today, this sort of timing was unpopular with marshals and increasing numbers were choosing to miss the race meetings organised by the worst culprits. Much of the blame then was a lack of a coordinated recovery service after incidents and the team had Robin Baxter's Blakesley Garage Land Rover on duty at the Paddock Exit at club meetings and on Copse Runway at major events to bring a consistency to what had always been considered an incidental part of an event.

The development of the team was supported by the BMRMC and, for more than twenty years, the team was restricted to BMRMC members. With the foundation of South Midlands region, links became closer and the ES team and the new region flourished. Phil Morom is remembered by probably few marshals still active today, other than by his Trophy which was awarded in his memory at club events, but his efforts in bringing up the standard of incident marshalling in Great Britain should not be underestimated. I think he often felt he should have started the team ten years earlier at the time the BMRMC was formed so that the two could develop together, or ten years later when safety was much more highly regarded by circuits, organisers and the sport's governing body. I remember him well long after his death not just for his passion about safety matters and good marshalling but also for his dry humour and his disgust at the large numbers of individuals and organisations who seemed, to him, to be determined to keep the status quo.

I am grateful to Mike Blakey for his detailed memories of the formation of the ES Team – in which he makes no mention of his own great influence on how well the team performed! Without doubt, Phil was the main inspiration behind the Team's formation but it was Mike who did all the behind-the-scenes admin work, so important to any organisation. I always saw the ES Team as the Phil and Mike Show! Mike, of course, has gone on to do an equally good job organising the marshals for Superbikes, where in many ways he has achieved a lot more for marshals than we have in motor racing.

My own memories of the ES Team, when I joined the Marshals' Club in 1970, were that while the Team was still somewhat in its infancy it was already well respected. More importantly, Phil Morom was well respected and such a good advert for marshalling that I am sure he brought into the sport just as many flag marshals, observers and other grades as he did ES Team members. Phil was just such an enthusiast for all things marshalling that it was impossible for anyone with the slightest interest not to be immediately enthused on meeting him. I know! That's why I started marshalling.

Another aspect of Phil's perspicacity was his common sense understanding of what was really needed on the grounds of safety. At the time, one of the fire extinguisher companies produced a film, *30 Seconds to Live*. This recommended that all fires should be attacked on the 2+2 or 4x4 method – four fire marshals, two with dry powder, and two with light water extinguishers. Phil's alternative view was that fire extinguishers should be at much more frequent intervals round the circuit – and by this time we had the number of ES marshals to man these points. Fire Marshals were able, therefore, to attend at incidents in a very short space of time. Using dry powder, they were able to arrest any fire before it became a major blaze and, in most cases, the need for foam or light water to cool hot surfaces (that could re-ignite gases) was eliminated. By this time, too, the fire tender would have arrived, with oodles of foam if any was required.

The 'professional' way – to await the attendance of all four marshals – risked too great a delay in that first, essential 'hit' on the fire, which more often than not got the driver released and the situation safely dealt with. Yet, with current marshalling numbers, the whole idea of having that number of marshals within the necessary strike time of any incident is clearly unachievable on many, many occasions.

This issue has been raised many times over recent years but has failed to rouse much reaction from those who run our sport. The reaction from fire professionals is often quite different. Most think that if you can get to a fire quickly enough, you could 'pee' on it to extinguish it and stop it becoming a major conflagration. That is principally why the fire brigade training concentrates on containment of fires, while we on the circuits need to major on instantaneous action to a car fire, to extinguish it instantly, and to better allow the driver to flee or be helped from the vehicle on fire.

Phil never really pushed his idea of fire fighting with the authorities but Silverstone management continued with his system while they had the marshals to man the many fire points. I firmly believe there are many, many drivers who escaped injury, or worse, because of Phil and his Team's belief in this method of fire fighting. As a Flag Marshal and Observer I witnessed several occasions when a car on fire ran to one of the marked fire points around the circuit and was extinguished almost as soon as it stopped.

Like his great friend, Jimmy Brown, Phil shunned any publicity of his efforts. He declined the opportunity to be our first representative on Race Committee and tried really hard to keep out of the limelight. It's a pity really because he deserved some formal recognition for all he did for the sport. If imitation truly is the sincerest form of flattery, then I suppose there is some consolation in the replica teams at circuits throughout the UK and elsewhere in the World. Remember, too, that all this was well before the dedicated teams we see in CART and IRL racing in the USA. These teams are perhaps now the best in the World, with total financial support from the race organisers, but what they now do originated in what Phil and his team did at Silverstone and how Phil saw his system develop over the years to come.

Like Mike, I still remember Phil Morom for all he did for the Marshals' Club and the sport in general. Even now, if you speak of Phil to Mike, Robin Baxter whom Mike has mentioned already, or Silverstone Syd, Syd Herbert, they all still hold Phil in some awe. I am sure there are many others among the multitude of young men he introduced to the joys of marshalling. One day there should be a plaque at Silverstone to mark how much he achieved for that fine circuit.

After Phil's sad death in 1987 the team continued under the stewardship of Mike Blakey and his team of helpers. Numbers peaked at around that time, too; as many as 600 ES marshals would turn out for a GP, most members of the Team, and for Club meetings ES numbers were sometimes embarrassingly large. Would that we could muster those sorts of numbers today. Not that members of the Team did only ES duties! Many organisers came to rely upon ES members volunteering to flag or observe when the Club's own marshals did not appear.

Today the Team still exists but under the aegis of the BRDC marshals' club rather than the BMRMC. Silverstone decided in 1992/3 to form its own marshalling section and, not unnaturally, the ES Team drifted that way, too. It is still a very professional organisation but, sadly, he numbers are down to about a third of what they were at the peak, as is pretty well the case throughout the sport.

The example set by Silverstone ES Team led to others making similar arrangements. The first was probably in the North East region of the Marshals' Club, remembered here by Chris Hobson.

By 1972 I had become the North East regional training officer for the club. I was commuting down to Silverstone virtually every other weekend to work on Phil Morom's incident team and we were eager to use the practices from Silverstone on the northern circuits and hills (Croft, Rufforth, Harewood etc.). We decided to set up a North East Incident team and started our planning.

No Probans in those days, so we bought ex-fire service uniforms, removed the shiny bits and sewed on BMRMC badges. Woollen roll neck sweaters, fire service boots and welders gloves completed the ensemble – topped off with a safety helmet and visor.

Each marshal was equipped with a trolley that carried two fire extinguishers (one dry powder one light water) and a wrecking bar. We placed long hooks with rope attached at strategic points around the circuits. Unsurprisingly, the trolleys proved of little use on the banks but were perfect for use in the pits – especially if anyone got in your way – a rap on the ankle from our trolley meant they were more alert next time!

At Silverstone, meanwhile, some bright spark had come up with the idea of a back pack instead of the trolleys. Two dry powder extinguishers in a back pack so we could move along the rough banks – unfortunately they had forgotten that we then had to jump off the top of the bank down to the circuit. Ever tried to jump off a four foot high wall with a heavy weight on your back? Onto hard ground you could break your leg or back, onto soft ground you sank in past your ankles; scrap that idea!

The teams were used around the North East for three years or so, to some considerable success, but first Rufforth closed down then Croft decided it no longer needed the teams, so we went back to simply providing the marshals for the organising clubs and Incident Team North East sadly disappeared.

Silverstone, Jimmy Brown and the Marshals' Club

To those around during Jimmy's long reign at Silverstone, he *was* Silverstone! He was appointed first Circuit Manager when Silverstone opened as a proper racing circuit just after WWII and remained there as Managing Director, then Chairman, until his untimely death in 1988. Jimmy saw Silverstone as his personal *fiefdom* and ran it accordingly. He sometimes might have seemed a bit autocratic, could be initially gruff but, like many Scots, his outward gruffness hid a much more mellow character and, certainly, as far as marshals were concerned, he always showed a heart of gold.

My first dealings with Jimmy were when I took over as Chairman of the South Midlands region of The Marshals' Club in the early 1970's. The South Midlands region was very much centred around Silverstone Circuit in those days and there were always a few marshalling 'whinges' to be dealt with. Jimmy used to say that so many of the complaints he received were contradictory, what pleased one marshal, displeased another. Our task, as the local committee, was to sift through the various complaints and sort the wheat from the chaff. As a result of this more reasoned approach we never failed to get a fair hearing and, almost inevitably, we came away with more than we asked for!

For instance, when Silverstone wanted to buy our marshals' hut to house their newly formed racing school, in 1983, Jimmy simply refused to pay more than it stood at in our books, despite the £400 we had just spent on renovations. Silverstone had given us the land, Nottingham

Sports Car Club had built the hut for us, we were no longer making any great use of it and Jimmy felt we were profiteering. So, we accepted his offer of book value. However.......... along with the cheque for the sale of the hut came a cheque for a further £400 as a donation to Club Funds! Once again, Jimmy did it his way but at no loss to us.

Elsewhere I cover Jimmy's great contribution to Phil Morom's initiative in setting up the Silverstone Emergency Services Team, very much a first at the time and now replicated at other circuits in the UK and abroad. As always, Jimmy never wanted special mention of his generosity, he would much rather it just happened without mention. He genuinely liked marshals, often asked those he trusted what more he could do to help but, always, on the condition that any help given should not result in too much fuss or over-effusive thanks!

Many of the marshals camped inside the circuit at that time for the big events and one night over a beer in the Silverstone Club Jimmy enquired after the welfare of the families who remained behind while we marshalled. What could Silverstone do to help them, he asked? My wife suggested it would be helpful for those who were camping, if a few food vans could call around to save the wives having to go outside the circuit during the day. Jimmy saw this as a good idea, not just for the marshals and their families, but to help Silverstone's relationship with the local villagers. So, at the next big meeting we had all the local butchers, bakers and grocery vans on site each day. Not a big issue in itself but another useful hint to the marshals that Silverstone cared about them.

On another occasion, we organised a drivers' forum for the Friday before the British GP. Silverstone very kindly offered the Silverstone Club as a venue. Then someone at the Silverstone Club advertised it in the Silverstone Club magazine as open to all and sundry! Fearing that marshals, for whom the event had been organised would be squeezed out, we hastily arranged a new venue, only for all Hell to break loose. George Smith, Silverstone Circuit Manager, was not well pleased!

I was in Scotland attending my Dad's funeral at the time. I rushed back earlier than planned for a meeting at Silverstone, which did not turn out very well. George was not to be appeased! I asked Keith Douglas to come with me to a meeting with Jimmy to try to sort things out. Jimmy gave us a hard time initially, as was his style, but, as was also his style, he came up trumps! By the end of our quite amiable discussions we had been allocated a marquee behind the Woodcote stands, big enough to take marshals and Silverstone Club members and the exclusive use of the BRDC suite to entertain our driver guests. Jimmy also offered to cover the cost of postage to our members to advise the new location but on the basis of what he had done already, we did not have the heart to send a bill!

When Jimmy retired, fellow circuit operator, John Webb, arranged for ex-Spitfire pilot Jimmy to have a fly past in a two-seater Spitfire, which I know he greatly enjoyed. The marshals' gift was nowhere near so grand but was still of some significance in the Brown household. Jimmy had an old Officers' Mess armchair, which was becoming a bit disreputable but he refused to get rid off it, despite much coaxing from the family to do so. In conspiracy with Jimmy's wife and family, we arranged for him to have a new armchair specially tailored for him by Watts of Northampton, which led to the eventual demise of the Mess chair – I think!

In his retirement speech – an achievement in itself to get Jimmy up on his feet to speak in public – he expressed his great regret that his old mate Phil Morom was not still around to share the day with him. We all felt that and Jimmy's was not the only eye with a tear in it at that statement.

Jimmy confessed to me when we first met that he had been one who was very suspicious when The Marshals' Club had been formed. Like many others, he feared it might become a marshals' union. This never became the case, of course, and Jimmy Brown became one of our staunchest supporters. He is sadly missed for his old-time, common sense, apolitical approach to everything he did in the sport, not just for the marshals.

He and Phil Morom had tremendous respect for each other. The Emergency Services Team at Silverstone at the height of its fame was a fitting tribute to both of them.

The Alternative ES Team – The Dirty Dozen

by John Staveley

There have always been rumours of an "alternative" ES Team in the North, famous (or infamous!) for having present Chairman Chris Hobson as one of the early members. I am grateful John Staveley for his memories of those early days.

Some thoughts on the N.E. Region of BMRMC in the years 1970 to 1975

I started marshalling at the age of 16 (Well 15) actually on a very cold January day at a Croft Rally cross. A group of us soon started to go to Silverstone and were welcomed by Phil Morom, who always made sure that we were made welcome. As a result of our journeys to Silverstone it was decided within the region that we should have our travelling version of the Silverstone incident team. The idea was that we would cover the North Eastern circuits (Croft, Rufforth and Cadwell) and the various hill climbs, kart meetings etc in the region.

Someone came up with the idea of modifying a welding trolley to carry two 20lb dry powder extinguishers and the team was set up. We had six (or maybe more trolleys) twelve fire extinguishers initially and a worthy bunch of incident trained 'bodies'. Additional training was undertaken by the team both in-house and at the West Yorkshire fire training school at Birkenshaw (near Bradford).

We attended many meetings with our trolleys and one of our achievements was getting organisers to allow us to be positioned where we were most likely to be effective, not just at a Marshal's post.

Les Bentley's wife, Jo came up with the idea of calling us the 'Dirty Dozen' and the name stuck. Les was at the time Chairman of the N.E. Region. I cannot remember all the names – but Chris Hobson was one of our number (Known as 'Cowboy Hobson' at the time because of the 'Dirty Dozen' connection – so he might remember some other names. However he goes:

Albert Clay
Barrie Blackburn
Chris Hobson
Ian Terry
Mick Starkey, still races occasionally and I understand a member of Darlington and District Motor Club.
Ken Martin
? Hartley
John Staveley
Don Staveley
(My Dad known by all the marshalling fraternity as 'Dad').

Some of the keen Geordie members set up their own branch called 'BMRMC Incident Team' – I had the honour of joining them on numerous occasions at Ingliston – where Caravan Corner became 'our own' and thanks to Graham Gauld's photos passed into Scottish Motor Racing folk lore.

These were: Graham Reeves (now a shooting fanatic)

Peter Clements (Bbecame a Dentist in York)

Steve Dresser

Bob ?

Harry ?

I cheekily wrote to the late Barry Foley to ask him if he would do a cartoon for us and to my surprise he did:

Training and Grading

The idea of a formal training and grading scheme for race marshals was proposed originally by our then National Chairman, Jack Lambert. Gary Davis as chairman of South Midlands region became the proposal's champion and all the initial discussion took place in South Midlands. It met with pretty well unanimous approval, *per se*, but some, myself included, wondered if it might not be a bit too rigid a scheme for something people do as a hobby. However, on the basis that some training had to be better than none, the proposal went forward to Council, after some healthy debate within the region.

Council approval was also pretty well unanimous and David Scott of Southern Region found himself 'volunteered' for the lead position in implementing the scheme. Dave remembers it well:

"At the time I was Southern Region Chairman and National Training Officer, tasked with putting together the formal training and grading scheme first proposed by Jack Lambert. My wife, Lynne, and I, over many months of 1974, put the scheme in place.

There was much to do; drafting and approving the structure and the way existing marshals would be graded. The detail of the upgrading through the categories and who would be the examining officials all had to be decided. The now familiar enamel badges of office needed to be designed and ordered, together with miles of Dymo tape for names!

There were plenty of members and committee members drafted in to help. It is difficult to recall everyone but I remember Judy Warby (now

Judy Spinks), Richard and Penny Green and Len and Anne Pullen all making significant contributions.

Lynne well remembers the final part of this long process when envelope stuffing was taking place and with boxes of envelopes sitting among our own packing cases – we were moving house at the time!

Over the years since, little has changed within the general format and the scheme has proved a great success. A testament to Jack Lambert, whose brainchild it was and the many members who nurtured it through its early stages."

As always, it has to be remembered that Dave was not only moving house during this time, he also had a "real" job! It is a tribute to all within the Club who take on tasks like the first Training and Grading Scheme that they find the time to do so. It is not widely known within the sport, even now, just how much work is done on a totally voluntary basis and it could be better recognised than it sometimes is.

Part of the success of the Training and Grading Scheme is, as Dave has already commented, that it remains pretty well as first formed, in general outline. Some detail has changed and, of course, it was fairly swiftly adapted to extend its use into rally marshalling first and then into speed, kart, hill-climbing and every other branch of the sport. Thanks to those marshals who travelled abroad, the Marshals' Club Training and Grading Scheme soon formed the basis of similar training schemes in Australia, New Zealand, the USA, Israel, various countries throughout mainland Europe and to the Scandinavian countries. It reached Hong Kong and was translated into several different Chinese dialects for marshals in Hong Kong, Macau and China.

This all took place while the Scheme was 'independent' and I have covered elsewhere the funding problems this created within the Marshals' Club, partially defrayed by the donations we eventually received from the MSA Training Trust. We remember especially in this context the generous donation we received each year from David Baxter of SUNBAC. This always went towards the cost of publishing updated training notes and, in effect, the supply of same to various motor sport organisations around the World. Let us hope that some at least noted the dedication contained within the notes of where the money to reprint them had come from.

While the system remained independent, the MSA were always there to offer help and advice. It was with MSA support and funding that we set up the first 'Train the Trainers' course, held at Birmingham University, under the close tutelage of our own Jim Whitaker. This was a popular and successful course, which saw around thirty Marshals' Club instructors formally recognised for their training skills.

Presentation was an important part of this training. As someone never comfortable speaking in public, despite years in business where I had to, I have nothing but admiration for those within our own Club who present so well. Jim Whitaker, already mentioned, is an excellent presenter, no doubt attributable to his formative years as a young Naval Officer. Chris Hobson presents for a living and added much to training sessions during his term as National Training Officer. John Felix, past Club Chairman, has become a past master at motor sport presentations both here in the UK and many countries abroad, as have Dave Pierre and Trevor Jackson as they took over some of the duties originated by John.

It was Chris Hobson, too, who took our training scheme into the computer age! Originally all the grading details were kept on manual record cards – with a wooden tray for each region, sorted in grade order plus another for lapsed members. Chris recalls that, when he took on the role of National Training and Grading officer (the posts were combined in those days) how shocked he was at the size of the task. It was almost a daily task to manually update the cards, produce the badge, send all the necessary forms to the member and then update the regions on a monthly basis.

Being a computer geek, Chris decided the system needed computerising and wrote his own program for the, then new, Dragon 32 home computer – linked it to an old black and white TV and stored the program together with each regions data on a selection of audio cassettes. These had to be rotated to keep a record of the grades and to ensure some safety when a tape inevitably snapped. However, it worked, and the club entered the computer era.

The records were maintained on the Dragon computer until the job was split up and training was taken on by Jeremy Edwards whilst his mother, Sylvia, took on the National Grading Officer role. Neither Sylvia, nor Laurie (her husband) had ever used a computer before and much fun was had in the transition. In fact they were given the computer to allow them to do the job.

When the new fangled IBM PC was released Chris rewrote the software program to run on that instead and the records were transferred to floppy discs – a much more robust storage media. So it continued until Dave Pierre assumed the role and changed the system to suit his way of working. It was changed yet again when Herman Ebner took over from Dave in 1996 and the records were migrated to Microsoft's Access database.

Others who contributed greatly to the advance of the Marshals' Training and Grading Scheme, were Jeremy Edwards, a school teacher by profession, Jon Cordery who led the team that adapted the training notes for rallying, Pete Cox who did the same for karting, Mike Farnworth who went on to lead a college course in the subject and many, many others over the years who have given up so much of their time to organise and improve the Scheme.

Dave Pierre was National Grading Officer for the Club at the time the Marshals' Club Training and Grading Scheme was 'nationalised' to become the MSA Training and Grading Scheme. Again, I have covered elsewhere that this was something of a mixed feast for the Marshals' Club but poor old Dave took the brunt of the confusion caused by the handover.

The MSA was going through a period of change at the time they took on the Training and Grading Scheme and the issue of National Grading Scheme cards to marshals fell seriously behind. Marshals who received cards discovered they were attributed to the wrong clubs and often the wrong grades. For instance, I had cards showing I was an AMOC and Bentley Drivers' Club marshal but apparently did not belong to the Marshals' Club, the only club I did belong to at the time. I did not take it personally that I was graded Course Marshal on one card, even though I was an Examining Observer/Senior Official and regular Clerk of the Course!

John Felix and then Dave Pierre volunteered to help out. John, initially, spent countless hours and days at Motorsports House, sorting out who belonged where and 'big Dave' took on the task of sorting out the issue of cards. I rather suspect he might not have done so, had he known what was in store!

Dave built himself a little office in the loft of his home. He had a separate telephone line installed there that was always busy. He spent every night there for months on end trying to sort out the unholy mess he had taken on. Eventually he succeeded and was able to pass on to the newly reorganised MSA a system that worked and a reasonably up to date marshals' register.

The Marshals' Training and Grading Scheme continues to flourish under MSA care, helped greatly by the fact that most of those concerned in updating the Scheme, as required, are Marshals' Club members. One major change, introduced in 2006, is the change to multi-skilling of marshals on post. This became necessary because of the reduced numbers of marshals now available to us. We can no longer afford the luxury of one-man-one-job approach and now propose to train marshals to be able to do several jobs on post, to allow a better response to any incident.

Even then, this is not new. In the late 1960's/early 1970's trainee marshals in many regions had to spend time on a training corner, trying out all the jobs – to see what they like best and were best (or worst!) at. Then the trainee went on to work with a (modern word!) mentor until thought competent to continue on his or her own. Many of the marshalling teams at Snetterton always rotated jobs on post, until quite recently when dwindling numbers made this no longer possible to do. Multi-skilling has also become common in modern industry and, from experience, is always appreciated by those who become multi-skilled and by the companies who benefit from the better contribution each person so "empowered" (another modern word!) is able to make.

Chris Whitlock, who with wife, Sue, travelled regularly to marshal at race circuits on the Continent, did several excellent newsletter articles on how marshals' training and grading differed abroad. In the main, marshals there worked more on the multi-skill basis and rotated jobs around the team. This approach seemed to work just as well as our own more specialised approach and perhaps explains why Chris was one of the early advocates of the multi-skilled approach for our own marshals, as numbers fell and our more specialised system made less good use of the reduced number of marshals generally available. Multi-skilling also featured prominently in our Alternative Marshalling proposals.

The existence of Volunteers in Motorsport and the government funding available to ViM has helped greatly in getting this sort of idea implemented speedily. For instance, multi-skilling of marshals to overcome some of the problems of shortage of marshals first appeared on the Marshals' Club's planning in 2000. However, without the funding to do it independently or funding support from the MSA the idea stayed on the planning board until picked up by ViM.

Hopefully, by the time government funding ends, ViM will have laid down a better process than now for the allocation of funds to worthy projects and that regular funds will remain within the sport to allow them to go ahead. Who knows, maybe we will get back to the idea of a (small!) levy on competition entry fees, ring-fenced for marshalling issues, that we finally persuaded the circuit owners and major organising clubs to accept, just before government funding became available.

They do it differently in France & Belgium

Chris Whitlock

Perhaps I should really title this piece "They DID it Differently" because it is sometime since we marshalled in France or Belgium. My experience is not exactly current; and another thing it was limited to endurance racing, so it's not necessarily typical or representative. So if your interested in some comments on how the French and Belgian's historically approached endurance racing read on.

Our experience at *Le Mans* was also coloured by the fact that on most occasions we were members of a British marshalling team and so it was hardly an authentic French experience. However, our first trip in 1984 was a small team that worked very closely with existing French Teams, and in 1989 we left the British Team and spent that year working on a French post. In 1991/92 we returned to the British Team, which was then working with a French Observer.

Le Mans is a unique experience and over the years we marshalled there we noticed a number of changes that altered the character and nature of the event. The most obvious being the introduction of the chicanes on the Hunadieres Straight (hope I got the spelling right). I well remember the *Chef De Poste's* dire statement when we first arrived in '84, that on average a marshal was killed each year on that section of track! Sadly the track lived up to this reputation when a French marshal was killed in the Nimrod accident that year; but luckily safety has improved significantly and the statement no longer holds true.

One thing that struck us was that marshalling in France seems to be a family affair, or then again that could be an aspect of Le Mans, where the family comes together for a camping weekend. Whatever, it was a very sociable occasion. It also seemed to be a very macho occupation; I don't recall seeing many, if any French female marshals. Maybe it's the geography of Le Mans, but there appeared to be long sections of track with no marshals present, or only stationed on one side. The French do not seem to have the same aversion to crossing the track as we do!

At Le Mans the marshalling force is made up from teams from around the country together with teams from across Europe, including Dutch, Belgium and German as well as British marshals. It was difficult to determine any logic or training structure, although marshals wearing FFSA overalls did appear more professional and were treated as an elite group. The French marshals we worked with did not seem to have any affinity to other circuits or organisations. The most experienced were given the job of Observer and the junior new members were allocated flagging duties. In '84 we saw no evidence of formal training or grading, in fact we were given the job of training their newest members in flagging. I remember one young lad who was terrified that he would cause an accident if he waved a blue flag, little realising he had more chance of causing one if he didn't wave it!

There's a strong sense of demarcation at Le Mans. Marshals are responsible for flagging, keeping the track clear of debris and dealing with stricken cars. The local Fire Brigade are responsible for fire fighting, and the Red Cross for First Aid and medical support. Gendarmes and the notorious CRS are responsible for crowd control, and they are not shy of using batons, CS gas or pistols if need be. Fire engines and ambulances are stationed at designated posts and Red Cross tents are set up for the medical teams. A small tent is provided as a concession for marshals to rest in when off shift, but most rely on their own camping equipment.

As British marshals, we sometimes experienced difficulties getting past the Gendarmes to access our posts, largely due to language difficulties. The French and their families seem to have no problems! We were sometimes amazed as to how close families and especially children were allowed to get to the action! We were also surprised at the French attitude to drinking on post. The Observers religiously chanted the mantra that drinking was prohibited, and then invited everyone to partake of a tumbler of pastis as an aperitif before Saturday lunch. The sight of firemen or marshals drinking wine with their meals is not uncommon and there was one memorable year when a Gendarme refused to let our French Observer back on post for the end of the race after his largely liquid lunch.

French marshals are as enthusiastic and dedicated as any British marshal and one cannot question their bravery. However, I do have some difficulty with their lack of imagination and discipline. I feel they sometimes do not appreciate the danger of a situation or exactly what is happening around them. There was the time a 956 locked its transmission and spun down the straight bouncing off the Armco and kicking up a huge cloud of dust. French marshals were over the barriers clearing debris before the dust settled and in their white overalls were invisible; they were ALL on track without any yellow flag cover! There was also the time a 934 stopped to change a flat tyre. The Observer insisted on a stationary yellow at the tail of the car and a green at the nose. Not much warning to Group C cars doing 200 +mph!

Our experience in Belgium was as you might expect a cross between our French and Dutch experiences. We were allocated to a team from Zolder who happened to be Flemish speakers, and Spa is in the French speaking area of Belgium. That introduced some interesting complications to begin with. The official language of the Spa circuit was French, yet most of the marshals were more comfortable speaking Flemish!

Our Belgium colleagues took pride in their marshalling skills and were a bit put out that our Observer insisted on us doing all the Flagging at the 1000kms meetings. Unfortunately, when he did let them have a go they did not rotate the flag duties amongst themselves, they lost concentration and consistency. Having said that though they did work together more than the French. They were always on duty and ready to respond to incidents. We got the impression that the Zolder marshals worked regularly together and had been trained as a team by the Observer. He was responsible for keeping the team together and up to strength.

Like the French, I was not always sure they were aware of the dangers around them. Half way through our first Group C practice at Spa we were asked to swap sides with the marshals opposite us. We were working on the approach to the Bus Stop, it was wet and the trees were retaining the spray thrown up as a fog. We could not see the next post for 20 seconds each time a car went by. I asked if they always changed sides in the middle of practice, they said yes except for F1 which were too fast. I pointed out that Group C were as fast as F1 and on considering this our Belgium friends decided it was unnecessary to change sides!

One thing about Spa, we got packed lunches. Some very good salads on hot sunny days and hot cans on cold days! The attitude towards smoking and drinking on post in Belgium seemed a bit ambivalent. Belgians who smoke are unlikely to stop when racing is going on and signing on took place in a bar at Stavelot. That on its own would not be a problem but the beers and brandies served with the coffee and croissants seemed a bit out of place.

BMMC MARSHALS GET CLOSER TO THE ACTION

George Copeland with Club President Barrie 'Whizzo' Williams.

Airedale & Pennine afternoon rally start from the George & Dragon
at Apperley Bridge, 1958.

Photograph by Tony Hodgetts

Judith learning navigation from Rob Gregson by YNW 422.

Photograph by Tony Hodgetts

Silverstone, 1958 British GP. This was the works Lotus F1 teams base!
The drivers were helping out with the work on the cars, the newly
announced Lotus 16s, which were rather temperamental.

Our paddock base was much tidier!

A Ferrari won the '58 British GP, but in the hands of a man who was a
pleasure to meet.

Photographs by Tony Hodgetts

Phil Morom founder of Silverstone Emergency Service Team.
Photograph by Syd Herbert

Cliff Hammond – One of marshallings' elder statesmen.

Graham Hill Bromham 1978 – David Collett, Alan Wooding.
June and George Copeland, David Jones

Erratum
Date should read 1973

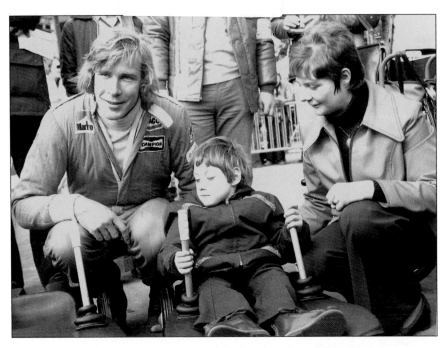

Mark from Hartwell accepting his kart from his hero James Hunt.

Dubai 1981
Standing: John Felix, Tony Iddon, Dick Moore, Cliff Wright, Wilf Nickson
Sitting: Dick Fraser, Richard Newton, Nevil Parker, Geoff Thomson, George Copeland.

Dubai 1981
Standing: Cliff Wright, John Felix, Wilf Nickson, Dick Moore
Sitting: Dick Fraser, Richard Newton, Nevil Parker, Geoff Thomson, Rob Adaway, George Copeland.

Air Crash Donnington – Award Ceremony.

Audrey Watt, Unipart Marshal of the year award winner, with
(left to right) John Felix, Derek Bell, Peter Cooper, Chris Kelf and
(centre) John Neil, Group Managing Director, Unipart.

Gleneagles 1987
The shooting party with host Jackie Stewart
(Left to right) David Darley, Mike Oxlade, George Copeland,
Jackie Stewart, Keith Douglas, Stuart Payne, John Watt.

Gleneagles 1987
Everyone in their finery
Standing: Stuart Payne, John Watt, Mike Oxlade, Keith Douglas,
George Copeland, David Darley
Sitting: Rosemary Darley, Joan Douglas, Audrey Watt, June Copeland,
Julia Oxlade.

Isle of Man first trip
At the back: John Watt, Julian Floyd, Tony Pernyes, Chris Hobson
On the steps: Brian Pearson
At the front: John Wood, Graeme Palmer, June Copeland,
Cliff Hammond, Rob Adaway, Derek Ongaro

Flag marshal in action – looks like Bill Turnbull.

Marshalling can take your breath away!

Photographs © Ken Gray

Marshals trying to separate a pair of Formula Palmer Audi's.

Kart marshals in action.

Marshalling can take your breath away – again at
Oulton Park

Northern marshals
John Philips,
Mike Patchett and
Phil Eddowes run
for cover under
attack from wayward
Ginetta.

… but return to douse the driver, Hunter Abbott.

Photographs by Paul Lawrence

-142-

Prince Michael of Kent Award 1992
– Tony Bird.

Prince Michael of Kent Award 1994
– John Felix.

Prince Michael of Kent Award 1996
– Tom Dooley.

Prince Michael of Kent Award 1998
– Keith Douglas.

Prince Michael of Kent Award 2000
– Bob Rae.

Prince Michael of Kent Award 2007
– Colin Rossborough.

Mike Newton at Daytona 2008.

Mike Newton at *Le Mans,* BMMC Badge on display.

John Felix with President 'Whizzo' at Goodwood.

The author on his way to his marshalling post at Silverstone.

Steve Tarrant at Kyalami.

They do it Differently in Germany

Before someone tells me that I have got it wrong, allow me to state that my experience of marshalling in Germany is limited to the Nürburgring and it is quite possible that elsewhere they have a different approach. In fact knowing the independent nature of the German Federal States I would not be surprised if there were variations on this theme.

The ASN in Germany is the Deutscher Motor Sport Bund, DMBS, and they have responsibility for overall safety (just like the MSA). The main difference is that they equip and support the Oberste Nationale Sportskommission, ONS. There are basically two major organising clubs in Germany; Allgemeiner Deutscher Automobil-Club (ADAC) and Automobilclub von Deutschland (AvD), and they are organised on a regional basis. Most of the meetings at the Nürburgring are organised by the ADAC, but the Oldtimer GP is organised by the AvD. I have marshalled at meetings organised by both and have found the ADAC to be the most welcoming and easiest to approach. The AvD seem to be reluctant to accept marshals outside their organisation; perhaps it is because they were playing away from home. The team for the Oldtimer GP were based in Frankfurt and Mainz; not exactly on the doorstep of the Nürburgring. AvD is the major organising club at Hockenheim.

I have marshalled at meetings organised by different regions of the ADAC at the 'Ring and there is a subtle difference in their approach, but basically the format is the same. There is great rivalry between marshalling teams from different clubs, regions and countries; each believing they are the best and the others are rubbish. Not much difference there then! ADAC Nord-Rhein is the home of the ADAC Marshals Club Nürburgring (AMCN). The ADAC marshals wear white or grey overalls and we were mistaken for Belgian on our first visit there, because we were dressed in orange. The reputation of British marshals had preceded us and once our true nationality was known the team were much friendlier. By the way AvD marshals wear red overalls, as do the ONS intervention/safety car teams.

As in Britain local motoring clubs affiliated to either ADAC or AvD can organise race meetings. Marshalling at the 'Ring seems to be a very sociable activity with most of the marshals having met each other through a local motor club. That club organised a meeting at the 'Ring and members of the club got into marshalling by supporting their local club and friends who were competing. The AMCN seems to be built around different groups of friends from local motoring clubs; the most enthusiastic being chosen as Observer for a sector of track. The Observers are responsible for organising their team and making sure their sector of the circuit is properly manned. This friendly team approach can lead to rivalries between different sectors and a disjointed approach to marshalling. Some sectors are better manned and trained than others and some are more enthusiastic and dedicated to the job in hand. Some are only there for the party and the money! Yes German marshals get paid! And despite being prohibited, drinking on post can be a problem. These differences become more apparent when the full Nordschleife (old) Nürburgring circuit is used.

There is no grading system in Germany and the marshalling job is much less sophisticated than it is in Great Britain. Basically the German marshal is expected to flag, sweep the track, clear up debris and report incidents. The Observer will be responsible for a number of posts and will be based at the 'High' Post. There will be a number of Posts reporting to the 'High' Post. Each Post will have a telephonist and two or three marshals, possibly manning points on both sides of the track. Each marshal will have flags at their disposal and there might be two or three fire extinguishers scattered around the manned points of the Post. The Observer usually has one or two deputies and they help him man the 'High' post, and train the marshals/telephonists on the Posts. The marshals are only expected to deal with minor incidents; their main role being flagging and track clearance.

The fact that every marshal is given a set of flags goes some way to accounting for why there is a proliferation of yellows at any incident. As the marshal on Post is also expected to deal with minor incidents it also goes some way to explaining why they are sometimes seen running along with a yellow in one hand and an extinguisher in the other. The marshals on post see it as a challenge to clear up the incident before the ONS have to get involved. Blue flagging in Germany is a 'black art'. Much depends on the Observers interpretation of the regulations! Some interpret the regulations too literally and insist that every attempt to overtake is blue flagged; others adopt the same approach as us and only want lapping flagged.

Major incidents are dealt with by the ONS who are professional marshals equipped and paid for by the governing body. They are stationed around the circuit in fast intervention vehicles and snatch vehicles. They are trained in First Aid, fire fighting and extraction. Their vehicles have some cutting equipment, fire extinguishers and medical support; but the doctors and local ambulance service are responsible for medical assistance and the local fire service is on hand for major conflagrations.

The ONS will use their Intervention Vehicles to deploy cones and close the track down to a single lane while cars are recovered from gravel beds or while Armco is repaired. Racing can continue whilst such activities are going on except where the track is closed down. The incident will be dealt with by the ONS, breakdown crews, medics and ambulance staff. The marshals in the sector form a line on track with yellow flags, maintaining the single file until the hazard is passed. This can be quite long if an oil slick is involved. Because there is always a shortage of marshals at the 'Ring, the AMCN maintains a reserve mobile squad of track marshals in a van equipped with brooms and "cement" ('oil' sand in Germany) to attend any oil spill. This is supposedly a fast response, but the van is the slowest thing on the circuit. If the van gets called to an incident at the 24 Hours, it can be a hazardous journey around the track.

We have been very lucky at the Nürburgring 24 Hours, in that we were assigned to a group of very enthusiastic and experienced marshals, possibly because we were an unknown quantity. Our Observer, Bernd Arnold, was elected Chief Marshal a few years after we first met him, but sadly he has now retired. During his time as Chief, Bernd tried to introduce a more structured marshalling regime. Training became important and experience and commitment were required before anyone qualified as an AMCN marshal. Every applicant has to attend the Nürburgring 24 Hours before they qualify. Not all his efforts were successful; surprisingly a number of marshals objected to the discipline he was trying to impose and resented being told what to do. It is not uncommon for a German marshal to leave his post to have his lunch, even if racing is going on. Our friends at the 24 hours have been impressed that we keep to a shift pattern throughout, never leaving the post unmanned. It has also been known for marshals to be caught drunk or drinking on Post. To our friends' credit they have always sent such miscreants packing, whether Belgian or German, even though it left the sector short-handed. Don't get me wrong, our friends love to party, (and how!) but I have never seen them worse for wear on circuit.

To sum up the Germans have adopted a two tier system of marshalling. Major incidents and safety work is carried out by full time professionals who are very well equipped. Flagging, Observing, incident reporting and track clearance are the responsibility of the volunteer, paid, marshals. This is one way of dealing with a shortage of volunteers, but it does lead to a them and us culture. The ONS marshals do not mix with the AMCN. The lack of formalised training and a structured marshalling system provides opportunities for an undisciplined approach which is exploited by some. The lure of lucre seems, on occasions, to attract the wrong element; but on the whole the enthusiastic German marshal is as dedicated as you or I.

They do it Differently in Holland

The ASN, equivalent to the MSA, in Holland is the Knac Nationale Autosport Federatie, KNAF. There are a number of clubs that organise race meetings, but there is only one marshals' organisation, the Officials Club Automobielsport (OCA). There are also only two motor racing circuits; Zandvoort and Assen, and the latter is primarily a bike circuit, only used occasionally for car racing and not every season, for reasons that will become clearer. This makes the organisation of marshalling much easier, but it does bring with it its own problems, as you will see.

Last September, following the DTM meeting at Zandvoort, I sat down and had a long chat with Hans Chow the Chief Marshal. He had asked for copies of our notes for new marshals so that he could crib some ideas for guidance that he was preparing. That Sunday evening he asked me to look at the result of his efforts while we waited for the traffic to clear. The subsequent discussion gave me a valuable insight into how marshals are trained and developed in Holland.

Trainee marshals spend a year on probation where their performance is constantly assessed by the Observers and Rescue Marshals. The trainees are given a number of different jobs during the year, startline, paddock or circuit marshal; but not Rescue Marshal. This is to assess what role they have an interest in or affinity for. If a trainee is mainly interested in meeting the drivers they are likely to be assigned to the Pits/Paddock; if they are interested in watching the cars and the racing they will be assigned as Circuit Marshals (Baancommissaris). If while working as Circuit Marshals they show ability for handling incidents safely, they will be given an opportunity to try as a Rescue Marshal. In the last couple of years the OCA has introduced a "new" role of Track Marshal. This is a potential Rescue Marshal who is assigned to the busier posts for incident work, when there are more Rescue Marshals available than vehicles for them. This happens rarely, usually the Sunday of a major meeting like DTMs or the F3 Masters. They are the equivalent of Incident Marshals. To complete their probation the trainees have to pass a written exam set by the KNAF, this then qualifies them as a Marshal and they get a licence from KNAF.

The Circuit Marshal role is a combination of Course Marshal and Flag Marshal. These marshals are expected to remain on post and attend incidents on the command of the Observer. Whilst on the post they carry out the flagging duties in turn, being allocated a particular flag according to their skill and the Observers assessment of their training need. The Dutch have wholeheartedly adopted the FIA flag signals, which means all flags are waved and waved Yellows are NOT preceded by stationary flags (this has resulted in some Rescue Trucks being written off). A multi car pile up, including two Rescue Trucks, occurred in a Renault Megane race; there was only one waved Yellow at the spot where the pile-up occurred – no prior warning]. Like us there is free use of the Blue flag during practice, but use of the Blue in racing is restricted to cars being lapped. In between races, if marshals are on the track, a Yellow flag is displayed to warn Rescue Units and Course Cars that may be circulating. A useful practice that we could adopt here?

The Rescue Marshals, however, work quite differently to rescue units in the UK. For a start the Rescue Truck is not a multi-purpose fire, ambulance and cutting vehicle as it is in Britain. Zandvoort has six or eight Nissan turbo diesel pick-up trucks, which are equipped with large foam bottles and four standard powder bottles (similar to the Land Rovers at Silverstone). One Nissan also carries hydraulic jaws for extraction work. They all carry tow ropes and are used primarily to clear cars from the track. They do not carry medical supplies. Each Nissan has a two man crew, a driver/radio operator and a Rescue Marshal. The Nissans are placed at strategic points around the circuit and are expected to attend any incidents in the next sector. They are expected to drag any damaged vehicles out of danger, rescue drivers, fight fires and call for medical support as necessary. Once they have dealt with an incident they will drive around the circuit, keeping out of the way of racing cars as far as possible, and return to their original position. You see a lot of white flags being used at Zandvoort. John Nicol had a problem with Nissans attending incidents without permission from Race Control during the F3 Masters; so now it is standard practice to radio in before joining the track! If there is a major fire the local fire brigade will attend the incident and the local Red Cross ambulance and circuit doctor are responsible for all medical issues. There is no insistence that walking wounded attend the medical centre for a check up.

The circuit owns and maintains the Nissans, which presents a problem if the OCA are asked to marshal a meeting at Assen. The OCA have to borrow the vehicles from Zandvoort, which can be politically difficult. The circuit also provides the Rescue Marshal's overalls, which are rather special. They have a removable fleece lining and a fully waterproof layer, beneath the flame proof outer. The suits are dark blue with reflective strips, as provided to the Dutch fire service. Orange cotton overalls are provided for the circuit marshals, but these are not flame retardant and many Dutch marshals have taken to purchasing and wearing British overalls. All marshals trackside have to wear a black & white chequered tabard.

The OCA has its own clubhouse at Zandvoort with a bar, changing rooms, showers and briefing rooms. After collecting passes at the reception outside the circuit gates, marshals congregate in the bar in the mornings to discover their post allocation, have a free cup of coffee and collect their packed lunch. The Observers and Rescue Marshals are given a pre-race briefing, which will include pointers about the trainee marshals allocated to Observers. The marshals are bussed from the Clubhouse to their posts and at the end of the day everyone returns to the Clubhouse. The bar is open for a bit of socialising and the Observers and Rescue Marshals retire to their briefing room to discuss the day, particular incidents and how marshals behaved. Reports on contentious incidents being considered by the Clerks will be written up as necessary and delivered to Race Control.

The Dutch have developed a system for dealing with a lack of marshals that works for them. Whether it would work here is another matter; the operation of the Nissans in particular could present problems!

They have the advantage that there is only one marshals club. There might not be a grading system as we know it but they do have a hierarchical structure and a method of progressing through it. But it is very dependent on who you know and how well you are known. If your face fits you can progress very rapidly. It is a result of having such a close knit community and might go some way to explaining why the OCA seems tied up in politics and suffers a succession of coups.

They do it Differently in Ireland (Eire)

by Chris Whitlock

Last year Sue and I accompanied Steve Davis on a weekend visit to Mondello for their last meeting. To say the Irish marshal differently from us is a bit of an understatement. Maybe it was a feature of the meeting, which being the final meeting was a "FUN" event, but their method of marshalling was very strange, at least to us. This difference in approach must be recognised by the Irish themselves for we received very comprehensive briefing instructions before we went!

So what is so strange about the way the Irish marshal? Well, for a start they don't have Observers! The posts are run by the Incident Officers who are in radio communication with Race Control. I was informed that the racing community is so closely knit in Ireland that the marshals found no action was taken in respect of written reports. In view of this there seemed little point wasting time writing them so they were abandoned. This was borne out to some extent by a curious event during the meeting. The Circuit Manager was taking the opportunity of the 'fun day' to have a go in someone else's car and in doing so was reported for a yellow flag infringement. By all accounts this presented the Clerk of the Course with a dilemma! He was reluctant to call the Circuit Manager up for a dressing down because the club was still waiting for the circuit to agree a date for a forthcoming Rally Cross meeting!

In fact I was told that the competitors virtually ran the meetings. I was informed that not long ago it was not uncommon for meetings to last as long as there was daylight, and sometimes longer! Practice was chaos as it was often held up for Seamus or Patrick to arrive, because they never miss a meeting. The introduction of a 6 p.m. curfew has at least forced the drivers to stick more or less to the timetable. Sounds like anarchy to me and so it proved at lunchtime. The drivers were offering marshals rides round the circuit in their race cars; Steve had a go with a borrowed helmet, in a competitor's Porsche. He came back grinning from ear to ear! Very nice of the drivers I thought and a useful experience for the marshals. Then I heard a marshal from my Post exclaim "Great fun, driver went faster than he'd gone in practice, lost it at the back there and spun across the gravel!" MAD!! When this madness finished the speakers in the paddock were calling all drivers to a mandatory briefing in Race Control. That is all drivers except the three that were still circulating flat out and getting more practice in, despite chequered and red flags being shown!

What else was strange? Well the Posts, or rather the lack of Posts. What I mean was the lack of definition of where the Post should be. If you were lucky there was a rickety platform, or paving slab for the Flag Marshal. They only have one Flag Marshal per Post (seem familiar?). The banks were uneven with little protection for marshals. I was given responsibility for two Posts and operated from a peninsula bank with a tyre wall one side and a gravel trap the other. The banks were steep and high with no easy access up or down. I had one course marshal, one flag and her young sister allocated to my Post. The sister was far too young and frightened to do course work so I made an arrangement that my Flag would help with course marshalling if needed and her sister would wave a yellow. Their rules are that only the Flag does not attend an incident. For some reason we were due to start practice when the Irish marshals had been asked to report for signing on! Somehow a few marshals, including us Brits had been asked to report an hour earlier. So we went out on Post hoping that our numbers would increase during the day. I did get another course marshal after lunch!

Their radio procedure was also strange. I know that radio conventions can vary, but I was always taught to announce where I was calling, to get their attention, and then say who was calling. The Irish wanted messages passed the other way around. Fair enough, just try and remember that, it happens! But if I got it wrong they just ignored the call; now that is different! At first I thought there was something wrong with my radio, but I found if I stuck to their conventions I had no problem passing messages.

So the Irish do things very differently. But they were some of the friendliest and helpful marshals I have come across, and just as enthusiastic as any I have met. The welcome pack we were sent beforehand included photos and short CVs of the main characters we were to meet and pointed out who to seek out for help and advice. Before signing on we were taken for a walk around the circuit and the idiosyncrasies of each corner and Post was explained to us. They are so hospitable that I was told they put out the Safety Car to control a support race at the BTCC meeting to allow a BTCC team out of the paddock and across the track to use the exit so that they did not miss their ferry. However they found more BTCC teams needed to leave at the same time so they decided to red flag the race. It could only happen in Ireland!

Keith Douglas

Where do I start, to record Keith Douglas's part in the history of the Marshals' Club and marshalling in general? He was there at the start; he was there until his sad death in August 2005. Throughout that time, Keith represented the Marshals' Club's interests, with his own brand of diplomatic skills and his enormous list of contacts within the sport and the governing hierarchy.

Keith's diplomatic skills were legendary, arising mainly from the amount of preparation that went ahead of any presentation. As a race commentator he spent the time going around the paddock, getting to know the teams and the competitors, so that he could impart this knowledge in his commentaries. It was the same with any new proposal for the Marshals' Club. Keith would quietly ask around for views on what he was proposing, before presenting a well rounded proposal to Council for approval.

His other great skill was 'networking' before that became a popular phrase! Keith travelled extensively in his position as Automotive Marketing Director for GKN and built up an enormous list of contacts throughout the World in the automotive industry and motorsport. I tapped into this list when my own business took me abroad and to this day we still visit Pocono Speedway in Pennsylvania where Keith introduced us to the owners many, many years ago.

Keith's other talent was to identify the strengths in those he met and to use their services accordingly. I first met him when he was trying to drum up some enthusiasm for the idea that we should seek to have a marshalling representative on the MSA Race Committee. From this initial contact we set up a good rapport and he and I would often discuss what the Marshals' Club needed to achieve in a business sense within the sport. We operated at similar levels in our business lives and seemed to share the same feelings on business ethics and what we thought the Marshals' Club should be doing to preserve its influence within the sport.

When it came to presentations, however, Keith found better strengths elsewhere! Chris Hobson, current Club Chairman, and Dave Darley, long time Chairman of Southern region, were and are very skilled presenters, whom Keith employed to good purpose on several occasions. Chris made several, well-received presentations to the MSA Board and to Motor Sports Council on what needed to be done to preserve the grass roots of motorsport and to keep up the number of volunteers, so essential to the eventual success of motorsport overall. Dave came in to Keith's last major presentation, People in Motor Sport (PIMS), which again outlined the challenges facing our sport and the danger of doing nothing.

Sadly, 'doing nothing' is largely what happened, despite how well Keith's Green Paper was received in 1989 and PIMS in 1998. We tried again in 2000 with a paper entitled the Marshalling Dilemma which won some support from the MSA-initiated Association of British Motor Racing Clubs, formed in 2001 to look at the future of Club racing in the UK for the next ten years. Many of the initiatives first mentioned in Keith's Green Paper in 1989 are now being acted upon, not least the £250,000 publicity campaign announced in Spring 2008. This contains so many echoes of Keith's and our own earlier papers, as did much of the Volunteers in Motorsport process.

History may or may not record Keith's part in so many worthwhile developments in motor sport. It may well not do so, since Keith never sought praise or recognition for what he achieved. He was happy for others, the Marshals' Club in particular, to take the credit.

Away from strictly marshalling matters, Keith was the innovator behind the idea of initial training for drivers before they ventured on track and the Association of Racing Drivers' Schools this idea gave rise to. In part, the idea came from observation that many drivers went racing without even the most basic idea of racing etiquette and what the various flag signals meant. The ARDS Scheme put paid to that; no driver can now go on track without having consulted the Blue Book and demonstrated a rudimentary knowledge of flag signals to the ARDS Examiner.

What is now the very successful Autosport International Show (AIS) is another idea that first germinated within a KHD initiative. I sat in on a couple of meetings with Haymarket in the early stages, when it was thought the Marshals' Club might become involved in the set up. We never did become directly involved but we have always had a presence at AIS, thanks to the ongoing generosity of Haymarket and Show Organiser, Bernie Cottrell. Outside of the BTCC initiative on recruiting in 2006/7/8 our presence at the AIS has been a steady source of new recruits to marshalling over many years.

Keith, as Chairman of the Society of Motor Manufacturers and Traders (SMMT), sat on the RAC Competitions Committee since 1972 and became a founder member of the RAC Motor Sports Council in 1975. He was part of the team that co-ordinated the setting up of the RAC Motor Sports Association (RACMSA) in 1978 and was an RACMSA main board Director until retirement. He was Chairman of the RACMSA Race Committee for many years and established a widely held regard for his calm and authoritative chairmanship style.

To many, Keith will be remembered as motor race commentator at Silverstone and elsewhere, a skill that seems to have passed on to sons Russell and Alistair, who both became race commentators in their own right. Keith first commentated at Silverstone in 1953 and commentated on more than twenty British Grands Prix there, plus countless other international and major national race meetings elsewhere.

He was also a prominent fund raiser and Life Governor of the Motor and Allied Trades Benevolent Fund (BEN). It was as Keith's guests at a BEN dinner that June and I first came across Stuart Turner, motor sport's Peter Ustinov. Stuart, that night, had strung together every cliché ever heard into a witty and entertaining after dinner address. It was one of those occasions when many appealed for a break from laughing so that they could get their breath back!

Keith's finest hour in motor sport was surely his Prince Michael of Kent Award in 1998. John Felix, then Club Chairman, delegated to me the job of making the proposal on behalf of the Marshals' Club and I was honoured to do so, with considerable assistance from son Russell.

The Marshals' Club greatly misses Keith's influence within 'the corridors of power' at Motor Sports House. My wife, June, and I miss him as a friend of some thirty years' standing. It was Keith's wife Joan who introduced June to timekeeping and from there to the Doghouse Club, where June was Secretary for many years following the sad death of Eba Grant, who had been Secretary from the very early days of the Doghouse Club when it was at full strength. We enjoyed many joint outings to the Doghouse Ball in London which, every other year, was the highlight of many motor sport enthusiast's year, the Doghouse Ladies Cabaret in particular.

History may or may not adequately credit Keith for all that he did for motor sport. Hopefully this chapter will and the Marshals' Club should always remember the best friend the Club ever had!

John Felix

No book on marshalling could be considered complete without a chapter on John Felix. John, Chairman of the Marshals' Club in probably its busiest and most innovative stage, has become *THE* complete marshal. Surely no one else has worked in so many different disciplines, held so many positions within MSA Steering Groups and visited quite so many countries on marshalling business, often representing the MSA. He has trained marshals in numerous countries around the World and is known and respected wherever he has been.

I have been lucky enough to understudy John on much of his officiating. I took over from him as Chief Marshal for Marshals' Club race meetings and later as Clerk of the Course. Later still, when we got into Thoroughbred Grand Prix racing with Steve Lydon, I shadowed John on many of the trips into Europe. It never ceased to impress me that wherever we turned up in Europe, marshals everywhere would rush to say hello, hola, ciao or bonjour, whatever was the language of the track we were at. Amazingly, John could almost always remember who these folks were and where and when he had worked with them in the past.

John started marshalling in 1962, going with a colleague from British Telecom to hill climbs at Shelsley Walsh. By 1964 he had discovered the Marshals' Club and was soon enrolled there, along with old school chum Cliff Wright. This led on to Nottingham Sports Car Club race meetings at Silverstone. NSCC had the monopoly on all the best dates at Silverstone then and their meetings, especially on Bank Holiday weekends, were the best around at the time. They were where I got my introduction to marshalling and I do recall later NSCC meetings as being the best recruiting ground at the time for marshals. Keith Douglas one of the founders of the Marshals' Club and then Chairman of the Marshals' Club, Jack Lambert, were both prominent members of NSCC and always allowed us space in the race day programme for recruiting ads and application forms. It helped, too, that Keith was then commentating at Silverstone and always gave us some good plugs throughout the day! I seem to remember a best ever total of 71 enquiries after one NSCC Bank Holiday race meeting.

As something of the new boy, John remembers being set up at one Silverstone race meeting. He was allocated to a post on the old Club straight and told that no one, but no one was allowed to cross the track at any time. No one told him that Jimmy Brown, who ran Silverstone at the time, had a regular route from his home at the Farm to Race Control, via the Club straight. So, there was the expected confrontation, which Jimmy never let John forget, even though they became firm friends for many years thereafter!

John and Cliff became Silverstone regulars and were among the early members of Silverstone ES Team, as Fire Tender drivers. Cliff and John decided to become a little more involved in the running of the Marshals' Club and both stood for election to the Midlands Region committee in 1974/75. Cliff was duly elected but it was next year before John joined him on the committee. Mike Cartwright stood down as Chairman soon afterwards and John found himself duly elected Chairman of Midlands Region, just as I was getting ready to stand down as Chairman of South Midlands region to start my business. Nevertheless, for the short time we sat on Council together, we found we agreed on many issues, although we both felt a sense of frustration when we could not win the vote on various matters at Council, despite the fact that between us we represented more than half the then total membership.

However, John's star was obviously very much in its ascendancy at the time and he was very soon afterwards elected National Chairman, when Jack Lambert retired. He took over at a time when the innovative Marshals' Training and Grading Scheme was just being introduced and he became deeply involved in that. Donington was just about to re-open, too, and through a contact made by Terry Farrell, was soon involved there as well. He, Rob Adaway and others helped lay out the new track and a new Emergency Services Team was formed, initially run by John himself but he as he became Clerk for the Donington Club, Jim Whitaker took over, followed by Alan Brown and then Diane Hardy who, of course is still there today.

Nottingham Sports Car Club ran the inaugural meeting at the new Donington and the Marshals' Club was offered two or three days that first season, which Ray Darvill our PRO readily accepted. Val Adaway and her team organised the races but with very short notice that the race days were on offer to us and few championship rounds still available, it was a bit of an uphill task to make the days we were offered very profitable. My own Company, BlowMocan, sponsored one day and several BlowMocan suppliers kindly offered awards for some of the races. I seem to remember that we made a small surplus but all enjoyed the involvement in setting up a new race circuit.

Running pretty much alongside all of this, John was heavily involved in setting up a new division of the British Motor Racing Marshals' Club to look after our burgeoning rally marshal section. It was decided this should be a separate club, the British Rally Marshals' Club, running as a subsidiary of BMRMC. The BRMC, under initial Chairman Adrian Breese, was pretty well an instant success. The hastily introduced Training and Grading Scheme for rally marshals was a big hit. Rally marshals from all over the British Isles joined up to take advantage of the training offered.

I did say in the opening paragraph that John came to office at a busy and innovative time. The Marshals' Club was going ahead in leaps and bounds. The Training and Grading Scheme was proving a big draw, with increasing encouragement from the MSA to extend the Scheme to other disciplines in UK motor sport. The Scheme was also becoming known abroad. Our National Training Day always had a fair sprinkling of visitors from foreign ASN's (invited by the MSA generally) and very soon John was on his travels abroad, spreading the word on training and marshalling matters generally.

John spent some time in Eire with the newly emerging Motor Race Marshals' Club of Ireland (MRCMI), set up by Eddie Fitzgerald. Marshals in Northern Ireland worked under the aegis of the Midland Region of the BMRMC but under John's tutelage they, too, soon had their own N Ireland region, under the initial chairmanship of Colin Rossborough.

The two organisations work well together to this day and John became a regular visitor to both ends of Ireland.

By now, John had taken a too-good-to-refuse offer of early retirement from British Telecom and it was now full throttle on motor sport business. He and a team of helpers that variously included Jim Whitaker, Jeremy Edwards, Dave Pierre and others visited Israel, Dubai, Sweden, India, China, Japan and the Isle of Man (!) to train marshals initially but then to train the trainers in those countries so that they could pass the message on. At one stage we recorded that our training notes had been translated into sixteen different languages, including we believe three different Chinese dialects. On a Clerking trip to Subic Bay in the Philippines, I spent some time with the marshals there and they, too, adopted our training notes; so yet another language to add to the list.

John's influence was much wider and grew as the years went on. He lectured on race organisation at an FIA conference held in Maranello. He has advised on safety at several circuits around the World and is a well-respected International Clerk and FIA Steward throughout Europe. His ability to consume alcohol and still come out the other end right as rain has proved a challenge to some of the local officials! When substituting for him I have often advised the first Stewards' meeting that I was there on health grounds – to save their livers!!

As race and track day organiser, he has organised many motor sport events in the Isle of Man and track days throughout Europe, usually with a group of marshalling buddies to help. Chris Ruddlesdin, a prominent orthopaedic surgeon in the North of England, regularly attends with his fully equipped Doctor's car. I have been on a couple of these outings with John and they are never, ever dull!

At Nürburgring for instance, I remember two most enjoyable days taking my turn at peddling an Avis hire car as fast as I could round the Nordschleife, as one of the rotating safety cars. Egged on by Herman Ebner and Martin Wotton, I eventually reached the target 100 mph on the final straight, helped by a tow from a 'proper' track day car – only to be chastised by Clerk of the Course, John Felix. It was not the done thing, it seems, to race the track day participants!

Herman, as a native Austrian and fluent German speaker, organised all our evening entertainment – including a 'last supper' event when thirteen of us sat down to individual à *la carte meals* Herman had arranged with the Austrian chef in one of Nürburgring's local hostelries!

John continues with those activities today and now has two companies organising race and track day events all around Europe, ably assisted by long time partner, Carolynn, who looks after all the administration and travel arrangements.

Despite all his grand jobs, John still turns out on the bank from time to time and can be found on various Rescue Units when required. Although no longer Chairman of the Marshals' Club (he stood down when he took on a Board position with BARC) John is known and respected by marshals everywhere.

Benefactors

When I first came into marshalling, our main benefactor was then Club Chairman, Jack Lambert. Jack and wife Irene very quietly took care of most of the Club postage account. Nothing was on record, so to speak, but it seems a batch of postage stamps would always appear just when they were needed.

Of course, as time went on, this sort of quiet 'sponsorship' of our activities by Club members became commonplace. As Treasurer, I was always very impressed by the number of people throughout the regions who found ways to subsidise our costs. In my own case, my company, BlowMocan, became the Marshals' Club's print shop during Ken James's reign as National Secretary. Ken had been our Receptionist's college lecturer and he would breeze into our office, bid Janet good day and then hog the photocopier for the next little while! There are many similar stories up and down the country where members quietly subsidised our costs.

From outside the Club, Jimmy Brown of Silverstone Circuits was principal benefactor when I joined. He worked very closely with Phil Morom and Mike Blakey who looked after the Silverstone Emergency Services Team. Phil's own company in Luton did its share, too. However, the greatest contribution was the race day Jimmie gave us at Silverstone each year. Initially, this was to allow our members to train as Clerks of the Course, etc but once Val Adaway and her team of helpers became involved, our race day became something of a money spinner. It was our most significant donation for many years.

When Donington first re-opened, we had a few race days there but the circumstances were slightly different and we struggled to make any significant surplus. For one Donington meeting, BlowMocan sponsored the day and two or three of BlowMocan's suppliers sponsored individual races. This included Ray Allen who remains as the Club's insurance broker to this day and rebates us a substantial part of his commission each year on our Personal Accident insurance.

We established an Emergency Services Team at Donington, under the Marshals' Club banner, and soon after Robert Fearnall took charge there we received a proportion of the fees the circuit charged for rescue units we manned. Robert was also quite generous with other benefits for the E S Team, now under the tutelage of Di Hardy.

John Kirkpatrick 'the Kilt' of Jim Russell Racing Drivers' School was another who quietly supported the marshals at Donington, in return for the support he received for his race days there.

Under the influence of David Baxter, SUNBAC Secretary and long-time scrutineer, SUNBAC became one of our most constant supporters over many years with a very generous donation from their annual race day at Silverstone. This stopped only when circuit hire charges went through the roof and few of the smaller organising clubs could afford to have race days there.

750 Motor Club was another who helped out with a sizeable donation to our training costs in one of the years we had been cut short of refund from the MSA. Top Hat Racing, whose championship then run under the 750 Motor Club banner heard of our 'plight' and immediately started a major donation each year to fund our training costs, becoming one of our most consistent and generous supporters during that time.

Currently, our longest-serving benefactor is Mike Newton, a prominent sports car driver long associated with our Northern Region. Mike's companies, first Dedicated Micros then Remguard, have been sponsoring marshals' overalls since 1994/95. This has allowed us to offer good quality overalls to marshals at prices that match those offered by the large organising clubs. Prior to this, Mike had very quietly been helping out with training day costs and the preparation of training videos.

Mike refuses all attempts to make him an Honorary Member of the Club and insists on being fully paid up! However, Eric Ridler eventually made the case for Mike to become Vice President of the Club and he was duly appointed during 2008. He is extremely generous with his time and efforts for the Marshals' Club. It seems we only have to ask for whichever of his precious cars Eric would like for one of the shows. Mike asks nothing in return and is a 'true gent'.

Eric's other regular contact is with Jim Bamber who has produced so many apt cartoons for us over the years. His cartoons in Autosport are always so topical; no less so for us and I have already sought permission to use some of his 50th Anniversary cartoons within this book.

Our most recent benefactor, in a variety of novel and interesting ways, has been Jonathan Palmer new circuit owner at Brands Hatch, Snetterton, Oulton, Cadwell Park and Bedford Autodrome. Dealing principally through Stephen Green, our priest-catching PRO, Jonathan came up with a few fresh ideas on how to reward marshals for their services on his circuits. By far the most popular has been the regular track days for marshals on all four race circuits. These are full blown track days, allowing marshals the opportunity to drive on the circuits they regularly marshal. 'Proper' instructors are there to offer help where required and discipline where necessary! I have done a couple in my BMW M5 and thoroughly enjoyed the outings – although it can be a little costly on tyres and brakes!

The motor racing shows we do attend (Autosport, Retro Show, the London Motorsport Show, etc) have proved to be quietly fertile recruiting grounds for new marshals. We do not always take names and subscriptions at these shows but now that Sue Whitlock has taken over as National Membership Secretary and attempts to find out where our new recruits come from, it is increasingly obvious that many come from our presence at these major shows, even if only to be there and register as part of the general motor sport scene. The organisers of all these shows have been exceedingly kind to us over the years in allowing us to be there and demonstrate our wares!

The Doghouse Owners' Club has been another steady supporter over the years, often helping out quietly in the background where marshals have been injured or otherwise suffered loss from a racing incident. The Doghouse Ladies generously donated the proceeds of their annual dinner to the Marshals' Club in 2007, money that we were able to dedicate right away towards the costs of our very successful Team Wilson/BTCC recruiting exercise that year.

Legacies have provided another source of financial support but we do not have very good records of all that we have received and I feel it would be wrong to list those we can recall for fear of offending those that have not been recorded. Suffice to say, perhaps, that all of these kind bequests have been put to good use and that all the families were thanked at the time.

To everyone who has helped out over the years, very many thanks from the Marshals' Club. If I have missed anyone, as is almost inevitable, please do forgive me. I have relied mostly on my own memory of who our many benefactors have been and there may well have been some I have forgotten or indeed never knew about, who worked away quite unrecognised in the background. Many thanks to you all.

Marshals in Motor Sport Jobs

Many marshals have gone on to make a career in motor sport.

George Smith became Circuit Manager at Silverstone when BRDC was at its height as an organising club. He became Director and then Director of Building when BRDC/Silverstone launched a new building plan for race teams to be based within Silverstone Circuit.

The Dickens family, Les and Rita, became full time employees there, too, and many others took jobs within the Silverstone/BRDC empire over many years. Pam Dearn and husband Gary took on various jobs at Silverstone. Pam is still 'mother hen' to all her marshals and Gary, as circuit manager was always ready to make what improvements he could to circuit facilities for the marshals. Sharon Bicknell, soon to marry fellow marshal, Matthew Smith, took over from Pam as Marshals' Secretary at the BRDC and went on to be Competitions Secretary at MG Car Club and then BRSCC. Diane Hardy, ably assisted by partner Steve Angel, continued to look after Donington Emergency Services Team after Di joined Donington full time.

The Management team at BARC – Dennis Carter, Dale Wells and Ian Watson – all started as marshals. The BRSCC management team is similarly sprinkled with those whose motor sport careers began in marshalling.

Bob Illman, regular Flag Marshal at Castle Combe, took early retirement during 2006 from many years as Financial Director at McLaren International, after similar posts at Fittipaldi and Wolf Engineering F1 teams. Very many others went on to work for major racing teams and it has been my pleasure to meet many of them in various countries around the World.

Don and Gwen Lawrence's wee boy Paul – all six feet whatever of him – went from being a brilliant Flag Marshal to part time motor sport journalist, then full time freelancing and the author of several important books on the sport and the personalities within the sport, including our own Barrie Williams.

Jonathan Noble, a young Silverstone ES team marshal whom we helped with the odd lift when he was still too young to drive, was one of the youngest winners ever of the prestigious Sir William Lyons award as the Guild of Motor Sport Writers' young journalist of the year and went on to join *Autosport*. There he became joint GP Editor with the renowned Nigel Roebuck before becoming Editor of Autosport.com.

One of June's timekeeping colleagues, young Marcus Simmons, went into journalism with *Motorsport News*, where he became Editor, then Editor of *Motor Sport Magazine*. Marcus also raced in Formula First for a while, with some success.

Many set up their own businesses in and around motorsport, with mixed results. One of the more interesting was Formula Services Limited, set up by Val Adaway. Val had organised successful race meetings for many years for the Marshals' Club, at Silverstone and Donington. She also helped with the race organising teams from other Clubs, at a variety of circuits around the country. During all of this, she became aware of the great difficulty some drivers had in getting their race entries in on time. It was often only a few days before the race that many drivers realised they had not made an entry and were now too late to get on the grid. This was not a problem that related solely to the Club driver, it was competitors at all levels who simply forgot there was essential paper work to be done if they wanted to race.

So, in 1979, amidst some scepticism from the establishment, Formula Services was born. John Webb of Brands Hatch was one who encouraged Val and gave her his support. Val advertised a complete race entry package – race entry (at the appropriate time!), help with preparation of commentators' sheets, collection of race and championship regulations and interpretation of same where necessary! All for a fee, of course. Many predicted that there were not going to be many competitors would pay for this service; how wrong they were.

Young drivers, old drivers, new drivers, experienced drivers, UK drivers and drivers from countries all around the World signed up with Formula Services. For many, it was a way of getting rid of a tiresome administrative task that interfered with their racing. For others it became a complete racing service, for overseas drivers in particular. Many seemed to arrive on these shores with Val's phone number and address ready to hand. She found them lodgings, directed them to the circuits, and introduced them to the organising staffs there and to Championship organisers. She even fed them at the circuit on many occasions!

Formula Services was very successful and despite the early cynicism, several imitators appeared but none was quite so popular with the drivers. However, once the likes of TOCA came along with, in effect, a race entry scheme included in the up front fee for entry to the Championship, business started to fall off. Other championship series began to follow the TOCA lead and Val wound down the business in the mid 1980's.

Val and Rob made many friends during this period, friends they still visit from time to time and hear from to this day. The list of drivers they helped over the years is long but it would be inappropriate to publish it here; suffice to say that the list contains many famous names.

Another aspect of marshals' work is what they do in their day jobs. A recent survey carried out by the Motorsports Safety Fund showed that a very large percentage of those who marshal hold down management jobs or senior positions in Information Technology. Within the Marshals' Club ranks we find F1 Team Directors, as noted above, many more who work at fairly high levels within the sport and numerous PhD's, MSc's and other well qualified scholars. We have several doctors and health care professionals, some who turn out in their chosen profession, others who prefer just to marshal. We even have a couple of millionaire businessmen, who managed to amass their fortunes in their time off from marshalling!

An excellent example of the wide variety of jobs held by marshals was when Val and Rob Adaway came across to lunch to let me have information for this book. At the time, we were struggling with a planned extension to our home. Every architect, every builder we spoke to wanted a twelve inch pillar each side of the planned opening to our new dining room, which quite frankly was putting us off the idea. We shared this story with Rob and Val, only for Rob to say, "I can fix that for you!" Despite all the years we have known Rob and Val and I worked with Rob on circuit, I had completely forgotten what he did for a living. Rob is a very experienced structural engineer and within a few days we had a scheme to present to our builders that totally eliminated the problem pillars! Job on, thank you, Rob.

Marshals really do come from all walks of life and bring with them an enormous depth of experience that serves the sport well.

1973 British Grand Prix

by Chris Hobson

In 1973 I was over the moon when I learned I had been accepted as an Incident Officer for the British Grand Prix at Silverstone. When I signed on I was given my usual post – Woodcote Tower. Fantastic – in those days the cars came straight out from Farm into Woodcote at absolute full speed then thundered off onto the main straight – no chicane, nothing to artificially slow them down, only a small amount of catch fencing up against the sleepers.

For the first time ever we had an 'Incident Vehicle' on the post – a pickup truck with a load of Tangy-Epco hydraulic gear in the back, manned by Paddy Kenshole.

All was peaceful until the GP itself. Having covered the grid for the start we returned to our positions to await the cars at the end of lap 1. Jody Schekter came into view, well ahead of all the others and going at a heck of a pace. I turned to the others and said "He'll never get round at that speed!" He must have heard me. Wide onto the grass, sideways, frantically trying to regain control, Jody swept past us, then, as sideways motion slowed, forward motion took over once again, as he hurtled across the track, bounced off the pit wall and landed in the middle of the main straight just as the rest of the pack came through Woodcote.

Our yellow flag made no difference whatsoever!

Sixteen cars either hit Jody or each other and came to a halt as mangled wrecks in the middle of the tarmac; we all leapt into action. Thankfully not one car caught fire, but poor Andrea De Adamich was trapped by his ankles in his; up against the sleepers and in agony. Paddy and the pickup truck were off like a startled rabbit, but it then took us almost and hour to cut the steering rack from the car and release the driver. Other North East region marshals were also involved, including one who told Barry Gill (reporting for the BBC and standing in the middle of all the carnage with a live mike and petrol all round him) to, "F**k off" just as he came on air saying "As I stand here the marshals are leaping into action…"

We tidied it all up and the race was restarted with a somewhat depleted field. We had proved how useful the rescue gear was, and from then on the incident vehicle became a standard part of the motor racing scene.

My memories of the 1973 British Grand Prix *(author speaking!)* were mainly that I missed it! I was on a trip to Zeltweg in Austria for a Formula 3 race, which was cancelled when we were halfway there! I heard about it when I came back, heard also that Dave Brodie was in Northampton General Hospital and set off there immediately with my Newsletter Editor's recording machine. Dave had an amazingly clear memory of the build up to the accident and then finding he could not breathe because of all the dry powder he had inhaled when his car caught fire. He wanted the names of the marshals who helped him and I know he went out of his way at future race meetings to find them and thank them for all their efforts that day.

Ballet Dancers!

Many times during this particular phase of my marshalling career I found myself asking, "How did I get myself involved in all this?" Here I was prancing about in a tutu to the strains of 'The Sugar Plum Fairy.' I who, despite years in business, remained in terror of speaking in public, much less making an exhibition of myself in this way! Pat Todd, you have a lot to answer for.

I joined South Mids Committee as Newsletter Editor soon after joining the Marshals' Club. In fact, it was at the first social event I attended that the then Chairman Pat Todd took me to one side to welcome me, discovered I could type – and before the end of the night I was South Mids Newsletter Editor. Isn't this always the way in the Marshals' Club?

However, worse was to come. Pat explained to me at one of my first committee meetings that it was the tradition in South Mids for the Committee to 'do a turn' at the annual dinner and all were expected to take part. Speaking or appearing in public is not something I have ever learned to enjoy. In business I did my fair share of speaking to new audiences and even did a couple of TV/radio shows, one with John Harvey-Jones, star of BBC's Trouble Shooter programme and ex-Chairman of ICI. This I did enjoy because he was such a great character to be around. For everything else I was always petrified. Yet, here I was under considerable pressure from Chairman Todd to become a ballet dancer!

As a quick aside, one of my fellow panellists on the John Harvey-Jones venture was Jon Dooley, a very quick and exciting driver to watch in a series of Alfa-Romeos over the years. The panel of four was chosen from a large number of business people in Milton Keynes and the surrounding areas. Two out of four from motor sport wasn't bad, I thought, reinforcing my long held view that many in authority in motor sport seriously underestimate the calibre of those they are dealing with at the average club race meeting.

As far as the ballet dancing was concerned it looked as if I was in. There was to be no escape for me. We were short of a place to meet and I offered the small canteen at Plysu in Woburn Sands, where I was then employed. Then I was asked if we could practise there as well. Perish the thought – but we did, with curtains very firmly closed! Plysu worked around the clock and I really did not want half the factory taking the p**s over my debut as a ballet star.

We practised once a week for ten or twelve weeks under the watchful eye of our ace choreographer, Patricia Smith. At first it was a bit of a laugh but as we got nearer the time, Pat got much less lenient with us and drove us hard to get the steps right, first time, every time (where have I heard that before?).

Then came the dresses! Pat told us what we needed and we had to beg, borrow or steal tights in colours to match all the flags. In my case, the biggest problem was finding tights big enough! John Gaddes, a good few inches taller than me but similarly built had his own problems. The rest, Pat Todd, Ricky Parnell and Colin Clapshoe found normal sizes a decent fit! We were not a pretty sight at the first dress rehearsal! Nevertheless, we ploughed on.

There was full attendance on the night of our annual dinner, as we crept away to get changed into our costumes, to launch ourselves on an unsuspecting audience. We got an absolutely hilarious reception. I remember seeing Bill Cox, very successful Ford Capri racer creased up with laughter and it was he and his driver mates who led the calls for an encore. I think we did two but by then we were completely knackered and could not wait to get to the bar for a drink. It was a riotous night which, in fact, I quite enjoyed in the end, despite my trepidation at first.

Interestingly, Pat Todd's wife, Marion, is the current Mayor of Peterborough. Pat has taken early retirement to be her 'consort' and I have threatened him with exposure as a past 'ballet dancer' if he steps out of line as Mayor's Consort!

BRSCC Bus – *Chris Whitlock*

Do you remember the BRSCC Green & Yellow double-decker promotion bus? If you look at pictures of it carefully you will see the roof line is a bit flat! BRSCC HQ decided to take it to Zandvoort on the *"BRSCC goes Dutch Tour"* in 1989 (still got the sweatshirt). Anne Rothburg and a couple of others were travelling in the double-decker, the rest of us, all marshals were travelling in a coach behind. Driving along the motorway up past Schiphol airport there was a flash of sparks from the bus as it passed under a bridge, next bridge there was a bang and a bigger shower of sparks and the bus pulled onto the hard shoulder; we followed. A very shaky Anne got off and came over to our coach, seems motorway bridges in Holland do not cater for British double-deckers. Anne and the passengers came and joined us in the coach leaving only the driver on the bus. On we went until! ... Approaching Schiphol there is a short tunnel under a canal, the headroom is lower than the bridges, in fact there were warning signs of the maximum headroom. There was no way a double-decker was going to get under! We left the bus and driver parked on the hard shoulder and continued on our way to Zandvoort – we were running late. We were planning to have a party and barbie in the paddock that night with the bus as the centre point. All the food and equipment was on the bus. All the best laid plans had gone awry because the bus was too tall.

When we got to Zandvoort practice was already underway, it was the last race meeting on the old GP circuit. When we eventually got off post at the end of the day we found the bus was in the paddock. Our driver had to wait for a police escort to take him off the motorway and lead him on a bridge free route to the circuit. Double-deckers are allowed in Holland, but it seems you need a special permit and agreed route before you can take them there. The bus was destined to remain at Zandvoort until such arrangements could be made for its return journey.

Marshals' Club 21st Anniversary Race Meeting Silverstone 19th August 1978

Ray Darvill, our then ever-active Public Relations Officer, was determined that our 21st Anniversary Race meeting at Silverstone should be a good one and that it should get some publicity in the motor racing Press. We did get coverage in the motoring Press but for all the wrong reasons.

The day started as normal. I was in my first year as the Club's Chief Marshal, replacing John Felix who had gone on to be a Clerk of the Course. When I look now at the number of meetings John has done as Clerk, in however many countries around the World it has been, I am reminded of how time flies. Time flies in another respect, too. We had a minimum of four to five Course Marshals, Flag Marshals and Observers at each post, plus the usual turn out of Silverstone ES personnel under the tutelage of their founder Phil Morom. Would that we could have similar numbers at a Saturday meeting now!

Andrew Kitson, well known motor sports artist, wrote a very lucid and respectful piece on the tragedy that was about to unfold on that day, for the Marshals' Forum on Ten-Tenths web site 26 years later which I reproduce with his permission.

"It was the BMRMC 21st Anniversary Meeting on 19th August 1978 on the Silverstone Club circuit. Some friends and I were watching from the Woodcote stands among the sparse crowd on this particular Saturday afternoon.

The third race of the day was the Lew Wooster Trophy for Modified Sports Cars. A car stalled on the grid, if I remember correctly, or it may have been hit by another at the green. However, the marshals could not move it. As the field thundered down the Club straight, crossed oil and yellow flags were shown to stop the race.

However, Reg Woodcock in his 3.8 Jag E-type was at the back of the field (Author's note: On the other side of the pack from the flag point) picking off the slower Midgets etc at an alarming speed difference down the straight and seemed to see the crossed flags and the slowing cars at the last minute.

Reg's car spun several times under heavy braking, from a point where the national circuit bridge crosses the circuit now. There was a marshals' post to the inside, protected by a small length of Armco. The marshals were slowing the field, waving arms, etc but a couple of them were beyond the Armco towards the track. Alas, Reg's car slammed into them and disintegrated, bodies flew through the air and there were fatalities. This tragedy made the TV news and of course the remaining race programme was cancelled. (Author's Note: In fact, we did resume racing; see later note.)

We drove home stunned but a couple of weeks later I was back at a race circuit. However, it did bring it home to me how dangerous a marshalling job can be, without you guys we would not have a sport and I am wondering if any of you remember this black day 26 years ago and if you can recall those who sadly fell for their sport?"

I was Chief Marshal that day, the saddest day of my marshalling life.

Graham Bond, regular BRDC Clerk, was our Clerk of the Course. (Graham sadly died a few years later on a cruise ship and was buried at sea.) John Felix was Deputy Clerk. Keith Douglas, BMRMC's 'founding father' was commentator; my son and daughter were helping him with lap charts and collecting result sheets, etc. The late Ray Darvill, Club PRO, had created some extra interest for this meeting, to celebrate our Anniversary.

My wife June was spectating by the paddock entrance/exit with some friends and June's sister, Lynn, who is a nursing professional. Lynn and John Huffer were among the first on the scene to attend to the injured. Club medic, the late Tom Dowell was the doctor in charge. Nigel Tan was killed instantly, John Baker was grievously injured, Dave Allen had a fractured femur (I think) and was reasonably relaxed on his way to hospital with Lynn in attendance. A South African marshal whose surname was Delahaye had minor injuries.

Lynn recalls how impressed she was with John Huffer and other marshals who attended the scene, how well they all coped with the tragedy and getting care to those who needed it.

In the meantime, the people in Race Control were having to find a Police Officer to act as Coroner's Officer and to decide what to do about the remainder of the race meeting. Drivers we spoke to left the decision to us; they would go along with anything we agreed to do. I consulted with Phil Morom (Mr BMRMC to many!) who suggested we continue, as much as a tribute to those who had fallen as anything else. Phil knew Nigel well and felt he would have wanted the race to continue. The injured marshals were being cared for and had by now left the circuit for the hospital in Northampton.

So, we continued and, even in hindsight, I think it was the right thing to do. It eased the tension for many although some of us in Race Control felt a bit jaded by the end of the day. Nothing, of course, to what the families felt and it was they who were constantly in our thoughts as we had to deal with the unfortunate formalities of such a tragic day.

Later that evening the hospital rang me at home to say that Dave Allen had died – which, at first, we felt was a case of mistaken identity and that it must have been John Baker who had died, because of the extent of his injuries assessed at the scene. Sadly for Dave's family, Dave had suffered an embolism while awaiting treatment at Northampton General.

Poor old John Baker was in and out of coma for eleven or twelve days. During this time we assisted with getting his parents up from Tunbridge Wells and we made sure that John had a regular rota of visitors to try to bring him around, including Frank Williams and Dave Brodie, who were visiting Jochen Mass who was in the General at the same time. Dave Brodie was particularly helpful in urging (almost lecturing!) John to get better. At some considerable risk, the decision was taken to transfer John to Tunbridge Wells hospital, on the basis that he might fare better amongst people he knew. Happily, this proved to be the case. One of the nursing Sisters was an old school mate, who helped greatly in John's recovery, slow and painful as it was.

Coincidentally, our Anniversary meeting was the same day we formally started BlowMocan, the plastics manufacturing company I co-founded in Milton Keynes. Much later than planned that evening, we held our inaugural Board Meeting to get things underway. BlowMocan was extremely successful but, as you might imagine, I remember that first day with some mixed emotions.

The highlight that lifts some of the sad memories for me, is how quickly John Baker got back to marshalling! Considering the extent of his injuries, it wasn't too long at all before John was back to regular marshalling and I speak to him regularly. John now puts in almost as many days as he did before his terrible injuries and has lots of marshalling friends who arrange lifts for him to other circuits. He, to me, epitomises what marshalling is all about, as do the numerous marshalling friends who help out.

Marshals are not a bad bunch of people to have as friends, are they?

21ˢᵀ Anniversary Race Meeting

John Baker's Memories

John has no clear recollection of the day; not too surprising, considering the extent of his injuries that sad day. However, I feel I can do no better than to give John's memories in his own words.

I set off from my home in Tunbridge Wells in the early hours of that day, little realising what would happen! It dawned sunny and bright as I recall; I remember the morning sunshine, a typically pleasant Summer's day. I was to flag at Woodcote Advance. My fellow Flag Marshal was Richard Delahaye, a friendly young man from South Africa. Our Observer was Don Baker – no relation, although Don sometimes would tell people he was my brother!

Practice and lunch completed, racing commenced with an event for motorcycles. Unfortunately, when it came to the Mod Sports race John Digby's Davrian was stuck on the grid. It could not be moved and the Clerk of the Course quickly made the decision to stop the race. As I recall, there was quite a breeze as Richard and I displayed crossed yellow and oil and yellow flags (the method in 1978 of letting drivers know that the Red Flag was being displayed at the start/finish line and the session had been stopped.) Two Silverstone ES marshals, Dave Allen and Nigel Tan came forward to help steady the flags.

That is about all I can remember until I woke up in Northampton General Hospital several days later, with both legs badly broken and several other injuries I will not bore you with. Apparently, the brake problem Reg Woodcock had in practice persisted. As he came to the end of the Club Straight, and belatedly saw the crossed oil and yellows, he braked hard and spun violently into our post.

Nigel Tan was killed instantly. Dave Allen passed away that same night in hospital. Richard was slightly hurt and quickly recovered.

Meanwhile, I was in a coma at Northampton General. George Copeland tells me I was in this state for over a week and even when I came round, I used to doze off in the middle of conversations but then I probably have always been a bit dozy! I do remember my legs being quite painful and as I gradually regained consciousness the decision was taken to transfer me to hospital in Tunbridge Wells.

My abiding memory of being in the Kent and Sussex Hospital is being in traction, my legs suspended and not being able to move much. Much later, I remember my first, laborious efforts in learning to walk again. In particular, the floor seemed so far away but slowly I progressed. Keep trying, I told myself. To relate another strange fact, I am now five feet eight inches tall, previously I was five feet ten inches. The doctors lowered me to make my poor legs equal!

After I left hospital and gradually got stronger, I had a strong desire to recommence marshalling. I undertook results score board duties in the early part of 1979 (A near miracle in my view and testament to John's quiet determination! – G.C) From there I moved on to paddock, paddock office, pits and start line – although, really, I could not wait to get back on the bank. Jim Keenan let me do flagging at Brands Hatch a few times. Jim had been a regular visitor while I was in hospital and knew how anxious I was to resume flag duties. Thanks, Jim; oh, the joy of being on a post again!

Much later, as my legs became stronger, I started to flag again as my main marshalling duty. I was determined to do it. So I have now enjoyed many years as a Flag Marshal. I have acted as a Judge with Don Baker's team in the 1990's at BRSCC meetings at Brands Hatch. I have also done Observer and Assistant Observer meetings but I must confess to not really enjoying the experience. Flag marshalling is what I want to do, even though this means I have to regularly exercise at a local gym to keep my battered legs up to it! As the man said, "Never give up!"

As to the accident – perhaps the post should have been better protected? Maybe we, the post marshals, should have been more circumspect? Unfortunately, as often happens with tragedies, several aspects link up to produce disaster.

Well, I am sure lessons have been learned and do get learned from all accidents. We now have better, more suitable barriers, more run-off areas, and repeater red lights around the circuit. The present red flag system is an improvement in itself. Time moves on and hopefully we improve all the time.

While writing this article, I must thank everyone who visited me, wrote to me, and gave me presents, sympathy and support. There were very many people, including George and June Copeland, whose help was enormous, Ray Darvill, Dave Sleeman, Chris and Sue Whitlock, Don Baker, Jim Keenan, Alec Spooner, Nick Adams (Sports 2000 star), Dave Brodie (Run, Baby, Run super saloon racer) Ricky Podmore, Reg Woodcock and everybody else, not forgetting the medical staff and my long-suffering family. Apologies if I have not mentioned you by name; my memory of that period is rather vague (probably no bad thing, John – G.C). However, your kindness is not forgotten.

As mentioned, the accident has not dimmed my passion for marshalling and racing. If anything, it has strengthened my resolve and determination. There is something very special about the camaraderie of our hobby.

Author's note:

Don Baker, veteran marshal and Brands Hatch regular died after a short illness in 1998. Richard Delahaye went back to South Africa soon after the incident.

Other Marhsalling Disciplines

Strictly speaking, *50 Years of Marshalling,* is to record the history of the British Motor *Racing* Marshals' Club, since it was the need to better organise and train race marshals that led to the Club being formed in 1957. However, it would be remiss of me not to record how the Marshals' Club's activities spread into all other disciplines in due course.

British Rally Marshals' Club

The first of these was the formation or the British Rally Marshals' Club in 1979/80. Encouraged by several people at the MSA, who wanted to see our training and grading procedures spread into rally marshalling, John Felix was encouraged to set up new company, the BRMC, as a subsidiary of BMRMC.

The Rally Marshals' Club got off to a flying start, vindicating those at the MSA who had seen the need. We very quickly had rally representatives in each of our then six regions, although some regions were always more active than others. The North East region in particular at that time, lead the way in number of rally marshalling days put in. That is not to say other regions were inactive, merely that many of the other regions' efforts were channelled through North East because so many Stage Commanders, etc came from North East region.

First Chairman was Adrian Breese, an active Silverstone Emergency Services Team member during the summer months but dedicated rally man during the winter months. The race and rally scenes then were a little more clearly defined in terms of their respective months of activity. Racing generally ran from March to early October and the principal rallies ran from October through to March. Adrian was a very effective Chairman during this early period – in his Lada car – but died of a heart attack at a cruelly young age. The Lada car was something of a trademark with Adrian; he used to say, "I am a Rally Marshal, usually plugging through forests on roads that would tear a normal car to shreds; my Lada suits me fine and I always got a good trade in price each year"

Jon Cordery took over from Adrian and has done a similarly competent job in keeping Marshals' Club influence to the fore in rally marshalling and at the MSA, through his membership of the Rallies Committee and various safety sub-committees. Membership has grown steadily but it seems to me there is not the degree of cross-fertilisation there used to be with marshals who regularly turned out for both rallying and racing. The two seasons now overlap much more than they used to – more rallies in the summer months, races now as early as February and as late as November, excluding the Boxing Day meetings that always took place as a chance to blow away the cobwebs after the festivities of the day before! Clearly, marshals cannot be in two places at once and even where dates do not clash, there is always the cost of attendance to consider and marshals have to choose carefully just how many days they can afford to do in any one season.

Karting

Next up, again inspired by comments from the MSA, was a move into karting. Marshals there were very often drawn from the Mums and Dads of young kart drivers. Emotions often overrode judgement with parents being too closely involved and the Marshals' Club sought to restore some order to the situation! Those involved, at karting venues up and down the country, had varying degrees of success at first but rather in the same way that the Marshals' Club had to gain acceptance over the years, so too did the Kart Section. Now, it is hard to remember those early days and the Marshals' Club kart people have brought significant improvement to the karting scene – and not always just in marshalling. Peter Cox, greatly aided by wife, Sue, and the team they have built up over the years, now advise on many aspects of track building, safety measures and, of course, the constant update of training schemes for

Kart Marshals. Brenda Catley was another who got involved in karting over the years, until her illness and sad death in 2007.

Hill Climbs and other Speed Events

Elsewhere I mention that John Felix was Chairman of the Marshals' Club during what was its busiest period of growth and innovation. It was John who oversaw the formation of the BMRMC Northern Ireland region that began the same year and the subsequent extension of our activities into karting, hill climbs and speed events. Marshals' Club members had always been involved in these activities outside of racing but as the Training and Grading Scheme became well known in circuit racing, many at the MSA and elsewhere saw the need for this to be extended into other disciplines. John was very much 'our man' at the MSA at this time and it always appeared to fall to him to start the initiation process. He always seemed able to pick the right people to help and it is a credit to John and the many people he enrolled to help him, that the Marshals' Club 'stamp', in Training and Grading especially, is still so evident in almost every discipline in motor sport.

BRMC Memories

Most of my recollections are from rallying in the late 80s and early 90s, when I was most active and doing more than forty marshalling days a year. I put a number of thoughts on paper at the time in the Marshal Law articles I wrote for the South Mids newsletter, but I now don't have many of these.

Inevitably, two characters no longer with us figure large – Adrian Breese and Ian Kellaway.

I am sure there will be many memories of Adrian – it hardly seems possible that he died so many years ago, in January 1995. I got to know him both from marshalling and from commuting with him into London when we both worked there in the early 90s. Amongst the many things that stay in my memory was the way, whilst Chairman of BRMC, he would personally call new members of the club to get them to training days and to rallies. The very thoughtful and caring way he approached his work with the rescue team at Silverstone – I remember him counting up the number of fatalities he had dealt with at the circuit over the years (which I recall ran well into double figures) and saying how much they had affected him.

His sense of humour will be widely mentioned I'm sure – on one rally he told the rescue vehicle to get ready to go in when a certain competitor was on the start line, so sure was he that it would crash. He was quite right of course.

Ian Kellaway also put in an outstanding amount of work to his support for the Club, active in all disciplines. Aside from having what must have been the most well-travelled Skoda in existence – doing 40,000 miles a year at one point. My abiding memory is from one of our trips to marshal the Tour of Mull, where I think Ian established the tradition of the BRMC providing a Stage Commander. When the rally first got permission to close public roads, there were strict instructions as to the need to tape off all means of access to the stage. On Ian's stage, these were followed to the letter – including the careful taping off of the local telephone box – a feat that rightly starred in the video of the rally. It also earned us the respect of the organisers and an invitation to run the stage in future years, representing as it did the fastidious way in which the Club's work was done.

There are many other memories from a time when the Club would put out marshals on rallies most weekends, including:

• The Club's own two single venue rallies run at Wilbaston in the late 80s, with Adrian acting as Clerk of the Course to the first

• Ian Hamer's exploits as a co-driver – crashing at the same point in both (or was it three?) runs through Pentimore woods on one event, and keeping up a tradition of failing to bring back a car in one piece whether marshalling or competing in five consecutive trips to Wales

• Dave King deciding to treat the timing crew to ice cream following a hard day's work on one stage at Weston Park – on the Network Q, in November…

• Coping with an entire field arriving back at Rally HQ simultaneously, following a stage cancellation on the Manx – the year that it was a round of the French championship. Anyone know the French for "please stop besieging our control while the organisers work out what to do?"

• Working on some of the smaller, club, rallies – including one Hella Stages where, as Stage Commander, I asked if I could have the stage plans a couple of days beforehand to set up our stage, only to be told that they weren't planning to recce the venue until the day before and hadn't worked out where it went yet…

One of the favourite memories of Adrian was his self-deprecating sense of humour. He liked to tell of one trip to Epynt on an icy December morning where his Lada had fallen foul of black ice on a bend, recounting that his passenger woke up at that point and asked what was happening, to which Adrian's response was "it's ok, we're just having an accident..."

Author's Note:

As well as writing for our newsletters, Richard has been our acting, unpaid legal adviser for many years. He was instrumental in the wholesale re-write of our rules during Ken James's term as Secretary, which still exist today, largely unaltered, except for those things that change through passage of time.

The Dubai Grand Prix

It was in early 1981 that John Felix started to ring around BMRMC Observers, to ask if they fancied a trip to Dubai to marshal the Dubai Grand Prix. I am not sure just how long a nanosecond is but I know it was less than that before I said yes!

Martin Hone and his International Festival Services organisation – who brought motor racing to the streets of Birmingham – had taken on the job of organising a race around the streets of Dubai as part of the celebration to commemorate the tenth anniversary of the formation of the United Arab Emirates. John Felix had been asked to supply marshals to run the event.

So it was that the following people assembled at Heathrow (and Manchester, I believe) during early December 1981 for the journey to Dubai.

Clerk of the Course	John Felix
Deputy Clerk of the Course	Tony Iddon
Observers and Trainers	Rob Adaway
	Reg Baines
	George Copeland
	Dick Fraser
	Chris Hobson
	Howard Houghton
	Cliff Hammond
	Don Lawrence

Dick Moore
Wilf Nickson
Nevil Parker
Brian Pearson
Tony Pernyes
Vic Sparkes
Harry Tinkler
Geoff Thomson
Cliff Wright
John Watt

Timekeepers   Brenda Catley
Joan Douglas
Roy Oates
Tony Daff

Commentators   Keith Douglas
Neville Hay

Scrutineers   Mike Garton
Robert Gibson-Phillips

First question on many lips was, "Is Dubai dry?" "No", we were reassured, "there will be plenty of opportunities for a pint or two." In fact, that proved to be something of an understatement!

The flight out was courtesy of Gulf Air and as guests of the ruler, we flew in Business Class. It appears that section ran out of Scotch during the flight but you may have to check the truth or otherwise of that rumour with Cliff Wright and John Felix!

Martin Hone and his party of helpers made us most welcome upon arrival. We would have some time to look around Dubai and it was perfectly safe to do so. So, off we went on a tour of this very interesting city. Dubai then was not as Dubai has now become. In 1981, many of the old traditions were still in place. Dhows still plied their trade to and from India and beyond. Much of Dubai's early wealth, prior to the discovery of oil, came from smuggling and ship repair. Ship repair remained and so did the odd bit of smuggling we were reliably informed. Of course Dubai is now one of the fastest developing countries in the World. The ruling family are preparing for the eventual reduction of oil revenues by transforming their country into one of the 'play capitals' of the World, for the rich and famous, and offering properties of exceptionally high standard to this same group. Meanwhile, they are spending oil revenue buying up well know companies such as P&O and various other blue chip UK companies. Most recently they are reputed to be trying to buy Turnberry and Gleneagles Hotels, two hotels near and dear to my heart! I earned my pocket money as a school boy caddy at Turnberry golf course (seven miles from my home in Girvan) and with a little more money available in later life, I have spent several enjoyable weekends at Gleneagles – the first on a Jackie Stewart Mechanics' Trust shoot.

Martin had made many friends within the ex-pat community there and they, in turn, were keen to become involved in the occasion. In the run up to the Grand Prix, many made themselves known to us and were keen to show us around, find us interesting places to visit and care for our welfare.

Then it was down to a little work to justify our trip. Martin's team had put together a fair sized group of volunteers, of all nationalities and levels of marshalling competence. Most had no experience whatsoever and it was our job to turn them into reasonably competent marshals in the two or three days we now had before the big event. They lacked nothing in enthusiasm and I think everyone agreed they acquitted themselves reasonably well on the day.

Medical cover was provided from a local, very modern and well-equipped hospital in Sharjah. Most of the nurses were from the UK, attracted by salaries, benefits and working conditions way beyond what was then available in the UK. One of the surgeons was a prominent military surgeon on something of a 'rest and recreation' period, following several years of duty in Northern Ireland during the worst of the troubles there. Again, they were all enthusiastic to help Martin's venture.

Competitors, too, were enthusiastic for an event outside the prior experience of most of them. Competing cars had been shipped out in containers immediately following the final round at Silverstone in October. Ford was still officially banned in the UAE and competitors had to be 'innovational' in devising similar blue ovals that did not say Ford. Gordon Spice Capri's became Spice Capri's, others simply had plain blue ovals.

Martin Hone's local contacts had got together a list of local folks who wanted to marshal, nearly all ex-pats, rather than Dubai Nationals. All the local volunteers assembled in a local cinema to be briefed on what was expected of them. Chris Hobson, then our Training Officer, gave a quite inspirational presentation, followed by Wilf Nickson as Chief Flag and John Felix as Clerk of the Course (the first of many overseas Clerking appearances for John!).

The local marshals were all very keen but the first practice day produced a few headaches with our volunteer force! Sometimes their enthusiasm was just a little bit beyond what was required and we had to issue a few "restraining orders" to keep their enthusiasm in check. All in all, things went well, though, and we were soon working as a team.

During racing, many of us were glad when it became our turn to be in the shade of the hotel complex. Not so the locals; they immediately donned every bit of clothing they had brought with them. The nurses on my post borrowed some of my spare clothing but only on the understanding they did not stretch it out of shape for me to wear afterwards!

For the main invitation race, Martin Hone had attracted a mouth-watering group of (truly!) famous drivers. In race entry order, they were:

John Watson	F1 Team Leader Marlboro McLaren
Sir Jack Brabham	World Champion 1959/60/66
Denny Hulme	World Champion 1967
Stirling Moss	Legendary F1 star
Carroll Shelby	Famed constructor and *Le Mans* winner 1959
Roy Salvadori	*Le Mans* winner 1959
Dickie Attwood	*Le Mans* winner 1970
Derek Bell	Five times *Le Mans* winner
Innes Ireland	Another legendary F1 star
John Fitzpatrick	Porsche IMSA Champion 1980
Dan Gurney	International GP winner

Late arrivals included James Hunt and Jody Scheckter. Jody was never there officially; he is Jewish and South African, both unpopular attributes in the Arab world at that particular time. So, Jody was picked up from his aeroplane on the tarmac and flown by helicopter on to the roof of the Hyatt Regency hotel and I suspect he never appeared on the immigration schedules!

Others there were Juan Manuel Fangio, John Harper and David Piper with his usual string of sports cars. Teddy Yip's Team Theodore F1 car was there for demonstration runs by popular F1 driver Patrick Tambay. Other notable drivers of the day included Nick Mason, Gerry Marshall, Mike Wheatley and Production Saloon Car aces Andy Rouse, Gordon Spice, Tom Walkinshaw, and Vince Woodman.

The fine gentlemen assembled to take part in the main invitation race then proceeded to drive like a bunch of rock apes. They demolished the rows of tyres we had installed to mark a chicane just down from where I was marshalling on the first lap. They then spent the rest of the race straight-lining the chicane and dragging stones and sand all across the carefully prepared circuit. Some had the good grace to apologise for the havoc they caused but always, it seems, with a wide grin on their faces! Frankly, we all enjoyed it, too.

Other races were much more genteel, with some valuable cars to be looked after. They were no less competitive, though, especially in the Production Saloon car race where the season long competition between the Spice and Walkinshaw teams was well to the fore!

I don't recall many race winners and in any event, the results were almost immaterial to enjoyment of the occasion, for all.

It all seemed a bit anti-climatic at the end of racing. Some of our Northern contingent were on their way home almost as soon as they had cleaned up and packed. The rest of us were able to contemplate the farewell dinner, after a few refreshments and into our dinner suits. (Marshals do scrub up well for parties!)

Dinners in this part of the world take something of a reverse order to those at home. Honoured guests file in once everyone is sat down – but there was nothing on any of the tables but a few pitchers of water and glasses. Was this going to be the 'dry' dinner we had feared??

Don Revie, ex-Manager of Leeds United and England, was star guest on behalf of the Al Nasr Sports Club of Dubai. He and other honoured guests had to be in place before the representative of the ruling family arrived – under heavily armed escort as there was some sort of security alarm going on at the time. All the marshals dived for cover as 'big' Cliff Wright decided to step out from his table to personally welcome the Sheikh! There was a distinct rattle of AK47's and a huge, collective intake of breath as we waited to see how this possible intrusion on the Sheikh's security would pan out. Fortunately, all was well.

There then followed speeches and votes of thanks from Don Revie and other honoured guests – who then departed the room, leaving the rest of us wondering quite what was going on. Our concerns were soon mollified by the appearance of hordes of waiters to set the tables and bring out the booze! We were very quickly tucking in to a gala feast, well lubricated by some excellent wines.

Our departure was planned on a 6.00 a.m. flight the next morning. A few of us decided it was hardly worth going to bed and spent the rest of the evening and the early hours of the next morning comfortably ensconced in one of the lounges downstairs, where the night staff kept us fed and watered.

Several of our volunteer marshals had come from the staff of the Hyatt, many of them from the kitchens. So, John Felix announced that two senior officials of the visiting party would be conducting an inspection of the kitchens. He and I, still in our dinner suits, then conducted a complete kitchen inspection at around 3.00 a.m. much to the amusement of those who had been marshalling with us over the weekend when they saw who was making the inspection!

Then it was up to our rooms for a quick shower, change out of evening wear and into our casuals for the flight home. It was a very subdued flight. My wife who came down with Val Adaway to pick up Rob and me declared straight away that she would be driving home!

One of the funniest stories concerning the aftermath of our visit to Dubai was when one of the marshals on my post said he would be coming to Britain for the next Grand Prix and could he camp with us at Silverstone. Spare tickets were easier to come by then and I was able to help him. However, as I was bicycling down to the gate to leave his tickets, I was hailed from this camper van heading up the Club Straight. Bill and his family were already in, without tickets. How did you manage to get in, I asked. "I just said I was visiting from Dubai and needed to meet George Copeland, and they let me in without question". Not a ticket to be seen; Heaven knows how he managed it!

All of us who attended that first major overseas outing for British marshals have fond memories of the occasion. So much so, that we managed a ten-year and a twenty-year reunion dinner. However, by the time twenty-five years came along, memories seemed to have dimmed a little and the occasion seems to have slipped into the backs of our minds. Maybe we will have to try again at thirty years!

Whatever the case, for me it was my first taste of the high life. I have had many subsequent visits abroad on motor race business but none that sticks in the mind like that first trip to Dubai. Thank you Martin Hone!

Since that time, of course, British marshals have travelled widely, both privately and as part of organised marshalling teams at new circuits around the World. John Felix is perhaps the most travelled, closely followed by The Race Gypsy (who writes of his exploits elsewhere) and John Tillott who managed to combine his business trips with marshalling in various countries around the globe. My own travels, mostly via introductions by John Felix, have taken me throughout Europe, to Japan and furthest of all, to Clerk an International meeting at a brand new circuit in the Philippines. Others now travel regularly to Australia, the USA and more recently to man new circuits in Bahrain and Dubai. There was a regular crew that went for many years to Korea and now to China for International F3 and GT meetings there.

Our marshals have always acquitted themselves well wherever they have been, evidenced by the large number of return invitations. It says a lot for our training methods and the enthusiasm and dedication of our 'Best of British' marshals!

Dubai Grand Prix – How it all came about

The idea of holding a major motor race in Dubai came about following Martin Hone's attempts over many years to have a motor race around the streets of Birmingham. The Birmingham event eventually took place after years of lobbying by Martin and his company International Festival Services. Sadly, when it did happen, IFS did not win the contract to organise it, which seems a great pity.

However, many in the know knew how much Martin and IFS had to do with the formation of the Birmingham race and when thoughts were first mooted about a similar event in Dubai, to celebrate the tenth anniversary of the United Arab Emirates, it was to Martin they came. The first approach came from head of Dubai Police, who was also a well known and relatively successful rally driver. The idea being to set up this event as the inaugural event in Dubai, heading towards a full blown Formula One Grand Prix in due course. Dubai was then already looking beyond existing on oil revenues alone and to develop other attractions to bring in revenue.

First surveys of the proposed site, around the Hyatt Regency Hotel in Dubai, called for considerable investment in the infrastructure around the hotel. Dubai was not nearly so well developed then and tarmac roads could become sand tracks almost without warning. Money was another issue. Rich as Dubai was, Martin would have to locate his own funding for the event itself. He did manage to find backers fairly quickly but in the longer term at least one never came up with the cash! What's new in that for motor race sponsorship?

The total budget, in 1981 values, was just under £1M, probably nearer £5M in today's terms. This had to include new roads around the hotel, with which there was some help from the Dubai government coffers.

However, the main issue was time! By the time everything was agreed IFS had 77 days to get the whole thing up and running! It is a matter of history that they managed to do so, even with this extremely short timescale. In that time, Martin and IFS had to engage all the guest drivers to come along (a *very* formidable and impressive list) for the main invitation race. British Leyland, as it was then, seemed uninterested in supplying cars for this race, despite the fact they were then trying to re-establish themselves in the UAE. Instead, Citroen took up the challenge of providing cars.

The organising team had to find and agree which cars would be appearing in the 'proper' races. This all had to be done at a fairly early stage as the cars were to be shipped by sea to Dubai and would leave the UK in October. Production Saloons, for instance, were into sea containers as soon as the last round of their championship was run at Silverstone in early October.

Again, it all happened. During this time, Martin was backwards and forward to Dubai on several occasions. Thankfully, he found in Dubai several people he knew from his renowned motor sports restaurant in Birmingham, The Steering Wheel Club, who came to his aid. Stan Robinson, there with the Al Futaim Honda agency, David Moody and Ian MacLeod of the Al Nasr Sports Club and Chris Davis, plus several Dubai dignitaries made up the local Race Committee – including Martin himself, of course! Permission came from the ruler himself, Shaikh Rashid Bin Said Al Maktoum, father of the present Maktoums who have so dominated horse racing in the UK over the past ten or fifteen years and presumably the grandfather of the Maktoum who founded A1GP!

Pre-event publicity for the event was enormous. Several TV companies took up the option to televise in various countries around the world. There were block bookings from all the surrounding Arab countries and an Austrian tour company booked 80 seats and used a special charter flight to bring the fans to Dubai. Sadly, there was not too much support from local spectators. Entrance fees were beyond many and there was rumoured to have been some 'local difficulty' which kept away ex-pats from Oman and other surrounding countries. We were never able to establish exactly what this local difficulty was but there was ample evidence that some who had intended to come, stayed away at the last minute.

So, with a vanishing sponsor as well, it proved to be something of a marginal return to International Festival Services after all the hard work they put in. Nevertheless, Martin says he would do the same thing again, any time! I know I speak for all the marshals and officials who attended by saying so would we!

Dubai Grand Prix – Chris Hobson's Memories

In 1981 I was nominated as National Training officer, and willingly took up the duties – which at that time also included grading administration.

I had only been in post a few weeks when I got a call from John Felix. "Are you busy the last week in November?"

"No why?"

"We're off to Dubai to run a race meeting there – since you are the National Training Officer you had better come along to train the marshals". Totally dumbfounded I arranged the time off from work.

The great day arrived and a coach took me down to London, then on to Heathrow where we all met up. Onto the plane and great mirth erupted when the stewardess asked Cliff Wright to, "Please return your seat to the upright position".

Cliff's reply? "I can't – I've broken it!"

On arrival at Dubai airport we were all subjected to security checks – no red and green channel then. All went well until my suitcase was searched. Suddenly my clothes were flying everywhere and I was ushered into a side-room at gunpoint. "Sign" they said and pushed a piece of paper at me. I signed – then realised it was a receipt for the training videos I was taking in – they had been confiscated in case they were pornographic! Released I joined the rest of the crew.

Felix met us at the hotel – annoyed at our delay. When told what had happened he introduced me to a very pleasant official – the chief of police! One radio call and fifteen minutes later a motorcycle courier arrived with my confiscated videos.

We arranged sessions to train all the local would-be marshals from scratch. It was great fun trying to explain the rules – especially the ones for flagging. I remember Wilf Nickson doing this bit but we were not sure at the end of it if the locals had really got the message. In the end we decided it would be better if we simply yelled when we wanted a flag displaying.

We had some R&R time and I again aroused the interest of the police when I was out taking photographs of the women shopping in the vegetable souk. I did not know I needed a husband's permission if the scene included his wife. After narrowly escaping arrest I returned to the hotel only to find there was no film in the camera! So I sneaked out the next day, this time with film, and got the photos I wanted.

Author's note:
Chris's mishap did not go unnoticed. Harry Tinkler well remembers Chris, armed with two or three cameras around his neck, snapping away at anything that moved, only to discover later his lack of film!

The event itself was different to say the least. The circuit had been constructed round our hotel and sand was everywhere – the main event saw Lolas, Astons and GT40s all trying to drive around on what resembled ball bearings! Things were more hilarious when it came to the "Celebrity Race". Citroen SMs provided by the local importer, driven by a bunch of hooligans (they made BTCC look like child's play). Cutting out the chicanes, driving across the sand, every car was dented, bashed and damaged – but they were all sold to the locals after the race! The saloon race featured "Spice" Capris – we could not call them Fords, because they were not allowed in the UAE. Reg Baines even had to remove his Ford T-shirt because of the offence it caused. (Woe betide anyone caught with M&S knickers!)

This was the first time BMRMC had ventured abroad *en masse*, and it proved a great success for us. Unfortunately the organisers made no money on it and the event was never repeated, although now of course there is a purpose built GP facility in Dubai).

Favourite Drivers

As I am sure is the case with all marshals, we have all had our favourite drivers over the years.

When I first became involved in marshalling, as plans to become the next Jackie Stewart foundered through lack of money and an even greater lack of talent, it was Club level drivers who made a hit with me first. Saloon drivers such as Bill Cox, Mick Hill and Ian Richardson were always so approachable. So, too, were other drivers at that level, Jim Walsh an all-time favourite in Formula Ford, his Irish mates, John Murphy, Bernard Devaney and Derek Daly. At that time we held monthly social meetings and it was always so easy to get drivers to come along to entertain us.

They also supported our Annual Dinners. The first one I attended in South Midlands region featured David Hobbs, no less, someone I now meet on occasion around the USA and who is a wonderfully irreverent commentator on Speed Channel in the USA. His off-the-cuff comments about the F1 circus are often very amusing and revealing. Steve Matchett, former Benetton mechanic is equally informative and observant on mechanical issues and he and David together make a formidable team on the GP races we watch when in the USA.

Jim Walsh, a very big favourite with Silverstone marshals in particular, for his exuberant but very successful driving style, tells a wonderful story of a big 'off' in private practice at Snetterton. He was trapped in the car, had broken hands and feet (very painful). Another driver stopped, was clearly alarmed at what he saw and immediately sped off for help. Jim, for something to do, decided to replace the glass in his spectacles that had become dislodged in the accident. Bearing in mind he had broken hands this was no small task but he did manage it. He put them to one side when help arrived – and the first person there stood on his newly-repaired spectacles and completely destroyed them! June and I went to visit Jim in Norwich Hospital the day after the accident and it is to Jim's credit that, although in considerable pain, he could gleefully relate this story to us at that time!

Internationally, I admired the driving skill of Ronnie Peterson and Giles Villeneuve. Weren't they exciting to watch? Emerson Fittipaldi was amazingly smooth and wonderfully laid back at times. I well recall one GP at Brands Hatch, while I was marshalling the flag point at the entrance to the pits, when Emerson came around to tell us that Café de Brasil, one of his sponsors, had a coffee kiosk behind the garage – with strict instructions to serve marshals first whenever there was a queue.

I remember with some amusement characters like Rupert Keegan and the somewhat risqué chat-show script he and Adrian Reynard developed over the years. I remember, too, Rupert's Dad who gave us five double return tickets anywhere on his British Air Ferries routes as a raffle prize and doubled that to ten when we said we were going to donate the proceeds to supplying mobility aids to children suffering from Spina Bifida.

In this respect I remember especially James Hunt, then with Hesketh and part-sponsored by Vauxhall Motors. James knew of these carts because they had been designed by Vauxhall apprentices and he readily agreed to present the carts for us. The first recipient, Mark from Hartwell, was severely disabled with Spina Bifida. He rarely, if ever, sat up on his own, something the carts were designed to help. Mark was also a great James Hunt fan; his eyes just lit up when his hero appeared and within minutes James had Mark scooting around the startline at Silverstone, sat bolt upright and steering his own way, with minimal assistance from James. This was one of the happiest moments of my life, just watching this youngster absolutely 'preen' under James's tutelage. James, who did not enjoy the best of Press at times, went on to present another five or so carts at various venues throughout the country, often at considerable expense for air fares from his then home in Spain.

There was another occasion when Peter Hunt rang to say that James was stuck in Spain because of strikes at some Spanish airports. I presumed Peter was ringing to say James would not be coming to our Grand Prix drivers' forum but, no, all he wanted us to do was make sure there was a sandwich or something for James when he arrived as he was going to get to us by a circuitous route, involving private airplane hire, and would not have time to eat *en route!* His comment when he arrived was that he didn't want to let the marshals down, as they always turned up for him!

In other areas, I enjoyed the saloon car contests between John Fitzpatrick, Hans Stuck, then Gordon Spice, Tom Walkinshaw and Andy Rouse. I enjoyed Dave Brodie's forceful style and did a newsletter interview with him following his big shunt at the 1973 British GP meeting at Silverstone.

Wot, no Scottish drivers? Well, yes, of course there were. I admired Innes Ireland for the character he was and Jim Clark as perhaps the most natural driver ever to come on the scene during my time as a marshal. Jackie Stewart was also a natural talent, instantly fast and very smooth, who went on to win three World Drivers' Championships. However, I admired Jackie as much for the way he chose to live his life. In a sport not renowned for total veracity, Jackie Stewart's transparency and honesty and that of his soul mate, Ken Tyrrell, shone out like a beacon. He has even managed to pass this attitude on to all those young drivers who passed through Team Stewart's Staircase of Talent – think David Coulthard, Allan McNish, Kelvin Burt, Dario Franchitti (who everyone we speak to in the USA believes to be Italian!) Gils de Ferran and many others. Jackie has been and still is a great ambassador for our sport

Latterly, I was always impressed by the quiet determination and maturity of Damon Hill. Having a son who suffers from Down's syndrome clearly gave Damon a better focus on life as a whole and I always felt he handled himself well, amongst the prima-donnas of F1. I wish him well in his new role as President of the British Racing Drivers' Club.

Currently, I will miss David Coulthard when he departs the scene and do so wish that Jensen Button could realise his full potential. Is he to be another Stirling Moss or Chris Amon? I find myself admiring Michael Schumacher for his special talent of binding a team around him and for the sheer number of wins and pole positions he has achieved. Sadly, his tendency to go too far on occasion will always taint the memory, just as it did, in my mind, with Ayrton Senna as well. (As a Clerk, I have had to explain to several drivers that what Senna and Schumacher got away with in Formula One has no bearing on my decision to penalise the same manoeuvre on a wet Saturday Club meeting at Silverstone!!) Alonso strikes me as the best of the bunch at the moment, at least until we see what Lewis Hamilton and others may bring to the scene in coming seasons.

Author's note:

I wrote the above paragraph in October 2006; who could have forecast Lewis Hamilton would do so well in his first year in F1 and that Alonso would take it so badly!

Away from Formula One, who could fail to be impressed by current drivers such as Allan McNish and Andy Wallace, who have both become sports car experts and still amongst the most approachable of drivers. In Historic F1 we have seen Duncan Dayton from the USA excel in everything he drives. Nearer to home, we have Michael Schryver and Simon Hadfield, both of whom seem able to drive and win in any car they take on. Simon runs a very successful restoration business and very often finishes up driving the finished product to victory.

At Club and National level we have drivers like Michael Hibberd who has been so successful in the very well supported Historic Formula Junior series run by the Historic Sports Car Club, which we 'badged' in 2007 to commemorate our 50th Anniversary. Currently he dominates the Historic Formula Junior series – when he can afford the time to race – and is now being closely followed by son Andrew.

For sheer exuberance, who can forget the antics of Gerry Marshall and his old sidekick, Barrie "Whizzo" Williams, who is still at it! The Hon Patrick Lindsay in his ERA was a sight to see and son Ludovic has carried on the same tradition. Willie Green always seemed a driver "out of his time" and who knows what he might have driven if he had been in the right place at the right time. There are so many others, it would take a book on its own to cover all the drivers who have given pleasure and interest to the marshals over the years.

Another aspect of some of my favourite drivers was how talented they were elsewhere. Jackie Stewart narrowly missed the cut to shoot for Great Britain in the 1960 Olympics in Rome. I have seen him shoot since and he still does not miss many but missed those few vital clays at selection time. Shooting's loss was motor sport's gain!

His team mate, the sadly missed Francois Cevert – my wife's favourite driver of all time – was a brilliant concert pianist. So, too, was Elio de Angelis, another whose life motor sport claimed at far too early an age.

Nigel Mansell was a scratch or better golfer, no doubt encouraged by his best mate Greg Norman. I am no musician but I am told both Damon Hill and Eddy Jordan could have had a future in the record business. As raconteur, few could match the droll, laid back style of Damon's Dad, Graham Hill, especially when teamed up with Jackie Stewart. Our own ex-President, Stuart Turner, is an equally gifted raconteur.

As is so often the case, those who rise to the top level in one activity, sport or business, are often equally talented in other areas too. Don't you just hate it when other people are so talented?

Gunfire at Gleneagles

The invitation for marshals to appear at the Jackie Stewart Mechanics' Trust shoots at Gleneagles in 1987 came right out of the blue. I had been on a business trip to Ireland, to be greeted on my return by a beaming wife, saying that Ruth Kinnear, Jackie's secretary, had been in touch asking if we could put a team together for the shoot in two weeks' time.

One of the main sponsors of the event, Goodyear, was having trouble with corporate raiders trying to unsettle the Company or, more precisely, upset the Company's share price so that they, the corporate raiders could benefit. In these circumstances, the directors of Goodyear who normally took part in the shoot felt they could not come to Gleneagles that year; rather they needed to stay home to fight off the corporate raiders, which I am pleased to say they did.

Jackie persuaded them to leave the team slot in place and he would find some marshals to fill their places. We were those marshals, "those other unsung heroes of our sport" as Jackie described us.

Mike Oxlade, Club PRO at the time, and Dave Darley put together the team. Keith and Joan Douglas, Mike and Julia Oxlade, Dave and Rosemary Darley, John and Audrey Watt, George and June Copeland and on his own Stuart Payne. We had to pay the air fare to take our wives but everything else was taken care of by the sponsors. Dave Darley brought along a rather ancient side-by-side shotgun and John Watt was resplendent in full Highland dress for the various functions we attended – a fine figure of a man!

First meeting place was Heathrow, to take the shuttle to Edinburgh. It was already shaping up to be a great event, standing in the queue with Ken Tyrrell, Derek Warwick and other "notables". When we arrived in Edinburgh, we were all greeted by Jackie himself. Then it was in to a fleet of motor coaches for a scenic drive to Gleneagles, all the time accompanied by the Grampian TV helicopter flying alongside filming our progress.

We arrived at Gleneagles to the skirl of the pipes from the resident piper and were individually announced and greeted off the bus by Jackie and Peter Lederer, General Manager of Gleneagles and still there twenty years later. A quick coffee and a chance to meet a few old friends from among the mechanics, in whose honour the event was being held. It is amazing how many marshals had gone on to be F1 team members and we recognised quite a few.

The shooters were then ushered into the equipment room, to be kitted out with Barbour jackets and over-trousers supplied by Barbour's Scottish Division and Hunter Wellington boots by Hunter Boots of Dumfries. We all felt we had moved up a step or two in society, in our new "Gatcombe Minks" and posh, green wellies!

Our wives, meantime, had been provided with various garments from the Boss range, including very fashionable sweaters, cashmere scarves and the like. Again, all rather posh!

Then we were invited to go to our rooms and unpack. There, the bed was absolutely covered with gifts from all the event sponsors. It was a bit like being in Aladdin's cave. Less than a day gone by and we were already feeling like all our Christmases had come at once! Thoughtfully, there was also a Jackie Stewart Shooting School holdall, to pack all these goodies in to go home.

Early next morning – early – we had to get down to the serious stuff, we were going to see how well we could shoot. None of our party was at all experienced, although some of us had handled a shotgun before. What we had not realised was just how much preparation the teams had put in. Lotus and Benetton were big rivals and they had been practising for months. Lotus started off with 100 hopefuls, whittled down over months of practice at the West London Shooting School to the final six. We had a lot of catching up to do.

The first day of practice was fun but very trying. The shooting instructors at Gleneagles were absolutely brilliant; we were hitting targets we never dreamed we would hit but I am not sure we always knew quite how we did it! Nevertheless, we were quite hopeful and thought we might acquit ourselves reasonably well, considering how little practice we'd had, compared to most of the other teams.

When not practising, we had the run of the hotel. Gleneagles is a truly first class resort. The weather, for February, was brilliant – bright sunshine to enhance the wonderful views of the Perthshire countryside. I spent a fair amount of time walking, and it was fascinating to tip my hat to all the famous drivers out on their keep fit runs when not practising on the butts. Gleneagles has become one of my favourite places in the World and I have been back several times since, both on business and with the family. It never fails to impress. This first time, however, there was no bill at the end of it, which was the most impressive thing of all!

Come Sunday morning and it was now getting really serious. This was Gunfight at O.K. Corral time for Lotus and Benetton, the rest of us were there to take minor places only it seemed! It was no less enjoyable for all that!

As a team we did reasonably well. Individually, we were missing targets we hit in practice and hitting those we had not. There was no rhythm to it. We were 16th or 18th out of 22 teams when regular competition came to an end – but then we faced the flurry! Two pairs of shooters from each team had to fire and load as a continual barrage of clays was thrown at us. I am afraid we did not do too well here and slipped to 20th out of 22. This still put us ahead of the Press team featuring our President, Murray Walker!

Then the two top teams showed us how it should be done. Regimented firing sequences, assisted loading and sheer precision saw the two top teams miss only one or two clays. Benetton won by about one clay and Roly Vincenzi was Top Gun. Roly's joy was unconstrained!

Final event of the day was a flurry shoot-off between the winning Benetton team and the Gleneagles Instructors, led by none other than Jackie Stewart himself, a very capable shot who missed selection for the Olympics only because of a totally out of character off day during the final selection process. Those responsible for releasing the clays tried everything to upset these last two teams. They released two or three clays at one time, a single the next time and at totally irregular times; nothing fazed these shooters! I seem to remember there was some debate over one nicked clay that was claimed as a hit but this was the only one in doubt. The two teams hit everything else and I think they eventually agreed to an honourable draw.

Then it was group photo time and into evening wear for the gala dinner and prize giving. What a night this proved to be.

The whole event is run in aid of the Grand Prix Mechanics' Trust, another JYS initiative to help out mechanics who fall on hard time because of work related injuries or other ill health. Over and above the costs of everyone attending the shoot (British Airways for instance provided all the air fares for the drivers from wherever they were in the World) the event raised £115,000 for the Trust. We had decided to contribute £25 a head, to repay in some small way for the most wonderful weekend we had enjoyed.

Jackie made a superbly witty speech after the awards had been made – including the fact that Innes Ireland had drunk the hotel dry of a particular brand of whisky after the first two days and fresh supplies had been rushed in! He listed all the sponsors, including BA as above, Barbour who kitted out all the shooters free of charge, Brierley Crystal who gave each shooter an engraved crystal decanter, Moet and Chandon who had donated gallons of free champagne and Gleneagles who had donated accommodation and other meals and entertainment. Then he paused. "But" he said, "the contribution that impressed me most was from those other unsung heroes of our sport, the marshals." We were called to stand up and be identified, to a standing ovation from everyone else there. A very moving tribute to marshals, I thought, one we will all savour for a long time to come.

This was a wholly remarkable weekend, all the more so for the short notice we had to attend. As I mentioned earlier, I have been to Gleneagles since but no visit will ever measure up to this first one. Jackie deserved his knighthood for this one act alone!

Plane Crash – Marshals to the Rescue

by Jim Whitaker

One of the most astonishing illustrations of the value of training motor sport's rescue teams undertake must surely be the case of British Midlands Airways Fokker Friendship aircraft which crashed on a training flight while trying to land at East Midlands Airport on 18th January 1987. Several rescue teams were training at Donington that day and rushed to the scene. Jim Whitaker describes the incident, with his usual brevity and conciseness!

A Practical Rescue Training Day

We were having a quiet, if cold, training day for rescue crews at Donington Park on Sunday 18th January in 1987. We were just about to start the after lunch session in Race Control when someone said "That plane's low". I intended to say "yes – they all look low from up here under the flight path for the airport" but on turning round saw a medium size airliner crash behind trees just outside the circuit perimeter fence.

Leaving someone to make a 999 call, the rest of the group set off for where we had seen the plane go down. Most of the group of twenty-three marshals were rescue crew from several different units together with some people who had come along to observe. One of the group was a doctor.

The plane was a British Midlands Fokker F27 which was on a training flight out of the nearby East Midlands airport. No passengers but three crew. The weather (subsequently implicated in the accident investigation) was cold (below zero) with a few inches of snow on the ground.

In spite of the spillage of some three tonnes of fuel there was no fire. Doubtless the low temperature assisted in reducing the fire risk but running through pools of fuel did cause some concerns. We rapidly removed one of the crew with leg injuries to one of our vehicles where first aid was given. One of the pilots was trapped in the left hand seat and the other required careful extrication from the right hand seat. Action started to cut free the trapped pilot. Treatment of all three casualties was started by the unit doctor and one of the rescue crew who was a paramedic

Airport and local authority fire services subsequently arrived. After about thirty minutes the team was able to rescue the other two pilots with the help of the fire services. All three pilots survived and we later had a very pleasant dinner with them. Subsequently the Royal Humane Society awarded its Commendation to the *Donington Park Race Circuit Rescue Unit and Marshals*. (The presence of individuals from Northern Race and Rally Rescue and BRSCC (Northern) should be noted.)

On the following pages are published the official report and letters and awards from the Civil Aviation Authority and the Humane Society – plus a team photograph of those concerned in the photograph section.

From: J.S.M.Whitaker,
Cockslan Cottage,
Banks Green,
Nr. Redditch,
Worcestershire,
B97 5SU.

Tel. [Home] Redditch (0527) 41285   19th October 1987
      [Business] 021-472 1301 Ext.2160

Participants in the Rescue of the Crew from British Midland Airways Fokker F27
Sunday 18th January 1987 near Donington Park

                                        Home Town

Mrs R Allison   Leicester
Mr SJV Allison   Leicester
Mr SH Angel   Burton on-Trent
Mr RF Ashton   Halifax
Mr AM Atkinson   Leicester
Mr PA Belcher   Bradford
Mr S Binns   Harrogate
Mr RM Blanklock   Ashby-de-la-Zouch
Mr P Broxup   Leeds
Mr A Carwithen   West Bromwich
Mr BH Commons   Chesterfield
Mr B Hodgkinson   Leeds
Mr AT Large   Matlock
Mr CR Mollart   Stoke-on-Trent
Mr JA Murdock   Harrogate
Dr PR Rayner   Chesterfield
Mr JK Riseley   Leicester
Mr TJ Sinclair   Long Eaton
Mr JJ Stewart-Bennett   Leeds
Mrs LP Welch   Leicester
Mr PJ Welch (Mr Welch died recently in an accident at Donington Park)
Mr JSM Whitaker   Redditch
Miss M Whitaker   Harrogate

Background

The above are volunteer Motor Race Marshals who specialize in the Emergency
Rescue and immediate care of racing drivers. On Sunday 18th January 1987 a
training session had been organised by Mr JSM Whitaker under the auspices of
The British Motor Racing Marshals Club (BMRMC)/Donington Emergency Services
Team. The Northern Race and Rally Rescue Marshals Club and the Rescue Crew
from The British Racing and Sports Car Club (Northern Center) had been
invited to participate. After lunch Dr PR Rayner, Honorary Medical Officer
to the BMRMC, was starting a lecture in advanced First Aid when the
participants saw the aircraft crash.

The Donington Emergency Services Team is run by the B.M.R.M.C. Ltd.

Page 1 of 3

Registered in England No. 962892   VAT No. 273 986702

ROYAL HUMANE SOCIETY.

INSTITUTED 1774.

PATRON

HER MAJESTY THE QUEEN

PRESIDENT

H.R.H. Princess Alexandra, the Hon. Mrs. Angus Ogilvy, G. C. V. O.

At a Meeting of the Committee of the Royal Humane Society

on the 2nd day of June 1987

Present   The Hon. E. L. Baillieu   in the Chair

It was Resolved Unanimously that

The Donington Park Race Circuit Rescue Unit and Marshals

be commended for their praiseworthy action

on the 18th January 1987

Chairman

Secretary

Case No. 60.434.

Airfield Duties

As well as becoming involved in other disciplines, early members of the British Motor Racing Marshals' Club became involved in what many might see as unrelated duties, namely, Airfield Control at Silverstone which on Grand Prix day often became the busiest airfield in the UK. Les Bentley, long time North East Chairman was part of that team and has allowed me some of his memories.

In 1973 the original team was Les, Gordon Hewitt, Peter Broxup, Maurice Smith and a couple of others for whom Les cannot now recall their names. Mike East (from nearby Oxford airport, I think) was the official Air Traffic Controller, ably assisted by his wife Carol. As aircraft movements increased, so too did the team from BMRMC North East. By 1980, the NE Team had grown to some 100, to cover a twin shift operation. They were now in sole charge of airfield security, including Customs and Excise considerations. The first Customs and Excise team who came to check arrangements found one of their own, Les, in charge! Les served his time with HM Customs and Excise and he and a couple of HMCE colleagues knew reasonably well what had to be done.

As Formula One wealth grew so, too, did the number of aircraft movements, until the absolute capacity of the Silverstone site was reached. To allow more helicopter landings, fixed wing landing were phased out. In 1999/2000 the Guinness Book of Records officially recognised a record number of aircraft movements in one day at Silverstone.

Les's team grew as well. It now numbered 200 marshals and five Air Traffic Controllers. There were now three separate heliports and sometimes up to 100 helicopters parked at any one time, something of a security headache for Les and his team. The team also doubled up on campsite security for the adjoining campsite – where theft became a bit of a problem from time to time.

On one occasion, someone stole a Marshal's rather expensive mountain bike. The thief was apprehended quite soon afterwards and happy to be passed over to the custody of Les and his team, as other airfield marshals prepared to lynch him! Another miscreant, ejected from being in the campsite without good reason, gained revenge by returning to pee in the on-site generator, which caused a fairly immediate technical hitch!

Like many marshalling activities, the time involved for the individuals concerned was quite horrendous and Les felt in 2001/02 that it was time for a rest and handed over to Richard Ashton, then NE Chairman. Sadly, the BMRMC involvement came to an end shortly afterwards, as Elf 'n' Safety rules began to bite and control had to pass to properly registered and approved company employees.

None of those who took part have any regrets and all of the team seem to have gone away with many happy memories of their days as Silverstone's Heathrow.

A Year in the Life of a Race Gypsy

Gypsy: a wanderer, member of a group or clan who move through settled societies and live off the land in return for labour or selling small goods or fortunes. Most commonly members of the Roma clan, usually known as Romany.

Most of you reading this enjoy being at race meetings, working as marshals, pit lane staff, scrutineers, in timing, etc. I expect you probably attend race events between ten and thirty days a year, constrained by factors such as work, money, and of course your family.

How would you like to spend eighty-five days a year at race events (forty percent outside the UK), and a further seventy days working drivers' schools, track days and corporate functions? This is the life of a race gypsy—and you can become one too.

I have always been a traveller. It is in my genes on both sides, from my father and maternal grandfather. By the time I started marshalling at the age of 19, I had already visited Toronto with my father and taken trips to Bordeaux and Hanover. I also explored England, Scotland and Wales: walking, climbing, sailing and caving my way round the island.

When I started marshalling at Castle Combe in 1966 I was surprised to find that most of my colleagues only ever worked Combe. It seemed if you were a Combe marshal you stayed there; if at Brands you stayed at Brands, etc.

By my second season I was bored with that attitude. Completely unannounced, I turned up at Brands and asked to marshal. No licences or grading cards in those days! After some surprise that as a complete stranger I already knew how to do the job I was accepted, and have never looked back. Soon I ventured to Silverstone (where I joined an emerging BMRMC), then Oulton Park and a newly-converted RAF airfield called Thruxton.

Fortunately, even at that age I had a job which paid well and gave me plenty of time off in addition to annual holidays. I had gone from working twelve days my first season to thirty-two the next. I finally settled on forty to fifty days a year for the next few years. There were far fewer multi-day meetings back in the '60s, though the BOAC 1000 KM at Brands and the Gold Cup at Oulton Park spring to mind, together with the GP of course. Easter could be fun, with Good Friday and Saturday at Oulton, driving through the night to Brands for Sunday (no direct motorway then—M1 was still being built, and M40 was a distant dream), then another overnight drive back up the A20 through the centre of London and down the Great West Road A4 to Chippenham for Castle Combe on the Monday. Three circuits in four days made a good break from work.

By 1969 I had teamed up with Barry "Tiny" Greenhill, and we both had itchy feet. Following a coach trip to *Le Mans* (the only time in 41 years I have paid to get into a race meeting!) we wanted to do more than just spectate at this event. We managed to evade the *gendarmerie* and found our way onto the Mulsanne straight. In broken schoolboy French we talked to the marshals there, and they directed us to an English-speaking post. The following year we marshalled.

Even now, becoming a race gypsy does not just happen. Preparation is required. My typical year starts with planning in November and finishes in March, fifteen months later. This is because some international events, including *Le Mans*, have very early deadlines for applications, and events in December through March have to be booked in time to arrange travel. The discipline (and savings!) needed for this advance planning do not suit everyone, and some people just do not like travelling. Still, attitudes have changed since I first started, helped by today's cheap travel, and, of course, the Internet.

I have worked *Le Mans* so many times now it is like second nature to me, but in the early days it was hard work to get in, and even now can be daunting for a 'virgin' at *La Sarthe*.

The *24 Heures du Mans* is the first date that goes into my diary spreadsheet every year. You must apply via the MSA (or the ASN for your country if you are not British) by the end of November if you are not already on the *Le Mans* list. Even then you can get caught out with holiday time or hotel or car bookings if the date changes later, which has happened to me on occasion. So hold off booking ferry or tunnel until early February, when the date is finalised. You will need to be at the circuit from 14.00 on the Wednesday to 16.00 on the Sunday, and the only really convenient way to do it is to camp at the post.

While Tiny and I were at *Le Mans* we met Dutch and Belgian marshals, and soon extended our foreign repertoire to Francorchamps for the Spa 24hr saloon race and to *Zandvoort* and *Zolder* for the GPs.

By this time I had moved on from what we now call incident grade to flagging. I still think that the old Stavelot Viaduct flag point at *Francorchamps* is the most demanding and exhilarating that I have ever worked. A downhill approach from *Malmédy* gave a perfect view and plenty of anticipation time, but the drivers could only see you when they actually arrived at the start of the viaduct about 80 yards away, so the actual flagging time was very short. Add to that the fact you were standing on a stone parapet about three feet wide, with the track about two feet below you on your left and a drop of thirty-odd feet on your right. It was one of only two places I have flagged where you could literally hit the driver on the helmet with the flag. The other is Cleveland post 10, just at pit entrance. I know that because I did it to Michael Andretti a few years back.

So the first half of the '70s was spent doing the grand tour of Europe. By now the BMRMC had started to talk seriously about marshal training, and I had progressed from being a flag marshal to both assistant observer and rescue. Rescue units at that time were based on old ambulances, with whatever cutting gear we could get our hands on.

A Grand Prix is another example of an event you need to plan early for (even the British one). These days I rarely do European GPs because I find they are too regimented for my taste. Instead I work the Canadian or US GP if they don't clash with *Le Mans*. These events are much more laid-back and seem, in my opinion, to have a more positive attitude to marshals. But if you want to "do the circuit" you need to contact the organisers early. Usually this is either the ASN of the country or a club designated on their behalf. If you are not sure who to ask, try talking to others who have travelled or put a message on the Ten-Tenths Marshals Forum. Remember that foreign workers are often not accepted for European GPs. It is difficult to get on the list for France, Italy or Monaco unless you already have personal contacts, but the Northern European events are easier. Australia, Canada and the USA are more used to foreign guest marshals, and working there can easily be arranged.

1976 was my GP year: six GPs in six countries and on two continents. Having done the European season in Germany, Holland, England and Monaco (never want to do that one again either) a colleague and I (armed with US visitors' visas) set off to my second cousin's in Washington, DC for a holiday. I already had contacts in Toronto through my father, and had written to BARC Station K about working the Canadian GP at Mosport. They also put me on to a contact in Binghampton, NY for the US GP a fortnight after, so we did the two back to back

We were trying to do the trip on the cheap (nothing new there), and stayed with my cousin in DC before getting a Greyhound bus up to Buffalo. We stayed with an ex-pat friend of mine in Dundas, Ontario, and had some misconceptions of life in that society. On being asked if we wanted to party one evening we agreed and so were driven well over two hundred miles for a bash, then back the same night!

It is worth remembering, when marshalling in the USA or Canada, that the place is big. We often forget how lucky we are with probably a dozen circuits within two hours' drive of our homes. Most of our North American fellows will have to travel twice that to get to their closest circuit. This means that you need to consider travel inside North America if you are doing more than one event there.

To get to Mosport we hired a car from a downtown rental. We asked for a compact and were told we could have a Ford Granada for the same price. Being used to a Cortina back home I agreed. The thing was like a tank: 6000cc engine and built like a battleship. Stupid car would not do more than sixty-five miles an hour flat out. When we took it back two weeks later the guy commented, "Ah, yeah, we set the limiter down because of the gas shortage and newly imposed speed limits in the US."

Mosport was fun, and this became the first of many visits over the years. The track always reminds me of Oulton Park with its combination of sweeping and tight bends and long straights and wooded scenery.

This trip was also my first experience with oval tracks, other than British stock car racing. After the USGP at Watkins Glen we had three weeks left of our holiday, so drove the Ocean Highway down to Florida, stopping at Daytona to talk our way into a USAC (predecessor of NASCAR) event.

It was a big learning curve. Marshalling in North America was, and is, organised in a much different way from Europe. As soon as I realised that hard-line communications allowed everyone to know what was going on all round the circuit I was hooked. It was also novel to be allowed to carry out all the duties on a post at the same meeting, not just one specific task like back home. More about that later!

Alas, that trip was the last trans-Atlantic trip for ten years. The following year I got married, and although Tiny and I did more events in Europe (hosting George Webster from Ontario who wanted to see *Spa*, *Nürburgring* and *Le Mans* at first hand) my marshalling dropped right off to only a dozen or so days a year as my family grew. My knowledge of Western Europe did come in useful for having cheap family holidays, though.

My interest in Indy Car began in 1992, and what a long, strange trip it was. My marriage had broken down in late '87, and my employers took advantage of my status, loaning me out to the British government for two years. I ended up in Jamaica in December '88 rebuilding their electrical power system, and marshalling dirt tracks at the weekends. I don't know about Jamaicans being good race drivers, but this group sure should have been winning the World Rally Championship!

When one of my Jamaican friends moved to Toronto in 1992 I rapidly accepted an invite to go and stay. Station K remained a contact, so I not only worked a club race at Mosport but my first Indy Car meeting at Toronto Exhibition Place. I had worked Birmingham for two years in the UK so street racing was not new to me, but the whole concept— 'talking' flagging, hard-line communications, and cars that actually overtook each other on the track—beat F1 hands down; really blew my mind.

Even now, the second event into my diary is always the Toronto Indy, as it still gets called. Technically it is now 'Toronto Champ Car' with about two hundred sponsors' names but no one remembers all of those.

What was Indy Car has now split into IRL on the ovals and Champ Car on the street circuits, though there is a lot of crossover. Both use some of the prestige circuits in the USA. Again, if you want to work these events I advise early planning, although usually an e-mail of intent is good enough to let the organisers or Flag Chief know you are interested. Application dates for working North American races are traditionally shorter than ours, and it is unusual to get a set of dates for the year such as BARC or BRSCC put out, except as a list of events for the big professional series. If you're looking at what's available in a particular area, monthly newsletters usually give dates for the next six weeks or so, together with contact details for the Chief Marshal.

My preference for Champ Car has to be Toronto, followed by Long Beach and the other Canadian races. Cleveland is fun in its own way (fancy racing round Stansted Airport—it is the equivalent). They shut the city airport for the weekend and use a combination of the main runway and taxiways.

That trip to Toronto kicked off a decade and a half of working tracks in North America at every opportunity. From Toronto I worked Mosport and the Toronto Indy. Then I branched out with lifts from Canadian friends into the US, to do Cleveland, Detroit and Michigan Speedway for CART, and hopped across to Montreal for the Canadian GP. Once I had enough contacts to create a base in Milwaukee I made it to the CART races at Road America, Mid-Ohio and Chicago.

When I was offered early retirement in 1999 I suddenly had both the time and money to join American and Canadian friends further south for the 24 Hours of Daytona, the 12 Hours of Sebring, and the *Petit Le Mans* at Road Atlanta. This opened up the Grand Am and American *Le Mans* series for me and gave me the opportunity to work another circuit I had always dreamed of doing—*Trois-Rivières* in Quebec— and eventually, with the return of F1 to the USA the following year, Indianapolis.

Meantime new ways to marshal abroad were opening up for other British marshals. As international championships began to be contested in second- and third-world countries, promoters looked for experienced people to mentor the local staff and volunteers. Subsequently both BRSCC and BARC sent senior officials and post chiefs abroad as expert trainers, expenses paid. As a result I worked the South Korean F3 race all five years (from '99 'til '03), and Bahrain and Dubai for a variety of events, including twenty-four-hour races. After the inaugural A1 race at Brands Hatch, British marshals (including me) provided marshalling staff for the Sheikh's home A1 event.

In 2002 I teamed up with a friend from St. Paul, Minnesota, which gave me access not only to club circuits in the US Midwest, but also to contacts at the Sports Car Club of America's Cal Club (Los Angeles) and San Francisco regions. At this point I realised that an SCCA flagging and communications (marshalling) membership would be cheaper than paying temporary membership fees at each meeting I worked in the USA.

Thus I can now add ALMS, Grand Am and SCCA club events into the planning spreadsheet. These dates, together with the UK club scene, mean that most weekends throughout the year there is a choice of which event to work. I simply decide for each weekend where I want to be.

So each year becomes a list of events: the Middle and Far East from November 'til February; Florida and California in March and April (Sebring, St. Petersburg, Long Beach and Las Vegas); back home for May and early June, then *Le Mans*. Deep breath, and then a North American GP plus Champ Car races in Canada during June and July; home again for August and September; then back to the USA for the *Petit Le Mans* at Atlanta. One thing I do try to do is to work a new circuit every year.

So if you want to travel, come and join me for one or more of these events. Many UK marshals are now working one-off races in North America. Flights are cheap and you will be made welcome.

Decide either on a particular event, or, if just visiting family and friends, where and when you will be in North America. It is easy to let the right people know you would like to attend an event. Either ask another marshal who travels, or use the Ten-Tenths Marshals' Forum to ask for advice. You will get the e-mail address of the appropriate flag chief back very quickly. There is always room for someone fitting a race into a family holiday as well as for the "pro" gypsies like me.

Applying for most events these days is done on line. The club will often publish an application form on its web site which you fill in with your details. Usually they give an e-mail address for the flag chief as well, in case you have queries. Most sign-on forms require an emergency contact name and brief medical details, including any allergies or physical issues, which you should fill in if you feel unable to carry out certain duties. For example, if you are not able to leap Armco, you can note that. Some organisations use a dedicated web site, much like Julian Floyd's site for BMMC www.marshals.org.uk in the UK. An equivalent site for SCCA club racing in America is www.dlbracing. com.

Here are some other pointers:

Planning your travel

Make and use contacts. Once you start travelling you will make new friends very quickly. Fellow travellers can offer advice on where to go and where to stay, etc. Many marshals at home who have travelled in the past will be glad to point you in the right direction. You will probably also find you are offered hospitality by local marshals, ranging from an invitation for a meal to sharing hire cars and motel rooms. Create business cards before you go, to give to people you'd like to remain in contact with. When planning your trips let these people know where you are thinking of going and tie in with plans they may be making to save money for both of you—or ask them who they know who might like to share. Be prepared to reciprocate with foreign marshals wanting to work events in Europe. If you have had good hospitality try and give some back. Just because you personally can't put up a foreign marshal, don't turn them down. Many UK marshals are more than willing to help return hospitality they have had in the past. Remember that what goes around comes around.

Plan for contingencies. Flights do get delayed. I always allow for a day at each end of the trip for unexpected issues, just in case. I can always find something to do near a racetrack if those extra days turn out to be truly extra. Hotels do double-book: you may find they have rebooked you twenty miles away. Luggage does get lost; in Europe and North America this is not too bad, since you can usually buy essentials; and luggage is usually recovered quickly. In the Far East, however, it often pays to pack two smaller bags with a distribution of essential items between them. You then have a chance that at least one will turn up.

Be flexible; direct flights are not always the cheapest. Staying further away from the track and using a hire car can work out to be cheaper than an expensive hotel close by. If your circumstances permit, you can even be flexible about which race you work when enquiring of foreign flag chiefs. While most people aim for a prestige event the little clubbie 'just up the road' can be just as much (or more) fun.

Make a reasonable budget. Remember that cheap air tickets are often non-refundable and non-transferable. If hiring a car, allow extra for local insurance. Check if motels include breakfast in the charge, and at what time. It is annoying to find you have paid for breakfast but the restaurant opens at 7.30 and you have to be at the track for 6.45. Always make a financial allowance for contingencies.

Know (or ask) what to bring (always have your towel....) and how to pack; try and pack as lightly as possible. Will you be expected to wear orange or white? Are steel toe-capped boots necessary on post, or can you wear shoes or trainers? Is the weather going to be hot, cold or merely temperate? Is there a large or small chance of rain? If the chance is slight go with the lightest rain gear available. Do not travel with knives, belt cutters or Leatherman, even in your checked luggage. Many security checks will confiscate them. NEVER carry illegal drugs or packages for another person. If you are not a frequent flyer become familiar with the luggage restrictions for flights out of all EU countries and OBEY them. Not doing so may lose you the flight.

Know what you need to do to meet each country's immigration requirements; for certain countries visitors' visas must be obtained in advance of travel or visa waivers must be purchased on arrival. Some countries have very strict rules about visitors not being allowed to work, including unpaid voluntary work. You have to decide why you are there before you are asked. "I am a motor race fan, and will be attending the race at…." will usually satisfy, but choose your words carefully. If caught out, lying will almost certainly mean you are refused admittance.

Buy good travel insurance, there are plenty of options from many outlets, including the Post Office and most supermarkets as well as high street brokers. Back that up with the BMMC FIO facility for track activity. (SCCA will insist you also have their insurance, paid for by a temporary membership, but will often refund the fee to visiting workers if there is no claim.)

Study how your event of choice will be run—what the flagging rules are, how workers rotate through the event, whether you are expected to bring your own meals. Most countries outside the UK do not use the grading system we are used to. You will probably be expected to rotate through all disciplines, so you will be flagging for one race and doing course (or response, as it is often called) for the next. Some series, notably Champ Car and IMSA, will designate dedicated blue flag marshals who will do each session for that series. In North America all communication to and from race control is on hard line. At the post communication will be under the control of a dedicated marshal. Some places will allow you to try this as part of the rotation, often with an experienced communications marshal on a second headset, while some will only allow specialists on 'comm'. North America uses a much stricter voice protocol than most UK marshals are used to—there is no room for 'storytelling', but a clipped set of standard phrases gets essential information back to Control very quickly. Many places use the term 'turn' or 'corner' instead of 'post' for marshal assignments.

A turn can often cover two or more actual posts, and you may be required to rotate through these over the course of the day.

Be prepared for different weather and different customs. Honour the other country's customs – when in Rome... Sadly, some countries are sexist in their outlook and female workers may be in for a difficult time in some Muslim countries, other Asian venues and even France (except for *Le Mans*).

Don't commit to iffy events, or if not getting time off from your job might cause you to renege. No chief likes last-minute dropouts who don't bother to call and say they can't make an event. At least try to e-mail if you have to abort. Above all, come prepared to learn, and realise that there are no right and wrong ways of organising marshals, just different ways.

Enjoy being a gypsy, see you at a circuit somewhere in the world!

Steve Tarrant

It was never the intention of this book to catalogue sad events but unfortunately there have been some in the Club's history. Silverstone was the first in my memory but uplifted by the swift return to marshalling of John Baker who was so grievously injured in that incident. Steve Tarrant has a similarly uplifting tale of his misadventure at the Goodwood Festival of Speed and it is his tale that makes interesting reading.

Steve writes:

Most people already know the circumstances of the accident that day.

How John Dawson-Damer, collector of classic Grand Prix cars, was driving the Lotus 63 4WD when competing at the 2000 Goodwood Festival of Speed.

Of how he crashed fatally at the finish line.

And that two marshals also were involved in the crash, Andy Carpenter succumbing from his injuries and myself becoming disabled.

Those were the headlines.

But after that, the story is less obvious but more significant – of how your comrades and friends trackside then rally around to help you get yourself back on your feet.

Sure, I'd made friends at the various tracks I'd visited most frequently before the accident, but once home from hospital and placed in front of a computer, I discovered a big wide world community of marshals, both within the UK and abroad.

I received emails of hope, support, encouragement, laughter and, above all, of still being part of a team whose bonds know no boundaries irrespective of race or nationality.

With support like this I have been able to return to the tracks, first as spectator and then as marshal, and work alongside these new friends, both in this country and further ashore. Internationally, Le Mans and Kyalami have already been visited, Daytona and Lausitzring are on the cards, and many more places I want and plan to visit over time. But always there is the same warmth of greeting, respect and mutual admiration for each other's abilities and contribution towards the bigger picture of marshalling alongside each other at a motorsport event.

I know I am lucky, both to be alive and to be part of the great fraternity of marshalling, and I look forward to maintaining this throughout the rest of my life, whatever other future challenges come my way.

Just look out for the flying wheelchair, or the flailing crutches!

Steve has been as good as his word. He travels widely and is known and welcomed at race circuits all around the World. His first major event was his excursion to *Kyalami* in 2005, described in the next chapter.

In November 2007 I met him in Daytona. He was on the third week of his trip, taking in race meetings at *Laguna Seca*, where he was a guest of Allan McNish, well known sports car driver, and two consecutive meetings at Daytona. The second of those was the Historic Sports Car meeting where Classic Sports Car Club brought out 30 cars and drivers to take part. In these litigious days, especially in the USA, there are limitations where Steve can officiate but the Central Florida Branch of the SCCA did their best to accommodate him.

Steve manages remarkably well and is amazingly independent! He seemed to enjoy the whole weekend despite staying at a s****y hotel on the beach! Regrettably, Daytona has some of the worst hotels in the USA and Steve found one of them! I know how he feels! We did the same thing fifteen years ago, on our first trip to Daytona, and have stayed away from those hotels ever since!

Best wishes, Steve, that you will continue to be able to do what you do in the way that you do it. You are an inspiration to us all!

Steve Tarrant at Kyalami

8PM, 8th November 2005 – Heathrow Airport Terminal 3. As most of British motorsport was coming to a close, so I was leaving on a jet plane for a three week holiday in the sun of South Africa. Nothing unusual there – except in my luggage were my overalls and boots as I was going to marshal at my favourite foreign circuit, *Kyalami*. And not just any old meeting, but the inaugural running of the GP Masters race, plus a fortnight later the final round of the 2005 Power Tour series (the SA equivalent of our TOCA meeting). The eleven hour flight went quite quickly, as I was in the company of commentator and journalist Bob Costanduros who was also flying down to cover the event.

After a day to acclimatise; it's amazing the effect of altitude has on your ability to do anything, as the circuit is 5500 feet above sea level and you run out of oxygen very quickly, it was off to the circuit on the Thursday for a 7am sign on. The reason for this was as well as testing at the circuit, they were running a couple of the GP Masters and F1x2 cars on the streets of Sandton to publicise the event, and therefore the marshals were divided into two teams; those staying at the circuit and those travelling. I remained behind and worked with Collin Richardson on the race control radio with much of the practice time given to the F1x2 cars. A fairly uneventful first day, except for when the UK officiating team arrived – from my home circuit, Thruxton! You travel 6000 miles to leave them behind, and they come looking for you!

I remained in race control for the Friday and Saturday practice days and enjoyed the company of the various officials that were running the meeting. Plus I bumped into my old friend Murray Walker, who was like a kid in a candy shop after a while away from there! He was so buoyed up with being back at a track and in the company of so many famous names, and it rubbed off on anyone with whom he came into contact.

Unfortunately, a side effect of hot weather and a prosthetic limb is that skin breaks down very quickly, and I was therefore reduced to the role of a spectator for raceday, as I needed to spend the day in my wheelchair and not wear the prosthetic leg. But that also meant I got to see the *Kyalami* Marshals' new clubhouse, as I was taken there to view for the day! It's a mighty impressive building in which to hold meetings and functions, plus it overlooks the track on the straight between Clubhouse corner and the Esses. I was able to see GP Masters relearning how to race as some of the drivers haven't raced for over ten years, plus the cars were all new and therefore no one knew how they would last.

The funniest sights were the passengers in the Minardi F1x2 cars who had been doing charity passenger rides all weekend, with drivers like Johnny Herbert taking it all very seriously. As the cars braked, so the passenger in the back seat would headbutt the cowling in front of them, as they weren't ready for the braking forces a modern car has! I would imagine all the physiotherapists in Johannesburg were very busy on the Monday, as over eighty fare paying passengers experienced F1 power and speed for the first time that weekend and would have the stresses and bruises to show for it!

I then had 10 days of rest and relaxation in the sun at my host's house in *Boksburg* (average daily temperature 30°C) before returning back to *Kyalami* for the 2 day Power Tour meeting. The meeting had a variety of races, from FFords and Production Saloons to Wesbank V8s and SA Superbikes, and several of the championships were going down to the wire. As the Friday was a normal working day, I volunteered to Flag Marshal at The Kink (after consultation with Tony Taylor, the Chief Marshal). This entailed getting my wheelchair up onto the rostrum, then clambering up myself so that I could then sit and watch, and then use the iron railing to haul myself up every time I needed to display a flag. But this was also magic for me – as this was the first time I could flag marshal since my accident in 2000! Despite the deluge of the daily 4pm thunderstorm, I came away from the stand feeling rather elated.

For race day itself, it was decided that I should join the pit lane crew and watch the personnel going about their tasks. But there was a further reason for being placed there as prior to the trip I had made contact with Chief mMarshal Tony Taylor and said I still had a dream of flying the chequered flag one more time, the very flag I was waving at the time of my accident.

So for the afternoon races, I found myself in the crow's nest at the startline, where I joined Lyn and Annemarie. I expected to just wave the flag for one race only, probably the last race of the day but suddenly, five races from the end of the programme, I had the flag thrust into my hand and told to get on with it! So I did, for each and every one of those five races!

What I was feeling at the end of the day is beyond words, as I had come full circle finally from being seriously injured and disabled, to retaking my place on the start gantry in just five years!

So this was very definitely a trip to remember for me, for all the RIGHT reasons!

PS I feel it is proper to say that I am currently not allowed to flag marshal whilst in the UK, following a directive in 2001 that I received from the MSA whilst I use a wheelchair for sitting, etc. The authorities in South Africa were fully aware of this in my discussions with them, and they deemed the practices I went through as being perfectly acceptable to them and their insurers. Therefore I do not want this to be seen as a slur against the MSA here in the UK, as they have been most supportive ever since the accident. However I suspect that in making their decision, they had to take counsel from outside bodies, like insurance companies, and this affects why I can do things in South Africa that I can't in the UK.

"Roundy-Roundy Racing"

Our introduction to 'roundy-roundy' racing, what road race aficionados called NASCAR, came in a discussion with Mark Donohue at Silverstone in 1975. Mark arrived hours early for our Grand Prix Drivers' Forum and June and I had to keep him company for that time. It was no problem, I can assure you and we very quickly became aware of why Mark was nicknamed 'Captain Nice' in US racing circles.

We were bemoaning the loss of the old Woodcote Corner and the new chicane, which was going to 'destroy' that year's British Grand Prix. Mark begged to differ and quoted how entertaining NASCAR had become simply racing round oval circuits. He perhaps detected some incredulity in my eyes and set out to persuade me that NASCAR racing was not only entertaining but just as skilful as road racing – different skills maybe but skilful nonetheless.

On the entertainment side, he thought that Bill France had got it just about right. Bill France knew what puts 'bums on seats', Mark said, and for that reason if they turned up at a circuit and Bill said, 'Guys, you are running on the rims today, no tyres', the drivers would have gone along with that. 'It is bums on seats that pay our wages,' said Mark, 'and we all have the utmost respect for what Bill France has achieved in making NASCAR so popular.'

I have to say that I was not totally persuaded by the end of Marks dissertation but I thought it would be worth seeing for myself if the opportunity presented itself. A few years later it did and courtesy of Keith Douglas, I attended my first NASCAR race at Michigan International Speedway as a guest of Chevrolet. It was quite an eye-opener. The first person I spoke to said the cars had achieved over 250 on the back straight in practice; when I asked if this was kilometres per hour he looked at me as if I had just fallen from a tree! It was a daft question of course, and he gave me a withering look as he explained very slowly (as I was clearly not all there!) that he meant 250 miles per hour and that most cars were doing that speed! The first twenty-eight cars on the grid were less than a second apart on lap times.

We were in the pit lane as the order to start engines was given. Forty-four big, unsilenced V8's starting all at once is quite an impressive noise! We could *feel* the noise through our feet and our bodies. It was almost a relief when the cars moved out on to the track.

Sadly, we could not stay until the finish of the race but John Bunker, my business partner who was with me, was quick to spot that 'debris on the back straight' took a long time to clear up if the pack was spread out but cleared up much more quickly if there was a good race going on! We travelled back to the airport with Lake Speed, one of the drivers who was out of the race early on, and I met Lake several times after that at Pocono. When Scott Speed appeared on the F1 scene we automatically assumed they were related but of course this was not the case; Scott comes from California, Lake from Missouri.

John and I attended several NASCAR races after Michigan and we became impressed by the closeness of the racing and the sheer speed, even when running two, three and sometimes four abreast. However, it was a visit to Pocono International Raceway in 1984 that lead to our closer contact with NASCAR racing. The introduction came again from Keith but this visit was to see an IMSA Sports Car race. We kept the contact with Doctor Joe and Doctor Rose, the owners of PIR, and later visited almost every year for one or other of their two NASCAR races. It was here that our better understanding of NASCAR racing grew.

At one of the early meetings there, June and I met up with Mary Marchman, wife of The Reverend Hal Marchman who was the vicar at Daytona and who had given the invocation there for the last thirty years or so. There was nothing Mary did not seem to know about racing tactics! She forecast who might come in for two tyres or four tyres, who might run a few laps longer, who would stay out just for the five points they got for leading the race and so on and so on. Invariably, she was right and we now much better understand what goes on in NASCAR racing.

NASCAR driving is another level of skill, of that there is no doubt. I have since had a go in one of the Petty Experience cars. I was marginally second fastest of around forty drivers and managed 125.8 mph against the all-time student lap record of 127.0 mph at that circuit. They are very, very agricultural vehicles compared to anything else I have driven. They are loud, heavy vehicles to drive but once up to proper, NASCAR-type speeds I am told they become quite delicate to drive. They have to be kept on line and in line because once they break away they are very, very difficult to recover.

Drafting is immensely important, as is the understanding of how one car can be unsettled by another running close by or overtaking and 'stealing your air'. Dario Franchitti has found this difficult to come to terms with in his first year in NASCAR; so has Sam Hornish Jr, another IRL/Indy 500 Champion who transferred to NASCAR in 2008. Juan Pablo Montoya has done rather better and the aforementioned Scott Speed, from F1, is beginning to do well in ARCA racing, the second league down from NASCAR Sprint Cup and in Pick Up Truck racing.

Because of my 'NASCAR experience', Dale Wells at BARC asked me to Clerk the SCSA cars at Rockingham in 2005. This had been running for a few years with mixed success. Now, the principal owner of the track, Gerry Forsythe who also part-owned CART in the USA, wanted one last attempt to really get it going. Mark Claussner was shipped across from the USA to coach the drivers and spotters and to be the 'front man' in the PR campaign to boost the number of drivers. My job was to make sure the races ran 'reasonably' within MSA regulations.

Mark was an excellent driver coach. We had one driver who could not get within three/four seconds of the qualification level and Mark took to coaching him by radio link from Race Control. I was so impressed; within two or three coaching sessions, this driver was inside the qualifying limit and went on to compete with us that season.

We were aided and abetted by the very capable Sonny Howard and wife Barbara, whose pick up truck racers were already putting on a show for the Rockingham crowds. They seemed to have picked up (horrible pun!) the advantages of drafting, including the bit of gentle bump-drafting that Sonny allowed, and were happy to run together side-by-side for lap after lap, without too many incidents.

We never quite got to that same level with the SCSA V8 'muscle cars'. I suspect there were bigger differences in the capabilities of each car and each driver and we never quite achieved the close running that makes oval racing so exciting. Neither did we reach the number of cars for each race to add to the spectacle, although Mark's PR campaign got us up to twenty-five potential starters during that first season we were involved.

This would have been something to build on for 2006 and 2007 if Gerry Forsythe had not sold the track towards the end of 2005! Clearly, he got an offer he could not refuse and at the time he was pouring funds into CART in the USA to keep that alive (against IRL). However, it did bring to an end the start money paid to every driver and the attractive prize money he had previously offered. Mark's contract for 2006 was cancelled and BRSCC took over the organisation of racing at Rockingham. SCSA sadly died during 2006 and 2007 and I suspect it will be a long time before NASCAR type racing returns to the UK as a regular feature.

Our own contact with NASCAR continues in the USA. If the Championship is close we like to do the last round at Homestead in Miami, which is not far from our second home in Sarasota and, of course, we always attend one of the Pocono 500 races in June or August. 'Doc' and Doctor Rose look after us very well and if we go to the June race we are flattered to be invited along with family and friends to the NASCAR presentation dinner that takes place then. This allows us to rub shoulders and talk to the 'big hitters' in NASCAR, like Bill France Jr until his death in 2007, Mike Helton, President of NASCAR, Jack Roush, Richard Childress, Joe Gibbs and Robert Yates from the team owners. On our latest visit we were honoured to meet James C France, the quiet man of the France family, now overseeing nephew Brian France in the CEO's chair he took over from his Dad, Bill France Jr. James has always kept out of the limelight, by his own choice, but has had a distinguished career racing and winning in Legend Cars and dirt track riding on motor bikes; he is also a Vietnam veteran.

All the NASCAR folks would like to know why SCSA did not quite make it in Europe. I am not sure I know the answer to that but I always promise them Marshals' Club help if they ever decide to bring a "proper" NASCAR to our shores! I suspect it will not happen any time soon, although James France is very much involved in the Daytona Prototype Series (DTP) which may venture further afield in due course.

Anyone who gets the chance should visit Pocono for one of the NASCAR events. Doctors Joe and Rose Mattioli bought into the circuit in the late 1960's as a part-time diversion from their medical practices. Soon it became a full time passion and commitment for them both and 'The Doc', Joe, became immersed in building a new race track. Broke a few times but "too dumb to know it", says Joe, it is now a very impressive facility in the Pocono Mountain area of Pennsylvania, just 100 miles from New York and the same from Philadelphia – a potential audience of some sixty million people!

The track is still wholly owned and run by the Mattioli family, with the eldest grandsons just appointed President and Senior Vice-President to become more involved the day-to-day running but it still has a distinctly family feel about it, something appreciated by the fans. There is a large corps of Goodwill Ambassadors, mostly Mattioli friends, who are very much in evidence at every race meeting. Their task is to make the fans feel comfortable and to listen to what the fans feel about circuit facilities. All those thoughts are relayed to 'Management' and it is impressive just how many have been acted upon over the years we have been attending Pocono International Raceway.

For instance, getting away from the circuit at the end of racing has improved immeasurably over the years, as Joe and his team work closely with local Police, the State Highway patrol and local inhabitants to devise better ways of routing traffic via single-track, country roads to the major Interstate highways back to New York and Philadelphia. The management team works very closely to avoid too much disturbance to local inhabitants who appreciate the income that the circuit brings throughout the Summer months to what was basically a Winter-only ski area before. It all seems to work very well and fans come back year after year. In fact, regular fans book their seats for next year within a very short time after the August NASCAR race when next year's ticket allocation sheets are distributed. There is a five or six year waiting list for the best mobile home positions in the infield.

I think I am still a road race fan, really, but there is something about the whole NASCAR scene that attracts us, not least the friendliness of all involved. NASCAR has the reputation of being a bit of a 'red neck' sport in the USA and some of our American friends look a bit askance at us when we say we are NASCAR fans. I suspect we will keep going while we share our time between the UK and the USA and maybe the two year contract with Sky TV to show NASCAR races live in the UK will help acceptance there, particularly with the insight provided by Keith Huwen, a knowledgeable commentator, and John Mickel who raced SCSA in the UK and Pick Up Trucks in the USA.

Finally, if anyone wants to better understand the history of motor sport in the USA, try the book by Chris Economaki (with Dave Argabright) called *Let 'Em All Go*. Chris is another regular at Pocono and is a most interesting character. He has been around racing in the USA *for ever* and is widely recognised as the doyen of American motor sports journalists. He commentated regularly with our own Jackie Stewart on ABC television and has many interesting stories to tell (some that did not make the book!). His book is an excellent history for anyone interested in oval racing.

Prince Michael of Kent Award

The Prince Michael of Kent award is presented annually for meritorious service to British motor sport. Marshals and members of the Marshals' Club, in particular, have done very well in being considered for this prestigious honour.

TONY BIRD – 1992

Tony was 80 years of age when he won this award as probably the longest-serving marshal in the UK at that time. He began his marshalling career when motor sport resumed after World War II, and became a founder member of The British Motor Racing Marshals' Club when that was founded in 1957. He also became BMRMC Competitions Secretary and ran the Marshals' Club's race meetings at Silverstone for many years. During all this time he remained active on the marshalling front and was widely recognised as the doyen of all marshals.

He was also a mine of good advice and it is thanks to Tony that we were alerted to the more beneficial treatment of VAT on race entries and club membership that helped greatly with Marshals' Club finances at a time when we were trying to rebuild reserves.

Sadly, Tony passed away a few years after his award but right up until his death he could be relied upon for regular articles for newsletters the odd word of guidance if he felt the Club was going about things in the wrong way.

JOHN FELIX – 1994

John Felix was the next marshal to win the award. Then Chairman of the BMRMC, John was and is perhaps the busiest marshal of his era! He regularly fulfils 100/120 marshalling days a year, in all capacities, everything from a marshal on the bank, to Rescue Operator, to Clerk of the Course or MSA Steward. John still turns out on the bank if he has nothing else to do! (There is a separate chapter earlier, on John's marshalling history.)

A worthy winner of this fine award.

TOM DOOLEY – 1996

Tom is perhaps best known for his activities with BRSCC in the North West but was previously a rally competitor – five times in the Monte Carlo rally – and President of the Lancashire and Cheshire Car Club. He remains active today in that same area and he regularly gets all the Chief Marshals from other clubs together to discuss marshalling issues at the start of each season.

He was founder member of the BRSCC North West Centre and long time member of the BMRMC, or the British Motorsport Marshals' Club as it has now become.

KEITH DOUGLAS – 1998

I am not sure there is much I can add here to the separate chapter and frequent mentions elsewhere on Keith's influence on motor sport and on marshalling in particular. The award citation said that Keith "had a long and distinguished history of achievement in motor sport". "Achievement" was the most important word there. Keith had no interest in empty words on how motor sport should progress; he got on and did something about it.

He always considered the Marshals' Club one of his proudest achievements and became a lifelong friend of marshals and all things marshalling right up until his sad death in August 2005.

BOB RAE – 2000

Keeping up the two-yearly award cycle, the Prince Michael of Kent Award went to Bob Rae, for "many years of outstanding contribution to safety in motor sport, notably his work for the British Motorsport Marshals' Club (BMMC)", something of an understatement perhaps!

Bob is a professional journalist and used his word-smith talents to write the *Pocket Guide to Rescue and Resuscitation*, followed by the *Pocket Guide to Marshalling*, both of which are published by the Motorsport Safety Fund and distributed around the World in several different languages. He regularly updates these very useful guides and is a regular contributor on marshalling issues in the various MSA and MSF publications.

COLIN ROSSBOROUGH

No award was made in 2001/3/5 but the marshals were back in 2007! This time it was Colin Rossborough, the very popular Chairman of the Northern Ireland region of the BMMC. Although the smallest of the BMMC regions it has always been very active, with the almost the whole membership turning out on a regular basis for rallies and race meetings on both sides of the North/South divide.

Colin was the original chairman of N Ireland region and built a strong team around him during his term of office. This team quickly regrouped without a hitch when Colin announced his intention to retire to Canada in 2007.

Looking through the various citations for this award, very kindly researched and provided by Margaret Forrest, PA to the Chairman and CEO of the MSA, it was very noticeable just how many of the other recipients started their motorsport careers as marshals. Many of those who now run circuits and race teams around the World also started as marshals. Marshals are a very talented bunch of people and have certainly made their mark on the Prince Michael of Kent award!

President – Raymond Baxter, OBE

Raymond Baxter was a Spitfire pilot during WWII, taking part in strafing raids on V1 and V2 rocket sites deep inside occupied Europe to try to stop the devastating effects of the rockets in raids on London. His last sortie was on 26th April, only a few days before the end of WWII in Europe on 5th May 1945. According to an interview in the Daily Telegraph on 5th May 2005, Raymond's recollections of VE Day are a little unclear. Locals carried Raymond and his Wing Commander shoulder high into the local pub that day and he is not sure if he may have hit his head on the low beams or whether he just had too much to drink! Whatever the case, his memory remained a bit hazy.

In the immediate aftermath of the War, Raymond joined the British Forces Network, a radio service that reached out troops all around the World. As a life long motor sport enthusiast and sometimes competitor in Monte Carlo rallies, it was a reasonably short step from the BFN to the BBC as motor sport commentator. By the time the Marshals' Club was formed in 1957, Raymond Baxter was very much the 'Voice of motor sport' and a natural choice as our first President.

He and Keith Douglas, both ex-RAF, both commentators were clearly well known to each other at the time, as Raymond recalls in a note he sent me only a few short months before his sad death at the age of 84 in September 2006.

"Keith Douglas and I, like all motoring enthusiasts of our generation, were lucky to enjoy the Golden Age of British motor sport. In the 1950's and 60's there were disused airfield circuits all over the country

and there was racing almost the whole year round, e.g. the famous BRSCC Boxing Day meetings at Brands Hatch. Every major club – and there were many – ran their own rallies on public roads and the 'plot and bash' era had headlights sweeping across the Yorkshire moors, the Dales, the Welsh lanes and the twisting byways of the Home Counties. The London Motor Club alone signed up more than 1,000 active members and the Monte Carlo Rally attracted more than 100 British competitors. Hill climbing sites included Bo'ness, the majestic Rest and Be Thankful and every major race meeting was like the Goodwood Revival of today.

Into this happily frenzied scene Keith brought authoritative PA commentary but with his professional background in engineering, a realisation of the necessity for responsible organisation.

At that time, I instigated the Federation of British Police Motor Clubs and Keith had spotted the requirement for the coordination of the army of happy volunteer marshals in every sector of the sport. It was all very well for mad keen individuals to offer to be on hand at midnight in the Kielder Forest but serious questions of safety were self-evident.

So, Keith Douglas and others, formed the British Motor Racing Marshals' Club and honoured me by his invitation to become the Founder President.

It was by no means plain sailing. The British Racing Drivers' Club, effectively the leading body of British motor racing did not want to know, nor did the British Automobile Racing Club. Gradually, through Keith's persistence and the establishment of the self-evident impact on the well-being and safety of the sport, the BMRMC became accepted as THE authority in marshalling.

Keith was rewarded with Associate Membership of the BRDC and was discreetly active there in later crisis meetings. He was a great chap, who concealed his driving purpose behind considerable charm and was the more influential for that."

A typically self-effacing contribution from Raymond Baxter, OBE. In fact, I know from talking to Keith over many years that he used Raymond as a sounding board for many of his ideas in the early years on where motor sport and marshalling should be going and that Raymond's reputation and contacts within the sport helped with the introduction of these ideas.

In later years, Raymond went on to other things within the BBC. He especially enjoyed his time as presenter of Tomorrow's World, at a time when technology was 'white hot', according to one commentator, which gave Raymond an outlet for his passion for all things technical. He commentated on the first live TV pictures from America, introduced Britain to the hovercraft and flew on the very first flight of Concorde.

One of his last public appearances was at the Goodwood Revival meeting just a short time before he died, when he did a wonderful joint interview with Murray Walker, who also became President of the British Motor Racing Marshals' Club and served almost as long has Raymond did.

A former deputy editor of Tomorrow's World remembers Raymond as, "Fearless in front of the camera, reporting around the World on important moments in history, he possessed authority, intelligence and charisma – and more than that, he was a true gentleman." A fitting epitaph I feel for someone in at the start of the Marshals' Club.

President Lord Hesketh

Lord Hesketh's reign as Club President was fairly brief. We were just getting to know him and he was just starting to make a contribution as President when his brief but hugely interesting foray into motor sport came to an abrupt end.

Team Hesketh was a sad loss to the sport. The Team had some interesting characters on board – Lord Hesketh, Bubbles Horsley and James Hunt – a remarkably aristocratic bunch who made a real impact on a rather staid sport, both in what the Team achieved in a remarkably short time but most of all, perhaps, because of the way it enjoyed itself after racing was done!

The Team laid on several memorable visits to the workshops and BMRMC marshals were always welcome in the pit garages, here or abroad. Ray and Gill Darvill, who introduced Lord Hesketh to the Marshals' Club, were in Holland for the team's first Grand Prix win. Lord Hesketh carried cases of champagne to each and every round, just in case they won, and when they did, it was champagne all round and lots of it. Ray and Gill remembered it as an amazing experience.

For what was a very young and inexperienced team, Team Hesketh achieved a lot. Lord Hesketh was only 22 when they started into F1. Bubbles was an ex-car salesman and James was (not always fondly!) known as 'Hunt the Shunt'. Still, they were able to attract one of F1's finest designers, Harvey Postlethwaite, to their cause and his designs surely proved their worth.

However, what success they had came at enormous cost and the Hesketh fortunes were soon depleted. Some reports say that the racing was funded from the slightly fortuitous sale of seaside property in Scotland when offshore drilling began and deep-water ports near to the shore were much in demand. F1 quickly ate up even this very large sum of money, for the times, and Team Hesketh, with one GP win, nine podiums and sixty-two championship points over three years was soon no more.

Lord Hesketh then had to turn his attentions to the family fortunes and took over from his mother running Easton Neston, the family estate near Towcester. Alongside this, he began to manufacture motor cycles – engineered to a fine degree but subsequently proved too expensive for the market.

A meeting with Prime Minister, Margaret Thatcher, got him interested in politics and he started to become a regular at the House of Lords. Under Margaret Thatcher, Lord Hesketh held several senior Government jobs, mainly to do with Trade and Industry.

Anyway, those who were around at the time remember Team Hesketh and Lord Hesketh in particular with considerable fondness. He was very British in his approach to everything he did – before it became unfashionable to be a patriot! I well remember how cross he was when 'some Dutchman' claimed that the team emblem bear infringed a Dutch patent. "Anyone can see this is a British bear", boomed Le Patron, "how can it be anything but with a great Union flag emblazoned on its chest?"

Happy times!

President Murray Walker, OBE

When Lord Hesketh dropped out of motor sport and asked to be relieved of his Presidency, the suggestion we approach Murray Walker met with unanimous approval. Murray said he would accept only if he felt he could do some good for marshals and we managed to persuade him that he would – and he surely did!

He was obviously very proud to be President of the Marshals' Club and took time, in the early years in particular, to attend all our major training sessions and to become acquainted with exactly what we did. He clearly took heed and would often drop snippets into his broadcasts of how marshals did this or that and how they trained for just such events, adding (Carlsberg style) that British Marshals were probably the best marshals in the World! Of course we are!

I suspect there is no need to itemise Murray's broadcasting career. No one with the slightest interest in motor sport, two wheels or four, can fail to have heard of Murray Walker. It is perhaps less well known that Murray's Dad was a championship motor bike trials rider and later a commentator. Murray followed on in both, not matching Dad's championship status in trials riding but surpassing him by miles in the commentator stakes! Not bad considering Murray did not get into full-time commentating until he retired from his day job in advertising.

He graduated from Sandhurst during WWII, first serving with a tank regiment and later as an officer in the Royal Scots Greys, made famous by our own John Watt, long time Chairman of North Region. John and his brother followed their father into the Greys, so quite a family connection there. Following demob Murray became assistant to the Advertising Director of Dunlop and stayed in advertising until eventual retirement to commentate full time.

Now, supposedly retired from previous BBC and ITV commentating duties, he is as busy as ever. He commentates regularly in Australia, is travelling Ambassador for the Honda F1 Racing Team and still finds time amidst all his other public speaking duties to take part in recent Targa rallies in Tasmania and New Zealand and the Classic Adelaide Rally – not bad for an old 'un!

To many, F1 races are nowhere near as exciting as they were when Murray was commentating. Murray's excitement could make even the most boring race seem interesting.

Murray's own contribution follows:

It was my honour and privilege to be the President of the British Motor Racing Marshals' Club, as it was then named, for a very long time. And for those of you who are saying "how long is long?" the answer is that I cannot remember. But it was a long time! To this day I have a guilty conscience about the fact that I did not do as much for the Club as I would have wished and that I was, frankly, more of a figurehead than a mover and shaker. However, I have an excuse. It is that, at the time I occupied the illustrious Presidential position, I was also first BBC TV's, and then ITV's, Motorsport commentator, was mostly out of the country and didn't exactly find time hanging heavily on my hands.

I certainly didn't get caught up in the minutiae of the Club's politics and I didn't have anything to do with the organisation and administration so what, you may ask, did I do to justify my role? Well the answer is that I thought the best way I could contribute to what is an absolutely crackerjack organisation was to point out, whenever I could in my commentaries, which went out to the whole of the English-speaking world except much of America (which mostly didn't give a damn about F1 anyway), that without the Marshals the sport wouldn't exist. I would emphasise that theirs was a vital role, that they did what they did out of sheer enthusiasm for the sport, that they didn't get paid for it, that they trained for and did it in their own time and that the multi-million pound drivers couldn't earn a penny if it wasn't for the bravery, skill and dedication of the Marshals. I also continually banged on about the fact that the best Marshals in the World were the British

Marshals and that this undeniable truth was underlined by the fact that foreign country after foreign country asked British Marshals to attend their event as skilled and experienced examples of the way to do it. Did it do any good? Well the answer is that I don't know but, believe me, it came from the heart.

For year after year I attended the annual training day, addressing the 'congregation' at the beginning of it and then showing the flag by appearing at the various sessions covering flag training, procedures and all the other things that Marshals have to master. I well remember climbing into a Michelin Man silver suit one year and plunging into a wall of flame to put out a petrol fire and thinking that I wouldn't very much like to be doing it for real. But my most vivid memory is of the time when I attended one of the advanced medical lectures on driver recovery from a crashed car. After sitting through a lot of medical detail about the gory and off-putting things that could happen the Doctor who was doing the lecture proceeded to show us a series of in-car photographs that I'd rather not have seen, like broken thigh bones sticking out of overall legs. So much so that, although I do not regard myself as a queasy chap, I began to feel very strange. Sort of dizzy and flushed. "My God ", I thought, " I'm going to faint. How incredibly embarrassing " I dimly remembered that the thing to do, allegedly, was to put your head between your knees so, dropping my handkerchief to give me an excuse to do so and to cover up my wimpishness, I did just that. Top Medico David Cranston was sitting next to me and as I straightened up I casually said " I think I'll go to the Flag Session now David" and wobbled out of the room. I was subsequently told that, as I did so, all the hardened veterans there burst out laughing for apparently I had literally gone green!

Happy days and I genuinely felt very honoured to be the Club's President but the time came for me to move on and be replaced by someone who has done an absolutely superb job - Stuart Turner - whose contacts, enthusiasm and tireless application must have been of immeasurable value to the BMMC.

In its fifty years the Club has been one of the pillars that have made British Motor Sport the envy of the world and a shining example of how to do a vital job with efficiency and good humour. Thank you for letting me be associated with you and my very best wishes for the continued success that you so richly deserve.

Murray is far too modest in his recollection of what he achieved for the Marshals' Club and marshalling in general. His constant mention of how much marshals contribute to the sport Worldwide was of immeasurable benefit in raising people's awareness of what it was marshals did. And, of course it kept us on our toes! We had to live up to Murray's proud boast that the British Marshals were the best in the World and we made sure our training and grading schemes kept us in the lead.

We thank Murray for his long stint as President, his continued interest in what we do – and we know folks who do a lot less in full time work than he does now 'in retirement!' Unless I am very much mistaken (who said that?) I suspect there will be no early bath for Graeme Murray Walker, OBE.

President Stuart Turner

Previous President, Murray Walker, went through several 'retirement phases' in his broadcasting career, first when BBC lost the F1 contract and again when he felt it was time to hang up the microphone and make way for the younger generation. None resulted in what most would recognise as 'retirement' and Murray is still very much involved in the sport. However, it was during one of these retirement phases that he told us he felt he should stand down as President of the Marshals' Club.

Peter Roberts was Chairman-elect at this time and I think it was he who first approached Stuart to be his 'running mate'. Murray felt Stuart would be an excellent choice and the rest of the Club agreed.

Stuart has spent his life in motorsport, a brilliant raconteur who has entertained many with his witty but always pertinent and topical after dinner speeches. Sports Editor of *Motoring News*, champion navigator and RAC Rally winner with Erik Carlsson, Stuart went on to be Competition Manager with BMC, and then had a spell at Castrol, before moving to Ford, where he was heavily involved in their motorsport programmes. He is a member of Motor Sports Council and prominent trustee of the Motorsport Safety Fund. By chance he was also peripherally in at the start of the Marshals' Club, as a member of the Club whence came the prime movers who saw the need for marshals to be properly organised and trained.

In his own memories of his term as President, Stuart records a feeling of mild frustration that the Marshals' Club was not yet ready for some of the changes he proposed. There is time yet, Stuart! Change can sometimes be slow in the Marshals' Club (it took seven years to win the case for centralised accounting and membership!) but we did go ahead with most of your proposals. However, it may be that we need better recognition nationally before we launch ourselves Internationally!

Although other priorities took Stuart away as our President, he still acts as our consultant from time to time and we are happy to seek his advice on a variety of motor sport topics. He keeps us 'in the news' when we have something to say, via *The Marshal*, the official newsletter of the Motorsport Safety Fund.

Stuart wrote of this time as President:

Being asked to contribute to this tome made an old but happy man feel even older and happier because it reminded me of just how involved I was in marshalling when I first joined a motor club back in 1953. It was the North Staffs Motor Club and I guess fairly typical of the day with a strong rally programme, an annual race meeting at Silverstone, several driving test events and a very strong ladies committee which ran a lively social programme.

I got heavily involved in organising rallies for the club and thus got directly immersed in finding marshals. It was the usual story – round up any and everybody you knew able to read a clock and write on a time card. As now, club magazines of the day were full of "please help" cries for marshals and this pressure may have actually led to the formation of the BMMC because one stalwart of the North Staffs, John Ashton, became involved with Keith Douglas in setting up the club. Another club member, Jack Bannister, was also involved with them and that helped me because when Jack gave up producing the club magazine to concentrate on the marshalling side, I took it over. If I hadn't done so, I don't think I'd have landed a job at what was then Motoring News *and maybe my life would have been a whole lot different.*

So I've always been grateful to the Marshals' Club and I was therefore very honoured when Peter Roberts asked me if I would become President. Whether he felt it had been such a wise move a couple of years later I'm not sure because I drove him mad campaigning for the BMRMC club to first of all drop the emphasis on racing – I based my view on experience with the Motor Racing Safety Fund which became even stronger when we streamlined its name to the Motorsport Safety Fund (in the process enabling us to approach rally enthusiasts for donations for the first time).

But I further argued that the club should really become the IMMC – the International Motorsport Marshals Club. I've been lucky enough to marshal on three continents and been involved in racing and rallying in even more and it's all left me convinced that the job's the same wherever it is. Therefore those involved should be united under one umbrella. The anti motorsport pressures around the world are much the same and I don't think it's the time for parochialism.

I lost the battle (the bruises have healed quite nicely now thank you) but I'd better stress that this wasn't the reason I asked to be relieved of the post – it was purely that my involvement with the Motorsport Safety Fund had started to take up much more time than I'd expected. I get great satisfaction that much of the printed material and DVDs we produce (with heavy input from BMMC stalwart Bob Rae) are now being used in several countries around the world.

Anyway, I was glad I'd stepped down when I saw that my successor was to be Barrie Williams. He seems like a nice young lad who should go far in the sport!

We are very grateful to Stuart for his time as President and continued interest in all things marshalling.

Barrie Williams

When work commitments in his 'real job' forced Peter Roberts to stand down as National Chairman, our President, Stuart Turner, announced that he, too, was proposing to give up office. Chris Stoddart, who was our National Secretary, was on 'away-a-day' duties for his employer at the time, leaving me in the driving seat, as it were, to find a new Chairman and President.

After some long discussions at a race meeting at Snetterton, where Chris Hobson was MSA Steward and I was Clerk, Chris (fairly willingly!) stepped up to the plate to be a candidate for Chairman. He is a long-time member of the Club (even longer than me!) and has held several positions on and around Council during that time, including a fairly productive term as National Training Officer. Training and Grading was once again in the forefront of our thoughts as we sought to change the present Scheme to make better use of the steadily dwindling number of marshals; Chris's experience in this area would be invaluable. So, Chris was duly elected and that was one position filled.

For the President's role, we chose this time to extend the invitation for nominations beyond Council and asked for suggestions from the membership. Barrie Williams, better known to many as Whizzo, was far and away the most popular choice. He was elected with a majority the politicians would have called 'landslide' and an inspired choice he has proven to be.

Irrepressible is the word that best describes Barrie and his attitude to motor sport. He seems able to get enjoyment out of anything he drives.

Put him in anything remotely competitive and he will be aiming for pole position, race win and fastest lap into the bargain. Give him a car that is fun to drive but unlikely to be a winner and he will entertain! As marshals, we have often had a cheery wave from Whizzo as progresses sideways through a corner.

Not too long after election as President he overcooked it and finished upside down in the gravel at Silverstone. Marshals, as always, were quickly on the scene, to be greeted with calls from underneath the car, "Quick, get me out of here, I'm your President!" Whether this entreaty had any real effect we do not know but he was released quickly and without injury. His only disappointment then was that it was a male medic who came forward to check him out rather than the bevy of pretty nurses he had envisaged would be there to take care of him!

Barrie has always been a great favourite with the marshals. He takes time to talk to them when he can, remembers who they are and is happier than many drivers to spend time in marshals' company. (The sadly departed David Leslie was another who regularly went out on the circuit to talk with marshals.) Since becoming our President he turns up at marshals' events throughout the country. He has presented marshalling awards in the North, done similar duty in the South and is a regular visitor at the recently revived monthly club nights in South Mids, his local region. At a recent club night, devoted to Historic Formula Junior racing, Barrie kept the whole thing moving along with his own vivid memories and knowledge of the Formula Junior scene.

My own special memory of Barrie goes back to when we lived near Salisbury, Wiltshire, in a village populated by Richard Longman, prominent Mini racer and preparer, and several other mini racers in adjoining villages. They all ran on shoestring budgets and as I had a tow bar on my car, I was occasionally called to help out with towing a trailer to Thruxton.

On one of these visits we espied someone hobbling about in the pits with his foot in plaster but dressed in racing overalls. "What a poser," we thought! Next thing we see is this same chap being manoeuvred into a race car. He then went out and won the race! It was Whizzo, of course! Talk about irrepressible!

Coincidentally, our 50th anniversary came in the same year as Barrie celebrated his 50 years in motorsport. Paul Lawrence took on the unenviable task of writing a book to commemorate Barrie's fifty years in racing – which Barrie wanted to call, 'Half Way There!'

I found it just as hard as Paul did, to tie Barrie down to get some real facts about his racing career. I managed some time with him at the MSA when I offered him a lift to a Race Committee meeting. Barrie started by saying he thought he had driven five or six or maybe seven significantly different cars so far that season (then less than half way through). Within ten minutes he listed nine different makes! He thinks he may have driven 180 or so different cars over the years.

He thinks he is getting close to 900 race starts and possibly 300 wins. Add to that some 300+ rallies, including twenty-eight International Rallies and you can see he has been a busy boy! He had one International Rally win and two class wins at the same level but has no idea how he performed in the others!

Currently, he enjoys the Classics at Goodwood and Silverstone. His most enjoyed moment from recent years was his titanic struggle with Frank Sytner last year and eventual win in the Richmond Trophy race at Goodwood. I have seen some film of that race and it did look to be a cracker!

When Barrie's book came out in the Spring of 2008 at the Retro Show, he spent a long time on the Marshals' Club stand, signing copies for members – and for many of his driving friends who bought from us because we were taking a small profit on each book sold. We sold out on all three days!

Barrie's career has been all about driving other people's cars and three days at the Retro Show brought home to all of us just how many driving friends he had! We met a dozen or more, all of whom had stories to tell about their driving experience with Whizzo. He is clearly a very able driving instructor and several of his driving partners commented upon how much they had gained from the experience.

As an instructor, Barrie is extremely proud of how many youngsters have been taught to drive at the Under17 Driving School he formed. Here he taught underage drivers road skills on marked out race circuits, the vast majority of whom went on to pass the official driving test first time. Some went on to race!

Barrie has very quickly become one of us. He seems to be just as happy in the company of a crowd of marshals as he does in some of the 'grander circles' in motor sport hierarchy. He has been an immensely popular President and I have no doubt we will want to keep him as long as he wants to be with us.

Stewards' Decisions

During the past little while, some of the Stewards' decisions in Formula One have received a bad Press, sometimes justified, sometimes in ignorance of the basic rules of F1. Various suggestions have been made but it seems the decisions get no better and there were some inexplicable judgements at the Belgian and Japanese Grands Prix in 2008.

One constant call has been for the appointment of permanent, paid Stewards to travel to all F1 races. In fact, this was tried during 2006/7, with one of the UK's most able Stewards (and regular race winning competitor!) appointed Chief Steward. I believe this turned out to be something of a 'poisoned chalice'. To my mind, it is the system that needs changing.

Up until around twelve years ago (I cannot remember exactly when) most judicial decisions in National car racing in the UK were taken by the Stewards – and every issue of the MSA news magazine, *Motorsports Now*, was filled with reports of long and expensive appeals heard at Motorsports House. The MSA decided that the system should change and Clerks were asked to be the first line in judicial matters at all National race meetings. The MSA also issued guidance notes and sentencing guidelines for various on-circuit misdemeanours.

This has been a huge success, in my view. A small percentage of Clerks' decisions are appealed to the Stewards of the Meeting but very, very few go beyond this stage; everything is almost always cleared up within the race meeting timetable. *Motorsports Now* has become a much slimmer magazine!

To my mind, Stewards, International or National are one stage removed from the actual running of the race meeting and are often asked to decide matters upon which they have too little up-to-the-minute or relevant information. Clerks or Race Directors, on the other hand, are up with the action, and much more likely to come up with the right decision, on the spot.

Added to this, most of the current Clerks and Race Directors in the UK came up the marshalling route; they have spent much of their life observing race behaviour from close quarters, on the bank. Many have been competitors; others are involved in race organisation and rule setting.

F1 and all International races should adopt the UK system of judicial process and I believe we could almost guarantee improved decision making. Let Charlie Whiting decide on the spot what punishment is due, if any, and leave the teams to appeal to the Stewards if they do not agree.

Failure to do something to improve the situation at International level can lead only to a continuation of inappropriate and inconsistent penalties such as those we saw at the *Spa* and *Fuji* races. As race officials, we need to stamp out 'rock ape' driving but we have also to allow racing to take place; that judgement comes best from those closely involved in the racing, as it happens.

I have not mentioned any driver involvement, I hear you say! It seems the obvious thing to do, to get some retired drivers to adjudge driving behaviour but frankly, this has seldom worked all that well. Drivers seem reluctant to become involved in being referees, just as football, rugby and other sports have found. Once a competitor always a competitor it seems.

During research for this book, there were several instances of drivers becoming involved in officialdom, from the early days when drivers would marshal if they did not have a drive, to the modern day, where some racing registers award championship points to drivers who do a day's marshalling. The early drivers seem to regard a day's marshalling as something of a jolly and were often reluctant to pass judgement on their peers. Today's drivers find the whole thing interesting but they very often conclude that marshalling is not something they really want to become involved in.

Back to my original suggestion, therefore; let the Clerk or Race Director come up with the on-the-spot judgement and let the appeal process take care of any complaints. This system is already well proven in the UK, where most Clerks are pretty well *au fait* with what passes for good driving and what does not. So, too, is Charlie Whiting and I think most F1 drivers would better accept his judgement than the judgement of Stewards from countries where very little motorsport of any kind takes place.

The Priest Catcher

When Father Patrick Horan decided to dice with the F1 cars on Hangar Straight at the British Grand Prix 2003, he was rescued by Stephen Green, at no small risk to himself. Stephen was presented with a special award by the MSA and received the BARC Browning Medal in recognition of his selfless act. Stephen is the Marshals' Club's Press Officer and some times correspondent to *Motor Sport News*.

As always, Jim Bamber produced an appropriate cartoon.

The Next Fifty Years

What will become of the Marshals' Club over the next fifty Years; who knows?

When first set up, the Marshals' Club had solid support from many in the sport who understood the need for motor race marshals to be better organised and trained than hitherto. The Club was misunderstood by others who feared it would be come some sort of union for marshals and in the mood of the day at that time, there would be strikes and walkouts and demands for 'rights'. Thankfully, this never became the case and many of those who first feared the Marshals' Club very quickly converted to become ardent supporters.

Those who better understood what the Club was trying to achieve pushed for recognition and although this was slow at first, the idea of an organisation dedicated to the recruitment and better organisation and training of marshals gained ground. There were some big hitters in the original team and they gradually won over most of the opposition, especially that from the ruling body of the day the RAC. Progress was steady rather than meteoric but numbers increased and new regions were formed as numbers grew all around the UK.

That same steady progress continued until the introduction of the Marshals' Training and Grading Scheme. This seemed to touch upon a pent up need for training in marshalling ranks and numbers grew rapidly as people joined to take advantage of the training we offered. The Training and Grading Scheme steadily spread to other disciplines. First into rallying via the British Rally Marshals' Club, set up as a subsidiary of BMRMC to deal with ever-increasing interest in rally marshalling. The MSA urged us to expand the Scheme elsewhere and over a period of three or four years it was extended into karting, hill climbs and all other speed events.

In my estimation, the Club's influence within the sport peaked around 1990. By then the Marshals' Club-inspired Train the Trainers programme was well underway, membership stood at something in excess of 2,800 and from insurance records kept at the time, Marshals' Club members put in over 40,000 marshalling days per season, out of a total of no more than 50,000. We supplied the vast majority of the marshalling effort at Silverstone/BRDC and enjoyed excellent working relationships with BRSCC and BARC, the other two main organising bodies at that time. BMRMC representatives were elected to Race Committee, Rallies Committee, Safety Committee and to all training and grading committees and steering groups. The Club's 'star' was very much at its zenith!

Then, in 1991/92, the MSA announced plans to introduce a National Training and Grading Scheme for marshals. We were persuaded to gift our scheme to become this MSA National Scheme. To a large extent, it was unavoidable that we should have gifted our Scheme but sadly it led to a fairly serious downturn in the Club's progress.

Other clubs with marshals could now do their own training and reclaim the costs of doing so direct from the MSA. With an eye for the bottom line several clubs began to actively recruit marshals to boost membership income. A regime change at Silverstone saw the formation of their own marshals' club and we lost our annual race day there that had been such a benefit to Club funds for many years. Marshals who had taken joint membership of the Marshals' Club to benefit from the then unique Training and Grading Scheme could now receive the same training (often given by BMRMC Instructors!) within their principal Club and withdrew from membership of BMRMC. Although many of these subsequently rejoined over a period of years the impact at the time was marked and we lost a considerable portion of our previous income.

To add to the financial 'calamity' a new management team at the MSA seemed unaware of the history of events and in the first year of operation of the new National Training and Grading Scheme, our training refund was cut back to 50% from the 100% we had enjoyed until then! This loss represented almost 50% of our subscription income at the time. It took considerable lobbying in the corridors of power at Motor Sports House to win back some of this loss and of course there was then the long struggle over ten years of so to get back to the 100% refund level we had enjoyed before the rules changed.

So, was this the Club's nadir? In my opinion, yes, it was. Balancing the books at the time was not easy but we had consciously, during the first five years of my Treasurer-ship, built up fairly healthy reserves to avoid ever being caught again, as we had been with the Personal Accident insurance increase. We weathered the storm, financially, and as a Club we simply dug deeper for ways to re-establish our place in the sport.

Keith Douglas was a great help at this time. He orchestrated our various presentations to recover the lost training refund and he and John Felix together (John was Chairman of the Club at the time) worked hard to maintain our influence on the various Committees and Sub-Committees at the MSA. With Keith gone and John having given up Chairmanship to join the BARC Board, there has been some slippage. Our influence within the MSA is not what it was and several of the hard won Committee appointments for Marshals' Club appointees have gone to others who, on the face of it, do not always seem to represent any great number of marshals at all. The current selection process lacks transparency and it seems there are no rights of appeal. Very few on the committees know how new members are selected and most claim they play no effective part in the selection. It does not seem a very democratic process, does it?

The Marshals' Club has also come under attack from some dodgy number crunching, from a similarly dodgy database. It is often quoted against us that we are only 1,300 or 1,400 marshals out of a total of 10,000 or 11,000 registered marshals. That total is made up of 6,000 to 7,000 rally marshals – and I will come back to that in a minute.

The remaining 4,000 are principally race marshals but the database is years out of date. The last time it was analysed properly, the total of *active* marshals came down to 2,650 and later to 2,350. From our own experience and that of other clubs, the first year drop out rate for new marshals is horrendous. No one ever 'joins' the MSA marshals' register; therefore, no one ever 'leaves', hence the number of largely redundant names listed there.

We have very few members who are rally marshals only and the fact that we have 1,400 or 1,500 of this reduced total of race marshals, plus another 200+ from other Clubs who have joint membership with the Marshals' Club, presents a totally different picture of the Marshals' Club's continuing influence where it counts, in marshalling days put in. We no longer keep the detailed records we once did but best estimates suggest that Marshals' Club members still put in some 70/80% of the total race marshalling days around UK circuits.

Rally marshal numbers are a different ball game. Many of those listed as marshals appear infrequently and the duties they undertake are quite different to circuit based tasks. Past-President Stuart Turner, still very much a rally man, reports that club magazines are full of requests for marshals, mainly for rallies, despite the high number of rally marshals recorded at Motor Sports House. Stuart sees no ready answer to this situation, nor does anyone else, it seems. The only thing to add is that most of the control points on most rallies are manned by BRMC marshals, past and present.

Circuit racing, with significantly lower total numbers, is much better served because individual race marshals tend to do many more days per season. Many race marshals do over sixty days a year, with a few who top 100 days per year. John Felix used to regularly do 100+ days marshalling, in all sorts of disciplines. Each of the organising clubs has its own nucleus of marshals, whom they look after fairly well and many of the Chief Marshals of the smaller organising clubs are BMMC members who can tap into the largest (real!) database of active marshals.

Regrettably, these points are not yet well made within Motor Sports House. Our 'promised' position on Motor Sports Council in 2007 was lost, largely, on the 'dodgy database number crunching' referred to above, when we were not there to defend ourselves. Clearly, we still have a persuasion task ahead of us.

It would help if we could win some public acknowledgement of what the Marshals' Club has achieved over the years and is still capable of doing if given the opportunity.

- The Marshals' Club pioneered on track personal accident insurance for marshals and – Heineken style – current PA insurance offered to members still affords benefits other insurance does not

- The Marshals' Club initiated and perfected what has become the National Training and Grading Scheme for marshals but there is scant public recognition of the BMMC initiative

- All major updates in the National T&G Scheme were written mainly by a succession of BMMC Training and Grading Officers

- Even after adoption by the MSA, extensions into other disciplines and/or to "offshore" locations were all conducted by BMMC personnel

- The Marshals' Club presented various reports on the marshalling dilemma in 1989, 1998 and 2000 containing suggestions for improvement that were largely repeated by the later Volunteers in Motorsport study

- Virtually all of the modules in the recently revised T&G Scheme, under the ViM banner, were written by BMMC members

- The multi-tasking approach contained within recent Training and Grading updates began with the Marshals' Club

- The recent initiative on Alternative Marshalling Methods started with the Marshals' Club

- The most recent and most successful recruiting effort originated within the Marshals' Club but announcement of the award to the team responsible managed to exclude all reference to the BMMC

I am conscious we must not simply 'whinge', nor must we complain publicly before we have taken adequate steps to correct some of the issues we complain of. I can assure you we have tried officially and formally to correct many of the issues listed, without too much success. The Marshals' Club has a proud record of achievement. The Club has been at the heart of every major advance in marshalling issues throughout the past fifty years. During that same time, the Marshals' Club has remained apolitical, has never become 'the union' some feared and remains today as the only club that exists solely to recruit, train and retain marshals, possibly the largest of its type in the World.

We understand that the governing body has a myriad of other priorities to take care of, bigger fish to fry and Heaven knows how they cope with the ever more restrictive legislation all businesses now run under. As the governing body it is damned if it does and damned if it does not. Yet, recent years have seen it less inclined to consult with the Marshals' Club *per se* and I for one feel this is a grave error.

People are the most important part of any successful organisation. Stuart Turner's questionnaire highlighted the fact that some 47% of marshals come from management or Information Technology backgrounds. Most of these people belong to the BMMC. Together we should be harnessing this talent instead of alienating it.

The Marshals' Club wants to be part of the solution in all things marshalling, as history shows it always has been in the past. The Marshals' Club still speaks for the very great majority of active marshals (race marshals in particular). We can be much more effective if we work together in a fairly equal partnership, free from the fear in some quarters that the Marshals' Club is some 'outside' influence just waiting to demand marshals' rights!

Volunteers in Motorsport was a fine initiative and, with the generous backing of Government finance and full support of the governing body, it became an excellent facilitator, enacting much of what the Marshals' Club had highlighted in prior reports to the MSA. With government funding now ceased, it will be back to getting things done without the benefit of ready cash. This is where the Marshals' Club has excelled and I am sure, if required, we could resurrect the idea of a ring-fenced levy on competition entry fees that AMRCO agreed to just before the arrival of government funding for ViM.

Volunteers in Motorsport is a catchy title and I am sure it will remain. However it is not something anyone can actually join. The Marshals' Club is and the feeling of belonging this provides is BMMC's biggest strength. It motivates the level of contribution noted above and I have no doubt this will continue provided, always, that credit is given where due.

The challenge for us as a Club – and for the sport as a whole – is to find ways to better retain the marshals we enrol. This is not unique to the Marshals' Club or even to motor sport. There are so many leisure opportunities these days it is not at all unusual for folks to try several before finding one they like – or simply go back to the sofa and their widescreen TV!

All voluntary activities suffer the same and in motor racing worldwide the constant features are reduced numbers of volunteers, an almost total dearth of young people coming along to participate and a steadily ageing list of volunteers at almost every event.

I have been Clerking at many of the Grand Prix circuits in Europe during 2008 and it is noticeable that on Fridays we are lucky if we have more than one marshal per post; Saturdays the number might double and we get to almost full manning by the Sunday. Lesser meetings struggle all weekend for numbers but in Continental Europe many of the circuits already adopt a system of incident handling and vehicle recovery similar to that contained within the Marshals' Club recommendations on Alternative Marshalling, which allows those meetings to go ahead with less than recommended manning.

Our own average age of a marshal in the UK increased recently from 49 years of age to 51 and has been growing steadily this way for years. The SCCA in America commented recently on the 'greying' of its marshalling force. Even more of a challenge is to get younger members to take on and maintain Committee posts. I took up a committee position within the Marshals' Club when I was still under 30 years of age; I was elected Chairman of South Mids regions, then the largest region, only a short time afterwards. Most of my fellow committee members were the same age or even slightly younger. Now, with increased pressures in the workplace, for those building a career in particular, it becomes increasingly difficult to recruit young men and women for committee positions.

The strongest 'pull' we have is that motorsport marshalling is still an attractive and entertaining occupation for anyone with real interest in motorsport – harking back to Sir Jackie's comments. Collectively, we still gain the greatest number of new members – and generally members who stay – from word of mouth. Marshals who enjoy what they are doing are the best advert possible to attract others – but this, in turn, increases the need to better look after those marshals we have, if we are not to be constantly recruiting new members, who may or may not stay the course and in any event, lack the experience of those we lose and, of course, need extra funding for training etc.

Many marshals belong to other organising clubs but still feel they should become members of the Marshals' Club, the British Motorsport Marshals' Club. They, in turn, recommend to marshalling colleagues that they, too, should join. Marshal to marshal contact works very well and the organising clubs are almost always happy to run articles on marshalling in race day programmes, periodicals and the like. It all helps Marshals' Club membership. I for one have always believed that anyone serious about marshalling should become a member of the Marshals' Club no matter how many other clubs he or she already belongs to!

During the early part of 2008, the MSA launched its GO Motorsport campaign, something else we had been harping on about for some time. We made a presentation on just this subject to the MSA Media Group in 2005. It is a costly exercise – with a budget of some £250,000 and we will do our level best, as a Club, to benefit from this new effort.

The only hesitation I have is that most of this funding and the funding for ViM was spent outside the sport, on consultants, media people, etc. I just wonder how much more benefit there might have been if some of this funding (not far short of £1M in total) had been spent on those already working within the sport. Existing marshals hear of all this money being spent and, quite frankly, wonder where it all went. (There is at least one circuit owner who shares this wonderment!) The existing marshals see no improvement in their working conditions, from all this cash. We must avoid spending everything on recruiting new participants, only to lose our more experienced regulars, through lack of proper care and attention.

We should also examine closely just how effective these 'big buck' campaigns have been and how much more productive it might be to support local efforts by the various clubs, like our own Team Wilson/ BTCC effort. This produced 1,400 new names in both 2007 and 2008, fot a total expenditure of £10,000 plus the free time put in by Team Wilson and other BMMC helpers. We took on 500+ new members and we know that BARC, BRSCC and other clubs also benefitted from the various Marshals' Club recruitment campaigns. However, these new members will slip away, too, if they are not looked after; some may slip away rather more quickly than our longer serving marshals who have become a little 'anaesthetised' over the years to the ongoing lack of care in some quarters. We really must concentrate on better looking after those we have!

Our own PR activities were stepped up in recent years and by and large this has been very successful. Stephen Green was 'marshalling correspondent' to *Motorsport News* for a while and Matt James, one of *Motorsport News'* editors, has remained an informed and helpful contributor to marshalling causes ever since.

Chris Hobson, current Chairman, 'locked into' much of the training re-writes under the ViM banner, is an excellent representative for the Marshals' Club and marshalling in general on Race Committee and several other MSA committees. His circuit walkabouts when acting as MSA Steward have greatly improved contact with the marshal on the bank.

Team Wilson, comprising Peter Wilson and wife Hilary, brother Ken Wilson and his partner Maureen, were jointly awarded the MSA Marshal of the Year award in 2007 for their sterling efforts on marshal recruitment at BTCC rounds. This was perhaps our best recruiting effort ever but that is not to talk down recruiting efforts elsewhere within the regions. North Region in particular has always had an excellent record at Oulton Park on recruitment and retention of marshals; the retention part being particularly valuable, as already mentioned. Other regions have not only participated with Team Wilson on BTCC recruitment but have all embarked on their own, local recruitment campaigns.

All of this helps keep our name to the fore. Drivers continually drop in to our recruiting tents to give their good wishes and thanks for services rendered. HSCC and other clubs regularly invite us to write about marshalling for their magazines.

I suspect the Club's name is now as well known as it has ever been and it is up to us to make the best of this over the next fifty years. We must remain positive about the benefits of motorsport marshalling as a hobby, continue to attract new members and hope that we can better persuade those who run our sport to become more effective in supporting those who are already here and contributing.

The global financial crisis that hit the World in Autumn 2008, just as this book was going to print, will make life no easier for any of us. Formula One cannot remain immune to the melt down in the banking/financial sector and there is no doubt in my mind that this will filter down through all levels of the sport during the next season or two. Sponsors for the professional registers (BTCC, F 3, F Renault, etc) will be harder to come by. Many, many competitors at national level will have to rethink their racing budgets, especially where the racing budget is part funded by companies they own/run. I very much suspect there will be shrinkage in all areas of motorsport – not least in marshalling, where marshals were already deciding to cut back, when petrol went through the £5 a gallon barrier earlier in 2008. The price of petrol may fall back momentarily but the overall financial picture remains gloomy.

With many marshals telling us they might have to quit marshalling because the costs had simply risen too high, we once again tried the competition levy route to subsidise marshals' costs. Sadly, this failed to excite any interest from the 'professionals' in our sport, leaving it to the smaller organising clubs and their largely amateur members as our principal supporters – but the potential loss of marshals was too serious for us to leave things there.

Mike Newton, our long-time supporter, gave us some new ideas on funding. Taking this on board, we hope to be able to offer further discounts on essential marshalling wear to our members and there will be valuable prizes to be won by those who renew for the new season. Some of this will be met from current reserves, in the hope that we can benefit in the future from the ideas Mike has put to us.

We are *THE* Marshals' Club. We still represent the very great majority of marshals in this country. We may not have won much support for our idea of a levy-funded travel allowance but, as always, we want to remain the leader in marshalling initiative and it seemed timely and appropriate that we should find some way of helping our members during a financial crisis, that most pundits say will not materially improve before 2010. Hopefully, these proposals will help and maybe a few others will follow our lead in due course.

There are some very challenging times ahead but I suspect no more challenging than those that faced our founders in 1957. I am sure we will cope!